19th Conference on Computational Natural Language Learning (CoNLL 2015)

Shared Task

Co-located with ACL-IJCNLP 2015

Beijing, China
30 – 31 July 2015

ISBN: 978-1-5108-0939-0

Printed from e-media with permission by:

Curran Associates, Inc.
57 Morehouse Lane
Red Hook, NY 12571

Some format issues inherent in the e-media version may also appear in this print version.

Printed by Curran Associates, Inc. (2015)

Association for Computational Linguistics
209 N. Eighth Street
Stroudsburg, Pennsylvania 18360

Phone: 1-570-476-8006
Fax: 1-570-476-0860

acl@aclweb.org

Additional copies of this publication are available from:

Curran Associates, Inc.
57 Morehouse Lane
Red Hook, NY 12571 USA
Phone: 845-758-0400
Fax: 845-758-2634
Email: curran@proceedings.com
Web: www.proceedings.com

CoNLL 2015

The Nineteenth Conference on Computational Natural Language Learning

Proceedings of the Shared Task

July 30-31, 2015
Beijing, China

Production and Manufacturing by
Taberg Media Group AB
Box 94, 562 02 Taberg
Sweden

Introduction

This volume contains papers describing the CoNLL-2015 Shared Task and the participating systems. This year, we continue the tradition of the Conference on Computational Natural Language Learning (CoNLL) of having a high profile shared task in Natural Language Processing (NLP), focusing on Shallow Discourse Parsing, which involves identifying individual discourse relations that are present in a natural language text. A discourse relation can be expressed explicitly or implicitly, and takes two arguments realized as sentences, clauses, or in some rare cases, phrases. Shallow Discourse Parsing is a fundamental NLP task and can potentially benefit a range of natural language applications such as Information Extraction, Text Summarization, Question Answering, Machine Translation, and Sentiment Analysis.

A total of sixteen teams from three continents participated in this task, and fourteen of them submitted system description papers. Many different approaches were adopted by the participants, and we hope that these approaches help to advance the state of the art in Shallow Discourse Parsing. The training, development, and test sets were adapted from the Penn Discourse TreeBank (PDTB). In addition, we also annotated a blind test set following the PDTB guidelines solely for the shared task. The results on the blind test set were used to rank the participating systems. The evaluation scorer, also developed for this shared task, adopts an F1 based metric that takes into account the accuracy of identifying the senses and arguments of discourse relations as well as explicit discourse connectives. We hope that the data sets and the scorer, which are freely available upon the completion of the shared task, will be a useful resource for researchers interested in discourse parsing.

For the first time in the history of the CoNLL shared tasks, participating teams, instead of running their systems on the test set and submitting the output, were asked to deploy their systems on a remote virtual machine and use a web-based evaluation platform to run their systems on the test set. This meant they were unable to actually see the data set, thus preserving its integrity and ensuring its replicability. We hope that the successful implementation of this new evaluation protocol in the shared task will encourage its adoption in future NLP evaluation campaigns.

Nianwen Xue, Hwee Tou Ng, Sameer Pradhan, Rashmi Prasad, Christopher Bryant, and Attapol Rutherford

Organizers of the CoNLL-2015 Shared Task
July 2015

Organizers:

Nianwen Xue, Brandeis University
Hwee Tou Ng, National University of Singapore
Sameer Pradhan, Boulder Language Technology
Rashmi Prasad, University of Wisconsin-Milwaukee
Christopher Bryant, National University of Singapore
Attapol Rutherford, Brandeis University

Program Committee:

Christopher Bryant, National University of Singapore
Jacob Eisenstein, Georgia Institute of Technology
Graeme Hirst, University of Toronto
Fang Kong, Soochow University
Man Lan, East China Normal University
Junyi Jessy Li, University of Pennsylvania
Annie Louis, University of Edinburgh
Hwee Tou Ng, National University of Singapore
Vincent Ng, University of Texas at Dallas
Sameer Pradhan, Boulder Language Technologies
Rashmi Prasad, University of Wisconsin-Milwaukee
Attapol Rutherford, Brandeis University
Mark Sammons, University of Illinois at Urbana-Champaign
Evgeny Stepanov, University of Trento
Yannick Versley, Universität Heidelberg
Bonnie Webber, University of Edinburgh
Nianwen Xue, Brandeis University

Table of Contents

The CoNLL-2015 Shared Task on Shallow Discourse Parsing
Nianwen Xue, Hwee Tou Ng, Sameer Pradhan, Rashmi Prasad, Christopher Bryant and Attapol Rutherford 1

A Refined End-to-End Discourse Parser
Jianxiang Wang and Man Lan 17

The UniTN Discourse Parser in CoNLL 2015 Shared Task: Token-level Sequence Labeling with Argument-specific Models
Evgeny Stepanov, Giuseppe Riccardi and Ali Orkan Bayer 25

The SoNLP-DP System in the CoNLL-2015 shared Task
Fang Kong, Sheng Li and Guodong Zhou 32

Shallow Discourse Parsing Using Constituent Parsing Tree
Changge Chen, Peilu Wang and Hai Zhao 37

A Minimalist Approach to Shallow Discourse Parsing and Implicit Relation Recognition
Christian Chiarcos and Niko Schenk 42

A Hybrid Discourse Relation Parser in CoNLL 2015
Sobha Lalitha Devi, Sindhuja Gopalan, Lakshmi S, Pattabhi RK Rao, Vijay Sundar Ram and Malarkodi C.S. 50

The CLaC Discourse Parser at CoNLL-2015
Majid Laali, Elnaz Davoodi and Leila Kosseim 56

Shallow Discourse Parsing with Syntactic and (a Few) Semantic Features
Shubham Mukherjee, Abhishek Tiwari, Mohit Gupta and Anil Kumar Singh 61

JAIST: A two-phase machine learning approach for identifying discourse relations in newswire texts
Son Nguyen, Quoc Ho and Minh Nguyen 66

The DCU Discourse Parser: A Sense Classification Task
Tsuyoshi Okita, Longyue Wang and Qun Liu 71

Improving a Pipeline Architecture for Shallow Discourse Parsing
Yangqiu Song, Haoruo Peng, Parisa Kordjamshidi, Mark Sammons and Dan Roth 78

A Shallow Discourse Parsing System Based On Maximum Entropy Model
Jia Sun, Peijia Li, Weiqun Xu and Yonghong Yan 84

The DCU Discourse Parser for Connective, Argument Identification and Explicit Sense Classification
Longyue Wang, Chris Hokamp, Tsuyoshi Okita, Xiaojun Zhang and Qun Liu 89

Hybrid Approach to PDTB-styled Discourse Parsing for CoNLL-2015
Yasuhisa Yoshida, Katsuhiko Hayashi, Tsutomu Hirao and Masaaki Nagata 95

Conference Program

Thursday, July 30, 2015

Session 3: 14:00–15:30 Shared Task oral presentations

The CoNLL-2015 Shared Task on Shallow Discourse Parsing
Nianwen Xue, Hwee Tou Ng, Sameer Pradhan, Rashmi Prasad, Christopher Bryant and Attapol Rutherford

A Refined End-to-End Discourse Parser
Jianxiang Wang and Man Lan

The UniTN Discourse Parser in CoNLL 2015 Shared Task: Token-level Sequence Labeling with Argument-specific Models
Evgeny Stepanov, Giuseppe Riccardi and Ali Orkan Bayer

The SoNLP-DP System in the CoNLL-2015 shared Task
Fang Kong, Sheng Li and Guodong Zhou

Friday, July 31, 2015

Session 8.a: 16:00–17:30 Shared Task poster presentations

Shallow Discourse Parsing Using Constituent Parsing Tree
Changge Chen, Peilu Wang and Hai Zhao

A Minimalist Approach to Shallow Discourse Parsing and Implicit Relation Recognition
Christian Chiarcos and Niko Schenk

A Hybrid Discourse Relation Parser in CoNLL 2015
Sobha Lalitha Devi, Sindhuja Gopalan, Lakshmi S, Pattabhi RK Rao, Vijay Sundar Ram and Malarkodi C.S.

The CLaC Discourse Parser at CoNLL-2015
Majid Laali, Elnaz Davoodi and Leila Kosseim

Shallow Discourse Parsing with Syntactic and (a Few) Semantic Features
Shubham Mukherjee, Abhishek Tiwari, Mohit Gupta and Anil Kumar Singh

JAIST: A two-phase machine learning approach for identifying discourse relations in newswire texts
Son Nguyen, Quoc Ho and Minh Nguyen

Friday, July 31, 2015 (continued)

The DCU Discourse Parser: A Sense Classification Task
Tsuyoshi Okita, Longyue Wang and Qun Liu

Improving a Pipeline Architecture for Shallow Discourse Parsing
Yangqiu Song, Haoruo Peng, Parisa Kordjamshidi, Mark Sammons and Dan Roth

A Shallow Discourse Parsing System Based On Maximum Entropy Model
Jia Sun, Peijia Li, Weiqun Xu and Yonghong Yan

The DCU Discourse Parser for Connective, Argument Identification and Explicit Sense Classification
Longyue Wang, Chris Hokamp, Tsuyoshi Okita, Xiaojun Zhang and Qun Liu

Hybrid Approach to PDTB-styled Discourse Parsing for CoNLL-2015
Yasuhisa Yoshida, Katsuhiko Hayashi, Tsutomu Hirao and Masaaki Nagata

The CoNLL-2015 Shared Task on Shallow Discourse Parsing

Nianwen Xue* Hwee Tou Ng† Sameer Pradhan‡
Rashmi Prasad◇ Christopher Bryant† Attapol T. Rutherford*
∗ Brandeis University
xuen,tet@brandeis.edu
† National University of Singapore
nght,bryant@comp.nus.edu.sg
‡ Boulder Language Technologies
pradhan@bltek.com
◇ University of Wisconsin-Milwaukee
prasadr@uwm.edu

Abstract

The CoNLL-2015 Shared Task is on Shallow Discourse Parsing, a task focusing on identifying individual discourse relations that are present in a natural language text. A discourse relation can be expressed explicitly or implicitly, and takes two arguments realized as sentences, clauses, or in some rare cases, phrases. Sixteen teams from three continents participated in this task. For the first time in the history of the CoNLL shared tasks, participating teams, instead of running their systems on the test set and submitting the output, were asked to deploy their systems on a remote virtual machine and use a web-based evaluation platform to run their systems on the test set. This meant they were unable to actually see the data set, thus preserving its integrity and ensuring its replicability. In this paper, we present the task definition, the training and test sets, and the evaluation protocol and metric used during this shared task. We also summarize the different approaches adopted by the participating teams, and present the evaluation results. The evaluation data sets and the scorer will serve as a benchmark for future research on shallow discourse parsing.

1 Introduction

The shared task for the Nineteenth Conference on Computational Natural Language Learning (CoNLL-2015) is on *Shallow Discourse Parsing* (SDP). In the course of the sixteen CoNLL shared tasks organized over the past two decades, progressing gradually to tackle phenomena at the word and phrase level phenomena and then the sentence and extra-sentential level, it was only very recently that discourse level processing has been addressed, with coreference resolution (Pradhan et al., 2011; Pradhan et al., 2012). The 2015 shared task takes the community a step further in that direction, with the potential to impact scores of richer language applications (Webber et al., 2012).

Given an English newswire text as input, the goal of the shared task is to detect and categorize discourse relations between discourse segments in the text. Just as there are different grammatical formalisms and representation frameworks in syntactic parsing, there are also different conceptions of the discourse structure of a text, and data sets annotated following these different theoretical frameworks (Stede, 2012; Webber et al., 2012; Prasad and Bunt, 2015). For example, the RST-DT Corpus (Carlson et al., 2003) is based on the Rhetorical Structure Theory of Mann and Thompson (1988) and produces a complete tree-structured RST analysis of a text, whereas the Penn Discourse TreeBank (PDTB) (Prasad et al., 2008; Prasad et al., 2014) provides a shallow representation of discourse structure, in that each discourse relation is annotated independently of other discourse relations, leaving room for a high-level analysis that may attempt to connect them. For the CoNLL-2015 shared task, we chose to use the PDTB, as it is currently the largest data set annotated with discourse relations.[1]

[1] http://www.seas.upenn.edu/~pdtb

Proceedings of the Nineteenth Conference on Computational Natural Language Learning: Shared Task, pages 1–16,
Beijing, China, July 26-31, 2015.

The necessary conditions are also in place for such a task. The release of the RST-DT and PDTB has attracted a significant amount of research on discourse parsing (Pitler et al., 2008; Duverle and Prendinger, 2009; Lin et al., 2009; Pitler et al., 2009; Subba and Di Eugenio, 2009; Zhou et al., 2010; Feng and Hirst, 2012; Ghosh et al., 2012; Park and Cardie, 2012; Wang et al., 2012; Biran and McKeown, 2013; Lan et al., 2013; Feng and Hirst, 2014; Ji and Eisenstein, 2014; Li and Nenkova, 2014; Li et al., 2014; Lin et al., 2014; Rutherford and Xue, 2014), and the momentum is building. Almost all of these recent attempts at discourse parsing use machine learning techniques, which is consistent with the theme of the CoNLL conference. The resurgence of deep learning techniques opens the door for innovative approaches to this problem. A shared task on shallow discourse parsing provides an ideal platform for the community to gain crucial insights on the relative strengths and weaknesses of "standard" feature-based learning techniques and "deep" representation learning techniques.

The rest of this overview paper is structured as follows. In Section 2, we provide a concise definition of the shared task. We describe how the training and test data are prepared in Section 3. In Section 4, we present the evaluation protocol, metric and scorer. The different approaches that participants took in the shared task are summarized in Section 5. In Section 6, we present the ranking of participating systems and analyze the evaluation results. We present our conclusions in Section 7.

2 Task Definition

The goal of the shared task on shallow discourse parsing is to detect and categorize individual discourse relations. Specifically, given a newswire article as input, a participating system is asked to return a set of discourse relations contained in the text. A discourse relation, as defined in the PDTB, from which the training data for the shared task is drawn, is a relation taking two abstract objects (events, states, facts, or propositions) as arguments. Discourse relations may be expressed with explicit connectives like *because*, *however*, *but*, or implicitly inferred between abstract object units. In the current version of the PDTB, non-explicit relations are inferred only between adjacent units. Each discourse relation is labeled with a sense selected from a sense hierarchy, and its arguments are generally in the form of sentences, clauses, or in some rare cases, noun phrases. To detect a discourse relation, a participating system needs to:

1. Identify the text span of an explicit discourse connective, if present;
2. Identify the spans of text that serve as the two arguments for each relation;
3. Label the arguments as (*Arg1* or *Arg2*) to indicate the order of the arguments;
4. Predict the sense of the discourse relation (e.g., "Cause", "Condition", "Contrast").

3 Data

3.1 Training and Development

The training data for the CoNLL-2015 Shared Task was adapted from the Penn Discourse TreeBank 2.0. (PDTB-2.0.) (Prasad et al., 2008; Prasad et al., 2014), annotated over the one million word Wall Street Journal (WSJ) corpus that has also been annotated with syntactic structures (the Penn TreeBank) (Marcus et al., 1993) and propositions (the Proposition Bank) (Palmer et al., 2005). The PDTB annotates discourse relations that hold between eventualities and propositions mentioned in text. Following a lexically grounded approach to annotation, the PDTB annotates relations realized explicitly by discourse connectives drawn from syntactically well-defined classes, as well as implicit relations between adjacent sentences when no explicit connective exists to relate the two. A limited but well-defined set of implicit relations are also annotated within sentences. Arguments of relations are annotated in each case, following the *minimality principle* for selecting all and only the material needed to interpret the relation. For explicit connectives, Arg2, which is defined as the argument with which the connective is syntactically associated, is in the same sentence as the connective (though not necessarily string adjacent), but Arg1, defined simply as the other argument, is unconstrained in terms of its distance from the connective and can be found anywhere in the text (Exs. 1-3). (All the following PDTB examples shown highlight Arg1 (in italics), Arg2 (in boldface), expressions realizing the relation (underlined), sense (in parentheses), and the WSJ file number for the text with the example (in square brackets)).

(1) GM officials want *to get their strategy to reduce capacity and the work force in place* <u>before</u> **those**

talks begin. (Temporal.Asynchronous.Precedence) [wsj_2338]

(2) But that ghost wouldn't settle for words, *he wanted money and people – lots*. So **Mr. Carter formed three new Army divisions and gave them to a new bureaucracy in Tampa called the Rapid Deployment Force**. (Contingency.Cause.Result) [wsj_2112]

(3) Big buyers like Procter & Gamble say *there are other spots on the globe, and in India, where the seed could be grown*. "It's not a crop that can't be doubled or tripled," says Mr. Krishnamurthy. But **no one has made a serious effort to transplant the crop**. (Comparison.Concession.Contra-expectation) [wsj_0515]

Between adjacent sentences unrelated by any explicit connective, four scenarios hold: (a) the sentences may be related by a discourse relation that has no lexical realization, in which case a connective (called an *Implicit* connective) is inserted to express the inferred relation (Ex. 4), (b) the sentences may be related by a discourse relation that is realized by some alternative non-connective expression (called *AltLex*), in which case these alternative lexicalizations are annotated as the carriers of the relation (Ex. 5), (c) the sentences may be related not by a discourse relation realizable by a connective or AltLex, but by an entity-based coherence relation, in which case the presence of such a relation is labeled *EntRel* (Ex 6), and (d) the sentences may not be related at all, in which case they are labeled *NoRel*. Relations annotated in these four scenarios are collectively referred to as *Non-Explicit* relations in this paper.

(4) *The Arabs had merely oil*. Implicit=while **These farmers may have a grip on the world's very heart**. (Comparison.Contrast) [wsj_0515]

(5) *Now, GM appears to be stepping up the pace of its factory consolidation to get in shape for the 1990s*. **One reason is mounting competition from new Japanese car plants in the U.S.** that are pouring out more than one million vehicles a year at costs lower than GM can match. (Contingency.Cause.Reason) [wsj_2338]

(6) *Pierre Vinken, 61 years old, will join the board as a nonexecutive director Nov. 29*. EntRel **Mr. Vinken is chairman of Elsevier N.V., the Dutch publishing group**. [wsj_0001]

In addition to the argument structure of relations, the PDTB provides sense annotation for each discourse relation, capturing the polysemy of connectives. Senses are organized in a three-level hierarchy, with 4 top-level semantic *classes*. For each class, a second level of *types* is defined, and there are 16 such types. There is a third level of *subtype* which provides further refinement to the second level *types*. In the PDTB annotation, annotators are allowed back off to a higher level in the sense hierarchy if they are not certain about a lower level sense. That is, if they cannot distinguish between the subtypes under a type sense, they can just annotate the type level sense, and if there is further uncertainty in choosing among the types under a class sense, they can just annotate the class level sense. Most of the discourse relation instances in the PDTB are annotated with at least a type level sense, but there are also a small number annotated with only a class level sense.

The PDTB also provides annotations of attribution over all discourse relations and each of their arguments, as well as of text spans considered as supplementary to arguments of relations. However, both of these annotation types are excluded from the shared task.

PDTB-2.0. contains annotations of 40,600 discourse relations, distributed into the following five types: 18,459 Explicit relations, 16,053 Implicit relations, 624 AltLex relations, 5,210 EntRel relations, and 254 NoRel relations. We provide Sections 2–21 of the PDTB 2.0 release as the training set, and Section 22 as the development set.

3.2 Test Data

We provide two test sets for the shared task: Section 23 of the PDTB, and a blind test set we prepared especially for the shared task. The official ranking of the systems is based on their performance on the *blind test set*. In this section, we provide a detailed description of how the blind test set was prepared.

3.2.1 Data Selection and Post-processing

For the blind test data, 30,158 words of untokenized English newswire texts were selected from a dump of English Wikinews[2], accessed 22nd October 2014, and annotated in accordance with PDTB 2.0 guidelines.

The raw Wikinews data was pre-processed as follows:

- News articles were extracted from the Wikinews XML dump[3] using the publicly available WikiExtractor.py script.[4]

[2] https://en.wikinews.org/

[3] https://dumps.wikimedia.org/enwikinews/20141119/enwikinews-20141119-pages-articles.xml.bz2

[4] http://medialab.di.unipi.it/wiki/Wikipedia_Extractor

- Additional processing was done to remove any remaining XML information and produce a raw text version of each article (including its title).
- All paragraphs were double spaced to ease paragraph boundary identification.
- Each article was named according to its unique Wikinews ID such that it is accessible online at `http://en.wikinews.org/wiki?curid=ID`.

Initially, 30k words of text were selected from this processed data at random. However, it soon became apparent that some texts were too short for PDTB-style annotation or otherwise still contained remnant XML errors. Another issue was that since Wikinews texts are written by members of the public, rather than professionally trained journalists, some articles were considered as not up to the same standards of spelling and grammar as the WSJ texts in the PDTB.

For these reasons, despite making the decision to allow the correction of extremely minor errors (such as obvious typos and occasional article or preposition errors), just under half of the original 30k word random selection was ultimately deemed unsuitable for annotation. Consequently, the remaining texts were selected manually from Wikinews, with a slight preference for longer articles with many multi-sentence paragraphs that are more consistent with WSJ-style texts.

3.2.2 Annotations

Annotation of the blind test set was carried out by two of the shared task organizers, one of whom (fifth author) was the main annotator (MA) while the other (fourth author), a lead developer of the PDTB, acted as the reviewing annotator (RA), reviewing each relation annotated by the MA and recording agreement or disagreement. Annotation involved marking the relation type (Explicit, Implicit, AltLex, EntRel, NoRel), relation realization (explicit connective, implicit connective, AltLex expression), arguments (Arg1 and Arg2), and sense of a discourse relation, using the PDTB annotation tool.[5] Unlike the PDTB guidelines, we did not allow back-off to the top class level during annotation. Every relation was annotated with a sense chosen from at least the second type level.

[5] `https://www.seas.upenn.edu/~pdtb/tools.shtml#annotator`

Also different from the PDTB, attribution spans or attribution features were not annotated.

Before commencing official annotation, MA was trained in PDTB-2.0. style annotation by RA. A review of the guidelines was followed by double blind annotation (by MA and RA) of a small number of WSJ texts not previously annotated in the PDTB, and differences were then compared and discussed. MA then also underwent self-training by first annotating some WSJ texts that were already annotated in the PDTB, and then comparing these annotations, to further strengthen knowledge of the guidelines.

After the training period, the entire blind test data was annotated by MA over a period of a few weeks, and then reviewed by RA. Disagreements during the review were manually recorded using a formal scheme addressing all aspects of the annotation, including relation type, explicit connective identification, senses, and each of the arguments. This was done to verify the integrity of the blind test data and keep a record of any confusion or difficulty encountered during annotation. Manual entry of disagreements was done within the tool interface, through its commenting feature. A recorded comment in the tool is unique to a relation token and is recorded in a stand-off style. Disagreements were later resolved by consensus between MA and RA.

3.2.3 Inter-annotator Agreement

The record of disagreements was utilized to compute inter-annotator agreement between MA and RA. The overall agreement was 76.5%, which represents the percentage of relations on which there was complete agreement. Agreement on explicit connective identification was 96.0%, representing the percentage of explicit connectives that both MA and RA identified as discourse connectives. We note here that if a connective was identified in the blind test data, but was not annotated in the PDTB despite its occurrence in the WSJ (e.g.,"after which time", "despite"), we did not consider it a potential connective and hence did not include it in the agreement calculation. When the textual context allowed it, such expressions were instead marked as AltLex.

We also did a more fine-grained assessment to determine agreement on Arg1, Arg2, Arg1+Arg2 (i.e., the number of relations on which the annotators agreed on both Arg1 and Arg2), and senses. This was done for all the relation types considered together, as well as for Explicit and Non-Explicit relation types separately. Sense disagreement was computed using the CoNLL sense classification scheme (see Section 3.3), even though the annotation was done using the full PDTB sense classification scheme (see Table 2). The agreement percentages are shown in Table 1. When multiple senses were provided for a relation, a disagreement on any of the senses was counted as disagreement for the relation; disagreement on more than one of the senses was counted only once. Absence of a second sense by one annotator when the other did provide one was also counted as disagreement.

As the table shows, agreement on senses was reasonably high overall (85.5%), with agreement for Explicit relations expectedly higher (91.0%) than for Non-Explicit relations (80.9%). Overall agreement on arguments was also high, but in contrast to the senses, agreement was generally higher for the Non-Explicit than for Explicit relations. Agreement on the Arg1 of Explicit relations (89.6%) is, not surprisingly, lower than for Arg2 (98.7%), because the Arg1 of Explicit relations can be non-adjacent to the connective's sentence or clause, and thus, harder to identify. For the Non-Explicit relations, in contrast, but again to be expected, because of the argument adjacency constraint for such relations, agreement on Arg1 (95.0%) and Arg2 (96.4%) shows minimal difference. Table 1 also provides the percentage of relations with agreement on both Arg1 and Arg2, showing this to be higher for Non-Explicit relations (92.4%) than for Explicit relations (88.7%).

Compared to the agreement reported for the PDTB (Prasad et al., 2008; Miltsakaki et al., 2004), the results obtained here (See Table 1) are slightly better. PDTB agreement on Arg1 and Arg2 of Explicit relations is reported to be 86.3% and 94.1%, respectively, whereas overall agreement on arguments of Non-Explicit relations is 85.1%. For the senses, although the CoNLL senses do not exactly align with the PDTB senses, a rough correspondence can be assumed between the CoNLL classification as a whole and the type and subtype levels of the PDTB classification, for which PDTB reports 84% and 80%, respectively.

3.3 Adapting the PDTB Annotation for the shared task

The discourse relations annotated in the PDTB have many different elements, and it is impractical to predict all of them in the context of a shared task where participants have a relatively short time frame in which to complete the task. As a result, we had to make a number of exclusions and simplifications, which we describe below.

The core elements of a discourse relation are the two abstract objects as its arguments. In addition to this, some discourse relations include supplementary information that is relevant but not necessary (as per the minimality principle) to the interpretation of a discourse relation. Supplementary information is associated with arguments, and optionally marked with the labels "Sup1", for material supplementary to Arg1, and "Sup2", for material supplementary to Arg2. An example of a Sup1 annotation is shown in (7). In the shared task, supplementary information is excluded from evaluation when computing argument spans.

(7) ($_{Sup1}$ Average maturity was as short as 29 days at the start of this year), *when short-term interest rates were moving steadily upward.* Implicit=for example **The average seven-day compound yield of the funds reached 9.62% in late April** . (Expansion.Instantiation) [wsj_0982]

Also excluded from evaluation, to make the shared task manageable, are attribution relations annotated in PDTB. An example of an explicit attribution is "he says" in (8), marked over Arg1.

(8) When **Mr. Green won a $240,000 verdict in a land condemnation case against the state in June 1983** , he says *Judge O'Kicki unexpectedly awarded him an additional $100,000* (Temporal.Synchrony) [wsj_0267]

The PDTB senses form a hierarchical system of three levels, consisting of 4 *classes*, 16 *types*, and 23 *subtypes*. While all classes are divided into multiple types, some types do not have subtypes. Previous work on PDTB sense classification has mostly focused on classes (Pitler et al., 2009; Zhou et al., 2010; Park and Cardie, 2012; Biran and McKeown, 2013; Li and Nenkova, 2014; Rutherford and Xue, 2014). The senses that are the target of prediction in the CoNLL-2015 shared task are primarily based on the second-level types and a selected number of third-level subtypes. We made a few modifications to make the distinctions clearer and their distributions more balanced, and these changes are presented in Table 2. First, senses in the PDTB that have distinctions that are too subtle and thus too difficult to predict are collapsed.

	Arg1 agr	Arg2 agr	Arg1+Arg2 agr	Sense agr
Explicit	89.6%	98.7%	88.7%	91.0%
Non-Explicit	95.0%	96.4%	92.4%	80.9%
Total	92.5%	97.4%	90.7%	85.5%

Table 1: Inter-annotator agreement on blind test data annotation in various conditions.

CoNLL senses	**PDTB senses**
Temporal.Synchronous	same
Temporal.Asynchronous.Precedence	same
Temporal.Asynchronous.Succession	same
∗ Contingency.Cause.Reason	Contingency.Cause.Reason + Contingency.Pragmatic cause
Contingency.Cause.Result	same
∗ Contingency.Condition	Contingency.Condition + Contingency.Pragmatic condition + Subtypes of Contingency.Condition + Subtypes of Contingency.Pragmatic Condition
∗ Comparison.Contrast	Comparison.Contrast + Comparison.Pragmatic contrast + Subtypes of Comparison.Contrast
∗ Comparison.Concession	Comparison.Concession + Comparison.Pragmatic concession + Subtypes of Comparison.Concession
∗ Expansion.Conjunction	Expansion.Conjunction + Expansion.List
Expansion.Instantiation	same
∗Expansion.Restatement	Expansion.Restatement + Subtypes of Expansion.Restatement
∗ Expansion.Alternative	Expansion.Alternative.Conjunctive + Expansion.Alternative.Disjunctive
Expansion.Alternative.Chosen alternative	same
Expansion.Exception	same
EntRel	same

Table 2: Flat list of 15 sense categories used in CoNLL-2015, with correspondences to PDTB senses. Senses that involve a change from the PDTB senses are marked ∗.

For example, "Contingency.Pragmatic cause" is merged into "Contingency.Cause.Reason", and "Contingency.Pragmatic condition" is merged into "Contingency.Condition". Second, the distinction between "Expansion.Conjunction" and "Expansion.List" is not clear in the PDTB and in fact, they seem very similar for the most part, so the latter is merged into the former. Third, while "Expansion.Alternative.Conjunctive" and "Expansion.Alternative.Disjunctive" are merged into "Expansion.Alternative", a third subtype of "Expansion.Alternative", "Expansion.Alternative.Chosen Alternative" is kept as a separate category as its meaning involves more than presentation of alternatives. Finally, while "EntRel" relations are not treated as discourse relations in the PDTB, we have included this category as a sense for sense classification since they are a kind of coherence relation and we require systems to label these relations in the shared task. In contrast, instances annotated with "NoRel" are not treated as discourse relations and are excluded from the training, development and test data sets. This means that a system needs to treat them as negative samples and *not* identify them as discourse relations. These changes have resulted in a *flat* list of 15 sense categories that need to be predicted in the shared task. A comparison of the PDTB senses and the senses used in the CoNLL shared task is presented in Table 2.

Relation	Sense	WSJ-Train	WSJ-Dev	WSJ-Test
Explicit	**Overall**	14722	680	923
	Expansion.Conjunction	4323	185	242
	Comparison.Contrast	2956	160	271
	Contingency.Condition	1148	50	63
	Temporal.Synchrony	1133	68	71
	Comparison.Concession	1080	12	27
	Contingency.Cause.Reason	943	38	74
	Temporal.Asynchronous.Succession	842	51	64
	Temporal.Asynchronous.Precedence	770	49	36
	Contingency.Cause.Result	487	19	38
	Comparison	347	20	1
	Expansion.Instantiation	236	9	21
	Expansion.Alternative	195	6	5
	Expansion.Restatement	121	6	7
	Expansion.Alternative.Chosen-alternative	96	6	3
	Expansion	24	0	0
	Expansion.Exception	13	0	0
	Temporal	4	1	0
	Temporal.Asynchronous	3	0	0
	Contingency	1	0	0
Implicit	**Overall**	13156	522	769
	Expansion.Conjunction	3227	120	141
	Expansion.Restatement	2486	101	190
	Contingency.Cause.Reason	2059	73	113
	Comparison.Contrast	1614	82	127
	Contingency.Cause.Result	1372	49	89
	Expansion.Instantiation	1132	47	69
	Temporal.Asynchronous.Precedence	418	25	7
	Comparison.Concession	193	5	5
	Temporal.Synchrony	153	8	5
	Comparison	145	1	0
	Expansion.Alternative.Chosen-alternative	142	2	15
	Temporal.Asynchronous.Succession	125	3	5
	Expansion	73	6	3
	Expansion.Alternative	11	0	0
	Contingency.Condition	2	0	0
	Temporal	1	0	0
	Expansion.Exception	1	0	0
	Contingency.Cause	1	0	0
	Contingency	1	0	0
EntRel	**Overall**	4133	215	217
	EntRel	4133	215	217
AltLex	**Overall**	524	19	19
	Contingency.Cause.Result	147	4	8
	Expansion.Conjunction	94	3	8
	Contingency.Cause.Reason	76	5	8
	Expansion.Restatement	57	0	1
	Temporal.Asynchronous.Precedence	42	2	2
	Expansion.Instantiation	33	1	1
	Comparison.Contrast	32	2	1
	Temporal.Asynchronous.Succession	18	0	0
	Temporal.Synchrony	16	1	0
	Comparison.Concession	4	0	1
	Expansion	2	0	0
	Contingency.Condition	2	0	0
	Expansion.Exception	1	0	0
	Expansion.Restatement	0	1	0
	Expansion.Alternative	0	0	0

Table 3: Distribution of senses across the four relation types in the WSJ PDTB data used for the shared task. The total numbers of the relations here are less than in the complete PDTB release because some sections (00, 01, and 24) are excluded for the shared task, following standard split of WSJ data in the evaluation community. We are intentionally withholding distribution over the blind test set in case there is a repeat of the SDP shared task using the same test set.

Table 3 shows the distribution of the senses across the four discourse relations within the WSJ PDTB data[6]. We are intentionally withholding the sense distribution across the blind test set in case there is a repeat of the SDP shared task using the same test set.

4 Evaluation

4.1 Closed and open tracks

In keeping with the CoNLL shared task tradition, participating systems were evaluated in two tracks, a *closed* track and an *open* track. A participating system in the closed track could only use the provided PDTB training set but was allowed to process the data using any publicly available (i.e., non-proprietary) natural language processing tools such as syntactic parsers and semantic role labelers. In contrast, in the open track, a participating system could not only use any publicly available NLP tools to process the data, but also any publicly available (i.e., non-proprietary) data for training. A participating team could choose to participate in the closed track or the open track, or both.

The motivation for having two tracks in CoNLL shared tasks was to isolate the contribution of algorithms and resources to a particular task. In the closed track, the resources are held constant so that the advantages of different algorithms and models can be more meaningfully compared. In the open track, the focus of the evaluation is on the overall performance and the use of all possible means to improve the performance of a task. This distinction was easier to maintain for early CoNLL tasks such as noun phrase chunking and named entity recognition, where competitive performance could be achieved without having to use resources other than the provided training set. However, this is no longer true for a high-level task like discourse parsing where external resources such as Brown clusters have proved to be useful (Rutherford and Xue, 2014). In addition, to be competitive in the discourse parsing task, one also has to process the data with syntactic and possibly semantic parsers, which may also be trained on data that is outside the training set. As a compromise, therefore, we allowed participants to use the following linguistic resources in the closed track, other than the training set:

- Brown clusters
- VerbNet
- Sentiment lexicon
- Word embeddings (word2vec)

To make the task more manageable for participants, we provided them with training and test data with the following layers of automatic linguistic annotation processed with state-of-the-art NLP tools:

- Phrase structure parses (predicted using the Berkeley parser (Petrov and Klein, 2007))
- Dependency parses (converted from phrase structure parses using the Stanford converter (Manning et al., 2014))

As it turned out, all of the teams this year chose to participate in the closed track.

4.2 Evaluation Platform: TIRA

We use a new web service called TIRA as the platform for system evaluation (Gollub et al., 2012; Potthast et al., 2014). Traditionally, participating teams were asked to manually run their system on the blind test set without the gold standard labels, and submit the output for evaluation. This year, however, we shifted this evaluation paradigm, asking participants to deploy their systems on a remote virtual machine, and to use the TIRA web platform (tira.io) to run their systems on the test sets without actually seeing the test sets. The organizers would then inspect the evaluation results, and verify that participating systems yielded acceptable output.

This evaluation protocol allowed us to maintain the integrity of the blind test set and reduce the organizational overhead. On TIRA, the blind test set can only be accessed in the evaluation environment, and the evaluation results are automatically collected. Participants cannot see any part of the test sets and hence cannot do iterative development based on the test set performance, which preserves the integrity of the evaluation. Most importantly, this evaluation platform promotes replicability, which is very crucial for proper evaluation of scientific progress. Reproducing all of the results is just a matter of a button click on TIRA. All of the results presented in this paper, along with the trained models and the software,

[6] There is a small number of instances in the PDTB training set that are only annotated with the class level sense. We did not take them out of the training set for the sake of completeness.

are archived and available for distribution upon request to the organizers and upon the permission of the participating team, who holds the copyrights to the software. Replicability also helps speed up the research and development in discourse parsing. Anyone wanting to extend or apply any of the approaches proposed by a shared task participant does not have to re-implement the model from scratch. They can request a clone of the virtual machine where the participating system is deployed, and then implement their extension based off the original source code. Any extension effort also benefits from the precise evaluation of the progress and improvement since the system is based off the exact same implementation.

4.3 Evaluation metrics and scorer

A shallow discourse parser is evaluated based on the end-to-end F_1 score on a per-discourse relation basis. The input to the system consists of documents with gold-standard word tokens along with their automatic parses. We do not pre-identify the discourse connectives or any other elements of the discourse annotation. The shallow discourse parser must output a list of discourse relations that consist of the argument spans and their labels, explicit discourse connectives where applicable, and the senses. The F_1 score is computed based on the number of predicted relations that match a gold standard relation exactly. A relation is correctly predicted if (a) the discourse connective is correctly detected (for Explicit discourse relations), (b) the sense of the discourse connective is correctly predicted, and (c) the text spans of its two arguments are correctly predicted (Arg1 and Arg2).

Although the submissions are ranked based on the relation F_1 score, the scorer also provides component-wise evaluation with error propagation. The scorer computes the precision, recall, and F_1 for the following[7]:

- Explicit discourse connective identification.
- Arg1 identification.
- Arg2 identification.
- Arg1 and Arg2 identification.
- Sense classification with error propagation from discourse connective and argument identification.

For purposes of evaluation, an explicit discourse connective predicted by the parser is considered correct if and only if the predicted raw connective includes the gold raw connective head, while allowing for the tokens of the predicted connective to be a subset of the tokens in the gold raw connective. We provide a function that maps discourse connectives to their corresponding heads. The notion of discourse connective head is not the same as its syntactic head. Rather, it is thought of as the part of the connective conveying its core meaning. For example, the head of the discourse connective "At least not when" is "when", and the head of "five minutes before" is "before". The non-head part of the connective serves to semantically restrict the interpretation of the connective.

Although Implicit discourse relations are annotated with an implicit connective inserted between adjacent sentences, participants are not required to provide the inserted connective. They only need to output the sense of the discourse relation. Similarly, for AltLex relations, which are also annotated between adjacent sentences, participants are not required to output the text span of the AltLex expression, but only the sense. The EntRel relation is included as a sense in the shared task, and here, systems are required to correctly label the EntRel relation between adjacent sentence pairs.

An argument is considered correctly identified if and only if it matches the corresponding gold standard argument span exactly, and is also correctly labeled (Arg1 or Arg2). Systems are not given any credit for partial match on argument spans.

Sense classification evaluation is less straightforward, since senses are sometimes annotated partially or annotated with two senses. To be considered correct, the predicted sense for a relation must match one of the two senses if there is more than one sense. If the gold standard is partially annotated, the sense must match with the partially annotated sense.

Additionally, the scorer provides a breakdown of the discourse parser performance for Explicit and Non-Explicit discourse relations.

5 Approaches

The Shallow Discourse Parsing (SDP) task this year requires the development of an end-to-end system that potentially involves many components. All participating systems adopt some variation of the pipeline architecture proposed by Lin et al (2014), which has components for identify-

[7] Available at: `http://www.github.com/attapol/conll15st`

System	learning methods	resources used	extra resources
ECNU	Naive Bayes, maxent	Brown clusters, MPQA subjectivity lexicon	no
Trento	CRF++, AdaBoost	Brown clusters, dependency/phrase structure parses	no
Soochow	Maxent in Open NLP	VerbNet, MPQA subjectivity lexicon, Brown clusters	no
JAIST	CRF++, LibSVM (SMO)	syntactic parses, Brown clusters	no
UIUC	Liblinear	Brown clusters, MPQA lexicon	no
Concordia	C4.5 (Weka)	ClearTK, syntactic parse	no
∗UT Dallas	-	-	-
NTT	Rule-based argument extraction and SVM based sense classification	Brown clusters, dependency trees	no
AU KBC	CRF++ for both arguments and sense, and rules	MPQA, VerbNet, Brown clusters	no
CAS	OpenNLP maxent	phrase structure trees	no
Dublin 1	RNN (Theano) for argument extraction, Maxent for others	syntactic features, skip-gram word embeddings	no
Dublin 2	LibSVM, Theano, word2vec	Brown clusters	no
Goethe University Frankfurt	SVM, rule-based	Brown clusters, word embeddings	no
IIT	Naive Bayes, Maxent	syntactic parses, Boxer	no
SJTU	Maxent	no external resource used	no
∗PKU	-	-	-

Table 4: Approaches of participating systems. Teams that have not submitted a system description paper are marked with ∗.

ing discourse connectives and extracting their arguments, for determining the presence or absence of discourse relations in a particular context, and for predicting the senses of the discourse relations. Most participating systems cast discourse connective identification and argument extraction as token-level sequence labeling tasks, while a few systems use rule-based approaches to extract the arguments. Sense determination is cast as a straightforward multi-category classification task. Most systems use machine learning techniques to determine the senses, but there are also systems that, due to lack of time, adopt a simple baseline approach that detects the most frequent sense based on the training data.

In terms of learning techniques, all participating systems except the two systems submitted by the Dublin team use standard "shallow" learning models that take binary features as input. For sequence labeling subtasks such as discourse connective identification and argument extraction, the preferred learning method is Conditional Random Fields (CRF). For sense determination, a variety of learning methods have been used, including Maximum Entropy, Support Vector Machines, and decision trees. In the last couple of years, neural networks have experienced a resurgence and have been shown to be effective in many natural language processing tasks. Neural network based models on discourse parsing have also started to appear (Ji and Eisenstein, 2014). The use of neural networks for the SDP task this year represents a minority, presumably because researchers are still less familiar with neural network based techniques, compared with standard "shallow" learning techniques, and it is difficult to use a new learning technique to good effect within a short time window. In this shared task, only the Dublin University team attempted to use neural networks as a learning approach in their system components. In their first submission (Dublin I), Recurrent Neural Networks (RNN) are used for token level sequence labeling in the argument extraction task. In their second submission, paragraph embeddings are used in a neural network model to determine the senses of discourse relations.

The discussion of learning techniques cannot be entirely separated from the use of features and the linguistic resources that are used to extract them. Standard "shallow" architectures typically make use of discrete features while neural networks generally use continuous real-valued features such as word and paragraph embeddings. For discourse connective and argument extraction, token level features extracted from a fixed window centered on the target word token are generally used, and so are features extracted from syntactic parses. Distributional representations such as Brown clusters have generally been used to determine the senses (Chiarcos and Schenk, 2015; Devi et al., 2015; Kong et al., 2015; Song et al., 2015; Stepanov et al., 2015; Wang and Lan, 2015; Wang et al., 2015; Yoshida et al., 2015), although one team also used them in the sequence labeling task for argument extraction (Nguyen et al., 2015). Additional resources used by some systems for sense determination include word embeddings (Chiarcos and Schenk, 2015; Wang et al., 2015), VerbNet classes (Devi et al., 2015; Kong et al., 2015), and the MPQA polarity lexicon (Devi et al., 2015; Kong et al., 2015; Wang and Lan, 2015). Table 4 provides a summary of the different approaches.

6 Results

Table 5 shows the performance of all participating systems across the three test evaluation sets: i) (Official) Blind test set; ii) Standard WSJ test set; iii) Standard WSJ development set. The official rankings are based on the blind test set annotated specifically for this shared task. The top-ranked system is the submission by East China Normal University (Wang and Lan, 2015). As discussed in Section 4, the evaluation metric is very strict, and is based on exact match for the extraction of argument spans. For the detection of discourse connectives, only the head of a discourse connective has to be correctly detected. Errors in the beginning of the pipeline will propagate to the end, and other than word tokenization, all input to the participating systems is automatically generated, so the overall accuracy reflects results in realistic situations. The scores are very low, with the top system achieving an overall parsing score of 24.00% (F1) on the blind test set and 29.69% (F1) on the Wall Street Journal (WSJ) test set. For comparison purposes, the National University of Singapore team re-implemented the state-of-the-art end-to-end parser described in (Lin et al., 2014), and this system achieves an F1 of 19.98% on the WSJ test set. This shows that a fair amount of progress has been made against the Lin et al baseline.

The rankings are generally consistent across the two test sets, with the largest change in ranking from the NTT team and the Goethe University team. This is perhaps not a coincidence: both teams used rule-based approaches to extract arguments. The rules worked well on the WSJ test set which draws from the same source as the development set, but might not adapt well to the blind test set, which is drawn from a different source. Machine-learning based approaches generally can better adapt to new data sets.

Due to the short time frame participants had to complete an end-to-end task, teams chose to focus on either argument extraction components or the sense classification components, or in the case of sense classification, either focus on the classification of senses for Explicit relations or senses for Non-Explicit relations. A detailed breakdown of the performance for Explicit versus Non-Explicit discourse relations is presented in Table 6. In general, parser performance for Explicit discourse relations is much higher than that of Non-Explicit discourse relations. The difficulty for Non-Explicit discourse relations mostly stems from Non-Explicit sense classification. This is evidenced by the fact that even for systems that achieve higher argument extraction accuracy for Non-Explicit discourse relations than Explicit discourse relations, the overall parser accuracy is still lower for Non-Explicit relations. The lower accuracy in sense classification thus drags down the overall parser accuracy for Non-Explicit discourse relations.

7 Conclusions

Sixteen teams from three continents participated in the CoNLL-2015 Shared Task on shallow dis-

Rank		Participant		Argument			Connective			Parser		
O	**L**	**Organization**	**ID**	**F**	**P**	**R**	**F**	**P**	**R**	**F**	**P**	**R**
				Blind Test								
1	1	East China Normal University	wangj	46.37	45.77	46.98	91.86	93.48	90.29	24.00	23.69	24.32
2	2	University of Trento	stepanov	38.86	37.25	40.61	89.92	92.57	87.41	21.84	20.94	22.83
3	3	Soochow University	kong	33.23	35.57	31.18	91.62	92.80	90.47	18.51	19.81	17.37
4	4	Japan Advanced Institute of Science and Tech.	nguyen	32.11	42.72	25.72	61.66	88.55	47.30	18.28	24.31	14.64
5	5	UIUC Cognitive Computing Group	song	41.31	40.48	42.18	87.98	89.11	86.87	17.98	17.62	18.36
6	6	Concordia University	laali	23.29	35.67	17.29	90.19	87.88	92.63	17.38	26.62	12.90
7	7	University of Texas Dallas	xue	30.22	31.70	28.87	89.90	92.73	87.23	17.06	17.89	16.29
8	8	Nippon Telegraph and Telephone Lab Japan	yoshida	35.55	52.16	26.96	51.04	92.45	35.25	15.70	23.04	11.91
9	9	AU KBC Research Center	devi	33.17	35.12	31.43	84.49	92.32	77.88	15.02	15.90	14.23
10	10	Chinese Academy of Sciences	xu15	21.95	28.88	17.70	82.60	93.02	74.28	12.62	16.60	10.17
11	11	Dublin City University 1	wangl	22.09	19.26	25.89	79.43	84.87	74.64	11.15	9.72	13.07
12	12	Dublin City University 2	okita	21.52	18.77	25.23	79.43	84.87	74.64	10.66	9.29	12.49
13	13	Goethe University Frankfurt	chiarcos	29.21	26.00	33.33	51.18	59.38	44.96	9.13	8.13	10.42
14	14	India Institute of Tech.	mukherjee	21.71	18.14	27.05	89.30	91.67	87.05	7.64	6.38	9.51
15	15	Shanghai Jiao Tong University 1	chen	4.70	4.53	4.88	81.68	81.17	82.19	3.58	3.46	3.72
16	16	Peking University	xu15b	12.70	10.54	15.96	59.11	58.69	59.53	0.92	0.76	1.16
				Standard WSJ Test (Section 23)								
1	1	East China Normal University	wangj	49.42	48.72	50.13	94.21	94.94	93.50	29.69	29.27	30.12
2	2	University of Trento	stepanov	40.71	39.71	41.77	92.77	93.80	91.77	25.33	24.71	25.99
8	3	Nippon Telegraph and Telephone Lab Japan	yoshida	43.77	48.83	39.66	89.12	91.84	86.57	24.99	27.87	22.64
7	4	University of Texas Dallas	xue	30.26	31.78	28.88	89.33	91.20	87.54	21.72	22.81	20.73
6	5	Concordia University	laali	24.81	36.98	18.67	91.38	88.76	94.15	21.25	31.66	15.99
3	6	Soochow University	kong	37.01	34.69	39.66	94.77	95.39	94.15	20.64	19.35	22.12
5	7	UIUC Cognitive Computing Group	song	38.18	35.73	41.00	91.83	92.33	91.33	20.27	18.97	21.76
4	8	Japan Advanced Institute of Science and Tech.	nguyen	35.43	52.98	26.61	63.89	91.87	48.97	20.25	30.29	15.21
13	9	Goethe University Frankfurt	chiarcos	36.78	36.58	36.98	68.19	71.96	64.79	15.23	15.15	15.32
10	10	Chinese Academy of Sciences	xu15	23.36	28.05	20.01	90.64	95.12	86.57	15.05	18.08	12.89
9	11	AU KBC Research Center	devi	31.26	31.76	30.79	86.44	94.36	79.74	14.61	14.84	14.39
11	12	Dublin City University 1	wangl	25.46	21.74	30.74	87.99	90.40	85.70	12.73	10.87	15.37
12	13	Dublin City University 2	okita	24.55	20.95	29.65	88.06	90.32	85.92	12.30	10.49	14.85
14	14	India Institute of Tech.	mukherjee	22.52	18.19	29.55	93.06	93.93	92.20	7.15	5.78	9.39
15	15	Shanghai Jiao Tong University 1	chen	4.57	4.24	4.95	78.67	77.84	79.52	4.43	4.11	4.80
16	16	Peking University	xu15b	13.24	10.65	17.48	58.04	57.28	58.83	2.11	1.70	2.78
				Development								
1	1	East China Normal University	wangj	57.21	56.84	57.59	95.14	95.28	95.00	37.84	37.59	38.09
8	2	Nippon Telegraph and Telephone Lab Japan	yoshida	51.42	56.56	47.14	88.94	92.39	85.74	31.60	34.75	28.97
2	3	University of Trento	stepanov	45.34	44.99	45.68	93.79	94.35	93.24	30.27	30.04	30.50
3	4	Soochow University	kong	43.12	41.06	45.40	94.22	94.93	93.53	26.32	25.06	27.72
4	5	Japan Advanced Institute of Science and Tech.	nguyen	40.07	58.92	30.36	65.53	91.56	51.03	26.10	38.38	19.78
9	6	AU KBC Research Center	devi	42.96	42.28	43.66	92.63	98.03	87.79	25.76	25.35	26.18
6	7	Concordia University	laali	29.87	44.43	22.49	92.25	89.27	95.44	25.71	38.24	19.36
5	8	UIUC Cognitive Computing Group	song	43.44	41.24	45.89	91.45	93.27	89.71	25.12	23.84	26.53
7	9	University of Texas Dallas	xue	35.78	37.77	33.98	93.43	94.85	92.06	24.19	25.54	22.98
10	10	Chinese Academy of Sciences	xu15	26.68	32.06	22.84	91.52	95.23	88.09	18.14	21.80	15.53
13	11	Goethe University Frankfurt	chiarcos	41.58	42.08	41.09	63.17	67.45	59.41	17.12	17.33	16.92
11	12	Dublin City University 1	wangl	29.75	25.59	35.52	85.65	90.10	81.62	16.51	14.20	19.71
12	13	Dublin City University 2	okita	29.09	24.98	34.82	86.33	90.35	82.65	15.36	13.19	18.38
14	14	India Institute of Technology	mukherjee	26.78	21.89	34.47	93.55	95.41	91.76	8.82	7.21	11.35
15	15	Shanghai Jiao Tong University 1	chen	6.81	6.43	7.24	86.09	85.28	86.91	6.55	6.18	6.96
16	16	Peking University	xu15b	12.64	9.00	21.24	51.54	42.64	65.15	1.49	1.06	2.51

Table 5: Scoreboard for the CoNLL-2015 shared task showing performance across the tasks and the three data partitions—blind test, standard test (WSJ-23) and development. The Column **O** and **L** refer to official and local ranks. The red highlighted rows indicate a system (JAIST) that performed poorly on the WSJ test set, but did much better on the blind test set. The blue highlighted rows indicate the opposite phenomena for a system (NTT) that ranked higher on the WSJ development and test partitions, but dropped in rank on the blind test set.

Rank			Participant		Explicit					Non-Explicit			
O	**E**	**I**	**Organization**	**ID**	**A12**	**A1**	**A2**	**Conn.**	**Parser**	**A12**	**A1**	**A2**	**Parser**
				Blind Test									
7	1	11	University of Texas Dallas	xue	40.04	49.68	70.06	89.90	30.58	21.61	25.02	34.77	5.20
1	2	1	East China Normal University	wangj	41.35	48.31	74.29	91.86	30.38	50.41	60.87	74.58	18.87
2	3	2	University of Trento	stepanov	39.59	49.03	70.68	89.92	29.97	38.31	43.29	56.57	15.77
6	4	15	Concordia University	laali	36.60	45.18	69.18	90.19	27.32	0.00	0.00	0.00	0.00
4	5	8	Japan Advanced Institute of Science and Tech.	nguyen	34.23	44.08	51.35	61.66	27.20	30.44	36.90	46.13	11.25
9	6	10	AU KBC Research Center	devi	34.73	44.49	64.20	84.49	26.73	31.91	35.70	46.60	5.53
5	7	5	UIUC Cognitive Computing Group	song	30.05	37.89	60.11	87.98	23.32	50.18	59.52	74.40	13.57
3	8	4	Soochow University	kong	30.42	36.43	73.04	91.62	22.95	35.87	49.87	51.07	14.35
10	9	13	Chinese Academy of Sciences	xu15	27.20	36.40	61.00	82.60	22.20	16.42	19.79	27.16	2.53
8	10	3	Nippon Telegraph and Telephone Lab Japan	yoshida	21.61	28.13	38.02	51.04	16.93	45.59	53.66	62.29	14.82
13	11	9	Goethe University Frankfurt	chiarcos	19.04	26.41	36.85	51.18	13.51	34.79	44.33	53.54	6.73
14	12	12	India Institute of Technology	mukherjee	13.65	22.32	61.99	89.30	12.36	26.24	37.03	41.49	4.98
11	13	6	Dublin City University 1	wangl	12.47	18.05	36.65	87.81	9.12	27.84	39.46	44.27	12.74
15	14	16	Shanghai Jiao Tong University 1	chen	10.55	13.94	48.97	81.68	8.04				0.00
12	15	7	Dublin City University 2	okita	11.10	16.65	28.13	79.43	7.85	27.61	39.24	44.05	12.30
16	16	14	Peking University	xu15b	3.57	6.07	20.89	59.11	2.32	18.02	26.46	28.85	0.10
				Standard WSJ Test (Section 23)									
1	1	1	East China Normal University	wangj	45.20	50.66	77.40	94.21	39.96	53.09	67.17	68.41	20.74
2	2	5	University of Trento	stepanov	44.58	50.05	76.23	92.77	39.54	37.44	44.50	47.56	13.28
7	3	10	University of Texas Dallas	xue	41.57	49.75	68.55	89.33	37.59	19.45	24.74	25.37	6.55
8	4	3	Nippon Telegraph and Telephone Lab Japan	yoshida	38.82	46.07	68.38	89.12	34.47	48.81	57.99	60.08	15.11
4	5	9	Japan Advanced Institute of Science and Tech.	nguyen	38.16	43.82	56.25	63.89	33.22	32.44	38.85	38.85	8.01
6	6	15	Concordia University	laali	38.07	44.69	72.34	91.38	32.60	0.00	0.00	0.00	0.00
5	7	4	UIUC Cognitive Computing Group	song	30.39	37.25	66.67	91.83	27.02	44.33	57.13	60.14	14.95
9	8	11	AU KBC Research Center	devi	30.77	36.64	49.68	86.44	26.78	31.66	38.28	43.29	4.82
10	9	13	Chinese Academy of Sciences	xu15	28.70	36.07	63.53	90.64	25.75	17.32	23.35	23.48	2.95
3	10	2	Soochow University	kong	30.21	34.02	74.48	94.77	25.30	42.38	57.71	54.95	16.97
13	11	8	Goethe University Frankfurt	chiarcos	25.20	30.79	50.74	68.19	21.89	46.25	62.84	63.50	9.79
11	12	7	Dublin City University 1	wangl	19.36	24.42	46.20	93.18	17.38	30.70	43.04	40.75	11.50
12	13	6	Dublin City University 2	okita	14.66	21.10	38.20	88.06	13.21	30.73	43.01	40.72	11.72
14	14	12	India Institute of Technology	mukherjee	13.78	20.34	59.38	93.06	12.90	27.42	38.47	36.44	3.93
15	15	16	Shanghai Jiao Tong University 1	chen	10.29	14.68	48.77	78.67	9.97		0.09		0.00
16	16	14	Peking University	xu15b	4.28	6.31	24.05	58.04	3.53	18.40	25.60	24.25	1.29
				Development									
9	1	10	AU KBC Research Center	devi	54.69	62.90	75.91	92.80	49.11	35.03	40.89	45.10	7.64
1	2	1	East China Normal University	wangj	54.05	61.56	80.56	95.14	48.16	60.01	70.32	74.23	28.70
2	3	6	University of Trento	stepanov	51.33	57.10	78.70	93.79	46.89	40.08	45.91	49.42	15.69
8	4	3	Nippon Telegraph and Telephone Lab Japan	yoshida	47.90	55.68	72.16	88.94	43.02	54.92	62.48	67.47	20.27
7	5	11	University of Texas Dallas	xue	48.51	57.46	72.24	93.43	41.49	23.49	27.67	29.83	7.49
4	6	8	Japan Advanced Institute of Science and Tech.	nguyen	45.14	51.56	57.79	65.53	41.17	35.09	40.29	40.29	11.82
6	7	15	Concordia University	laali	45.91	53.16	75.34	92.25	39.52	0.00	0.00	0.00	0.00
5	8	4	UIUC Cognitive Computing Group	song	34.78	43.18	65.97	91.45	31.18	49.88	60.59	64.47	20.00
10	9	13	Chinese Academy of Sciences	xu15	33.16	41.71	67.99	91.52	30.25	19.30	23.13	23.83	4.35
3	10	2	Soochow University	kong	34.67	38.67	74.37	94.22	29.78	49.94	62.13	62.37	23.54
13	11	9	Goethe University Frankfurt	chiarcos	27.37	33.93	48.32	63.17	23.77	53.24	66.71	70.69	11.67
11	12	5	Dublin City University 1	wangl	20.52	28.55	41.78	93.23	17.70	35.49	45.26	45.16	15.96
12	13	7	Dublin City University 2	okita	18.59	26.27	37.33	86.33	15.82	35.49	45.32	45.13	15.07
14	14	12	India Institute of Technology	mukherjee	17.09	25.94	65.52	93.55	15.59	32.25	41.22	40.96	4.99
15	15	16	Shanghai Jiao Tong University 1	chen	15.15	18.35	58.27	86.09	14.57			0.36	0.00
16	16	14	Peking University	xu15b	3.14	4.77	19.08	51.54	2.79	17.90	22.92	23.76	0.77

Table 6: Scoreboard for the CoNLL-2015 shared task showing performance split across Explicit and Non-Explicit subtasks on the three data partitions—blind test, standard test (WSJ-23) and development. The rows are sorted by the parser performance of the participating systems on the Explicit task. The Column **O**, **E**, **I** refer to official, Explicit and Non-Explicit task ranks respectively. The blue highlighted rows indicate participants that did not attempt the Non-Explicit relation subtask. The green highlighted row shows a team that probably overfitted the development set. Finally, the red highlighted row indicates a team that possibly focused on the Explicit relations task and even though their overall rank was lower, they did very well on the Explicit relations subtask. This is also the system that did not submit a paper, so we do not know more details.

course parsing. The shared task required the development of an end-to-end system, and the best system achieved an F1 score of 24.0% on the blind test set, reflecting the serious error propagation problem in such a system. The shared task exposed the most challenging aspect of shallow discourse parsing as a research problem, helping future research better calibrate their efforts. The evaluation data sets and the scorer we prepared for the shared task will be a useful benchmark for future research on shallow discourse parsing.

Acknowledgments

We would like to thank the Penn Discourse TreeBank team, in particular Aravind Joshi and Bonnie Webber, for allowing us to use the PDTB corpus for the shared task. Thanks also go the LDC (Linguistic Data Consortium), who helped distribute the training and development data to participating teams. We are also very grateful to the TIRA team, who provided their evaluation platform, and especially to Martin Potthast for his technical assistance in using the TIRA platform and countless hours of troubleshooting.

This work was partially supported by the National Science Foundation via Grant Nos. 0910532 and IIS-1421067 and by the Singapore Ministry of Education Academic Research Fund Tier 2 grant MOE2013-T2-1-150.

References

Or Biran and Kathleen McKeown. 2013. Aggregated word pair features for implicit discourse relation disambiguation. In *Proceedings of the 51st Annual Meeting of the Association for Computational Linguistics*.

Lynn Carlson, Daniel Marcu, and Mary Ellen Okurowski. 2003. Building a discourse-tagged corpus in the framework of Rhetorical Structure Theory. In *Current Directions in Discourse and Dialogue*.

Christian Chiarcos and Niko Schenk. 2015. A minimalist approach to shallow discourse parsing and implicit relation recognition. In *Proceedings of the Nineteenth Conference on Computational Natural Language Learning: Shared Task*.

Sobha Lalitha Devi, Sindhuja Gopalan, Lakshmi S, Pattabhi RK Rao, Vijay Sundar Ram R., and Malarkodi C.S. 2015. A hybrid discourse relation parser in CoNLL 2015. In *Proceedings of the Nineteenth Conference on Computational Natural Language Learning: Shared Task*.

David A Duverle and Helmut Prendinger. 2009. A novel discourse parser based on support vector machine classification. In *Proceedings of the Joint Conference of the 47th Annual Meeting of the Association of Computational Linguistics and the 4th International Joint Conference on Natural Language Processing of the AFNLP*.

Vanessa Wei Feng and Graeme Hirst. 2012. Text-level discourse parsing with rich linguistic features. In *Proceedings of the 50th Annual Meeting of the Association for Computational Linguistics*.

Vanessa Wei Feng and Graeme Hirst. 2014. A linear-time bottom-up discourse parser with constraints and post-editing. In *Proceedings of the 52nd Annual Meeting of the Association for Computational Linguistics*.

Sucheta Ghosh, Giuseppe Riccardi, and Richard Johansson. 2012. Global features for shallow discourse parsing. In *Proceedings of the 13th Annual Meeting of the Special Interest Group on Discourse and Dialogue*.

Tim Gollub, Benno Stein, and Steven Burrows. 2012. Ousting Ivory Tower Research: Towards a Web Framework for Providing Experiments as a Service. In Bill Hersh, Jamie Callan, Yoelle Maarek, and Mark Sanderson, editors, *35th International ACM Conference on Research and Development in Information Retrieval (SIGIR 12)*, pages 1125–1126. ACM, August.

Yangfeng Ji and Jacob Eisenstein. 2014. Representation learning for text-level discourse parsing. In *Proceedings of the 52nd Annual Meeting of the Association for Computational Linguistics*.

Fang Kong, Sheng Li, and Guodong Zhou. 2015. The SoNLP-DP system in the CoNLL-2015 shared task. In *Proceedings of the Nineteenth Conference on Computational Natural Language Learning: Shared Task*.

Man Lan, Yu Xu, and Zhengyu Niu. 2013. Leveraging synthetic discourse data via multi-task learning for implicit discourse relation recognition. In *Proceedings of the 51st Annual Meeting of the Association for Computational Linguistics*.

Junyi Jessy Li and Ani Nenkova. 2014. Addressing class imbalance for improved recognition of implicit discourse relations. In *Proceedings of the 15th Annual Meeting of the Special Interest Group on Discourse and Dialogue*.

Sujian Li, Liang Wang, Ziqiang Cao, and Wenjie Li. 2014. Text-level discourse dependency parsing. In *Proceedings of the 52nd Annual Meeting of the Association for Computational Linguistics*.

Ziheng Lin, Min-Yen Kan, and Hwee Tou Ng. 2009. Recognizing implicit discourse relations in the Penn Discourse Treebank. In *Proceedings of the 2009 Conference on Empirical Methods in Natural Language Processing*.

Ziheng Lin, Hwee Tou Ng, and Min-Yen Kan. 2014. A PDTB-styled end-to-end discourse parser. *Natural Language Engineering*, 20(2):151–184.

William C Mann and Sandra A Thompson. 1988. Rhetorical Structure Theory: Toward a functional theory of text organization. *Text*, 8(3):243–281.

Christopher D. Manning, Mihai Surdeanu, John Bauer, Jenny Finkel, Steven J. Bethard, and David McClosky. 2014. The Stanford CoreNLP natural language processing toolkit. In *Proceedings of the 52nd Annual Meeting of the Association for Computational Linguistics*.

Mitchell P. Marcus, Beatrice Santorini, and Mary Ann Marcinkiewicz. 1993. Building a large annotated corpus of English: The Penn Treebank. *Computational Linguistics*, 19(2):313–330.

Eleni Miltsakaki, Rashmi Prasad, Aravind Joshi, and Bonnie Webber. 2004. Annotating discourse connectives and their arguments. In *Proceedings of the Human Language Technology/North American Chapter of the Association for Computational Linguistics Workshop on Frontiers in Corpus Annotation*.

Truong Son Nguyen, Bao Quoc Ho, and Le Minh Nguyen. 2015. JAIST: A two-phase machine learning approach for identifying discourse relations in newswire texts. In *Proceedings of the Nineteenth Conference on Computational Natural Language Learning: Shared Task*.

Martha Palmer, Daniel Gildea, and Paul Kingsbury. 2005. The Proposition Bank: An annotated corpus of semantic roles. *Computational Linguistics*, 31(1):71–106.

Joonsuk Park and Claire Cardie. 2012. Improving implicit discourse relation recognition through feature set optimization. In *Proceedings of the 13th Annual Meeting of the Special Interest Group on Discourse and Dialogue*.

Slav Petrov and Dan Klein. 2007. Improved inferencing for unlexicalized parsing. In *Proceedings of the Human Language Technology/North American Chapter of the Association for Computational Linguistics*.

Emily Pitler, Mridhula Raghupathy, Hena Mehta, Ani Nenkova, Alan Lee, and Aravind K Joshi. 2008. Easily identifiable discourse relations. Technical report, University of Pennsylvania.

Emily Pitler, Annie Louis, and Ani Nenkova. 2009. Automatic sense prediction for implicit discourse relations in text. In *Proceedings of the Joint Conference of the 47th Annual Meeting of the ACL and the 4th International Joint Conference on Natural Language Processing of the AFNLP*.

Martin Potthast, Tim Gollub, Francisco Rangel, Paolo Rosso, Efstathios Stamatatos, and Benno Stein. 2014. Improving the Reproducibility of PAN's Shared Tasks: Plagiarism Detection, Author Identification, and Author Profiling. In Evangelos Kanoulas, Mihai Lupu, Paul Clough, Mark Sanderson, Mark Hall, Allan Hanbury, and Elaine Toms, editors, *Information Access Evaluation meets Multilinguality, Multimodality, and Visualization. 5th International Conference of the CLEF Initiative (CLEF 14)*, pages 268–299, Berlin Heidelberg New York, September. Springer.

Sameer Pradhan, Lance Ramshaw, Mitchell Marcus, Martha Palmer, Ralph Weischedel, and Nianwen Xue. 2011. CoNLL-2011 shared task: Modeling unrestricted coreference in OntoNotes. In *Proceedings of the Fifteenth Conference on Computation Natural Language Learining: Shared Task*.

Sameer Pradhan, Alessandro Moschitti, Nianwen Xue, Olga Uryupina, and Yuchen Zhang. 2012. CoNLL-2012 Shared Task: Modeling multilingual unrestricted coreference in OntoNotes. In *Proceedings of the Sixteenth Conference on Computation Natural Language Learining: Shared Task*.

Rashmi Prasad and Harry Bunt. 2015. Semantic relations in discourse: The current state of ISO 24617-8. In *Proceedings of the 11th Joint ACL-ISO Workshop on Interoperable Semantic Annotation*.

Rashmi Prasad, Nikhil Dinesh, Alan Lee, Eleni Miltsakaki, Livio Robaldo, Aravind Joshi, and Bonnie Webber. 2008. The Penn Discourse Treebank 2.0. In *Proceedings of the 6th International Conference on Language Resources and Evaluation*.

Rashmi Prasad, Bonnie Webber, and Aravind Joshi. 2014. Reflections on the Penn Discourse Treebank, comparable corpora, and complementary annotation. *Computational Linguistics*, 40(4):921–950.

Attapol Rutherford and Nianwen Xue. 2014. Discovering implicit discourse relations through Brown cluster pair representation and coreference patterns. In *Proceedings of the 14th Conference of the European Chapter of the Association for Computational Linguistics*.

Yangqiu Song, Haoruo Peng, Parisa Kordjamshidi, Mark Sammons, and Dan Roth. 2015. Improving a pipeline architecture for shallow discourse parsing. In *Proceedings of the Nineteenth Conference on Computational Natural Language Learning: Shared Task*.

Manfred Stede. 2012. *Discourse Processing*. Morgan & Claypool Publishers.

Evgeny Stepanov, Giuseppe Riccardi, and Ali Orkan Bayer. 2015. The UniTN discourse parser in CoNLL 2015 shared task: Token-level sequence labeling with argument-specific models. In *Proceedings of the Nineteenth Conference on Computational Natural Language Learning: Shared Task*.

Rajen Subba and Barbara Di Eugenio. 2009. An effective discourse parser that uses rich linguistic information. In *Proceedings of Human Language Technologies: The 2009 Annual Conference of the North American Chapter of the Association for Computational Linguistics*.

Jianxiang Wang and Man Lan. 2015. A refined end-to-end discourse parser. In *Proceedings of the Nineteenth Conference on Computational Natural Language Learning: Shared Task*.

Xun Wang, Sujian Li, Jiwei Li, and Wenjie Li. 2012. Implicit discourse relation recognition by selecting typical training examples. In *Proceedings of the 24th International Conference on Computational Linguistics*.

Longyue Wang, Chris Hokamp, Tsuyoshi Okita, Xiaojun Zhang, and Qun Liu. 2015. The DCU discourse parser for connective, argument identification and explicit sense classification. In *Proceedings of the Nineteenth Conference on Computational Natural Language Learning: Shared Task*.

Bonnie Webber, Markus Egg, and Valia Kordoni. 2012. Discourse structure and language technology. *Natural Language Engineering*, 18(4):437–490.

Yasuhisa Yoshida, Katsuhiko Hayashi, Tsutomu Hirao, and Masaaki Nagata. 2015. Hybrid approach to PDTB-styled discourse parsing for CoNLL-2015. In *Proceedings of the Nineteenth Conference on Computational Natural Language Learning: Shared Task*.

Zhi-Min Zhou, Yu Xu, Zheng-Yu Niu, Man Lan, Jian Su, and Chew Lim Tan. 2010. Predicting discourse connectives for implicit discourse relation recognition. In *Proceedings of the 23rd International Conference on Computational Linguistics*.

A Refined End-to-End Discourse Parser

Jianxiang Wang, Man Lan*
Shanghai Key Laboratory of Multidimensional Information Processing
Department of Computer Science and Technology,
East China Normal University, Shanghai 200241, P. R. China
51141201062@ecnu.cn, mlan@cs.ecnu.edu.cn*

Abstract

The CoNLL-2015 shared task focuses on shallow discourse parsing, which takes a piece of newswire text as input and returns the discourse relations in a PDTB style. In this paper, we describe our discourse parser that participated in the shared task. We use 9 components to construct the whole parser to identify discourse connectives, label arguments and classify the sense of Explicit or Non-Explicit relations in free texts. Compared to previous discourse parser, new components and features are added in our system, which further improves the overall performance of the discourse parser. Our parser ranks the first on two test datasets, i.e., PDTB Section 23 and a blind test dataset.

1 Introduction

An end-to-end discourse parser is given free texts as input and returns discourse relations in a PDTB style, where a connective acts as a predicate that takes two text spans as its arguments. It can benefit many downstream NLP applications, such as information retrieval, question answering and automatic summarization, etc. The extraction of exact argument spans and Non-Explicit sense identification have been shown to be the main challenges of the discourse parsing (Lin et al., 2014).

Since the release of Penn Discourse Treebank (PDTB) (Prasad et al., 2008), much research has been carried out on PDTB to perform the subtasks of a full end-to-end parser, such as identifying discourse connectives, labeling arguments and classifying Explicit or Implicit relations. To identify discourse connectives from non-discourse ones and to classify the Explicit relations, (Pitler and Nenkova, 2009) extracted syntactic features of connectives from the constituent parses, and showed that syntactic features improved performance in both subtasks. For the argument labeling subtask, (Ghosh et al., 2011) regarded it as a token-level sequence labeling task using conditional random fields (CRFs). (Lin et al., 2014) proposed a tree subtraction algorithm to extract the arguments. (Kong et al., 2014) adopted a constituent-based approach to label arguments. As for Implicit sense classification, (Pitler et al., 2009), (Lin et al., 2009) and (Rutherford and Xue, 2014) performed the classification using several linguistically-informed features, such as verb classes, production rules and Brown cluster pair. (Lan et al., 2013) presented a multi-task learning framework with the use of the prediction of explicit discourse connective as auxiliary learning tasks to improve the performance.

All of these research focus on the subtasks of the PDTB, and can be viewed as isolated components of a full parser. (Lin et al., 2014) constructed a full parser on the top of these subtasks, which contained multiple components joined in a sequential pipeline architecture including a connective classifier, argument labeler, explicit classifier, non-explicit classifier, and attribution span labeler. In this paper, we followed the framework of (Lin et al., 2014) to construct a discourse parser. However, our work differs from that of Lin's in that our system introduces new components and features to improve the overall performance. Specifically, (1) we build two different

Proceedings of the Nineteenth Conference on Computational Natural Language Learning: Shared Task, pages 17–24,
Beijing, China, July 26-31, 2015.

extractors for Arg1 and Arg2 respectively for labeling Explicit arguments in the case of PS (i.e., Arg1 is located in some previous sentences of the connective); (2) we add new features to capture more information for classification or recognition; (3) we build two different argument extractors for Non-EntRel relations in Non-Explicit; (4) we use the refined arguments to improve the Non-Explicit sense classification.

The organization of this work is as follows. Section 2 gives a sketch description of our parser in a flow chart and the function of every component in this architecture. Section 3 describes the components and features in detail. Section 4 reports the preliminary experimental results on the training and development dataset, and the final results on two test datasets are shown in Section 5. Section 6 concludes this work.

2 System Overview

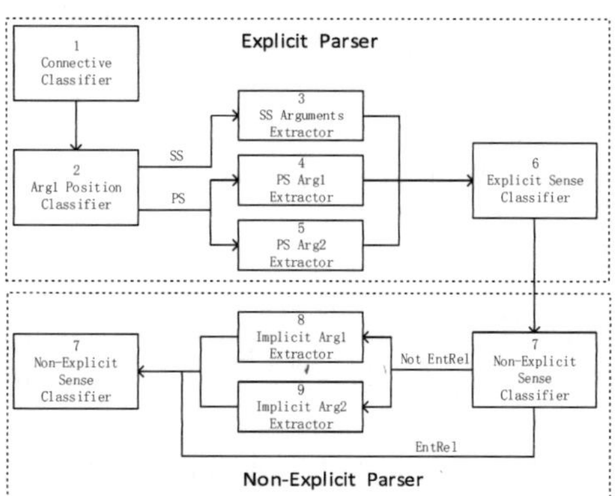

Figure 1: System pipeline for the discourse parser

We design the discourse parser as a sequential pipeline, shown in Figure 1, and the 9 components of our parser are listed as follows.

First, for texts with Explicit connective words:

(1) **Connective Classifier** is to identify the discourse connectives from non-discourse ones.

(2) **Arg1 Position Classifier** is to decide the relative position of Arg1 – whether it is located within the same sentence as the connective (SS) or in some previous sentence of the connective (PS).

(3) **SS Arguments Extractor** is to extract the spans of Arg1 and Arg2 in the SS case.

In the PS case, we build two extractors to identify the text spans for PS Arg1 and PS Arg2 respectively.

(4) **PS Arg1 Extractor** is to extract Arg1 for PS.

(5) **PS Arg2 Extractor** is to extract Arg2 for PS.

(6) **Explicit Sense Classifier** is to identify the sense that this Explicit connective conveys.

Second, for all adjacent sentence pairs within each paragraph, but not identified in any Explicit relation:

(7) **Non-Explicit Sense Classifier** is to classify the sense of each sentence pair into one of the Non-Explicit relation senses.

Since attribution is not annotated for EntRel relations, if the output of the above Non-Explict sense classifier is EntRel, we regard the previous sentence as Arg1 and the next one as Arg2. Otherwise, we build the following two argument extractors to label Arg1 and Arg2.

(8) **Implicit Arg1 Extractor** and (9) **Implicit Arg2 Extractor** extract Arg1 and Arg2 for Non-EntRel relations in Non-explicit, respectively.

3 Components and Features

Generally, our parser consists of 9 components, which compose an Explicit parser and a Non-Explicit parser. Most of features used in our parser are borrowed from previous work (Kong et al., 2014; Lin et al., 2014; Pitler et al., 2009; Pitler and Nenkova, 2009; Rutherford and Xue, 2014).

3.1 Explicit Parser

3.1.1 Connective Classifier

Since the input of the discourse parser is free text, the first thing we need to do is to identify all connective occurrences in text, and then to use the connective classifier to decide whether they function as discourse connectives or not.

For each connective occurrence *C*, we extract features from its context, part-of-speech (POS) and the parse tree of the connective's sentence. Note that $prev_1$ and $next_1$ indicate the first previous word and the first next word of connective *C* respectively. For a node in the parse tree, we use the POS combinations of the node, its parent, its children to represent the *linked context*.

The features we used for connective classsification consist of the following: (1) Pitler's: *C string* (case-sensitive), *self-category* (the highest node in the parse tree that covers only the connective words), *parent-category* (the parent of the *self-category*), *left-sibling-category* (the left sibling of the *self-category*), *right-sibling-category* (the right sibling of the *self-category*), *C*-Syn interaction (the pairwise interaction features between the connective *C* and each category feature (i.e., self-category, parent-category, left-sibling-category, right-sibling-category)) , Syn-Syn interaction (the interaction features between pairs of category features); (2) Lin's: *C* POS, $prev_1$ + *C* string, $prev_1$ POS, $prev_1$ POS + *C* POS, *C* string + $next_1$, $next_1$ POS, *C* POS + $next_1$ POS, path of *C*'s parent $\rightarrow$ root, compressed path of *C*'s parent $\rightarrow$ root; (3) our new proposed features: the POS tags of nodes from *C*'s parent $\rightarrow$ root, *parent-category linked context, right-sibling-category linked context*. Our three new features are considered to capture more syntactic context information of the connective *C* for connective classification.

3.1.2 Arg1 Position Classifier

After identifying the discourse connectives from the texts, we come to locate the positions of Arg1 and Arg2 of the connective *C*. Since Arg2 is defined as the argument with which the connective is syntactically associated, its position is fixed once we locate the discourse connective *C*. So we only need to identify the relative position of Arg1 as whether it is located within the same sentence as the connective (SS) or in some previous sentences of the connective (PS). We do not identify the case which Arg2 is located in some sentences following the sentence containing the connective (FS), because the statistical distribution of (Prasad et al., 2008) shows that less than 0.1% are FS for Explicit relations.

The features consist of the following: (1) Lin's: *C* string, *C* position (the position of connective *C* in the sentence: start, middle, or end), *C* POS, $prev_1$, $prev_1$ POS, $prev_1 + C$, $prev_1$ POS + *C* POS, $prev_2$, $prev_2$ POS, $prev_2 + C$, $prev_2$ POS + *C* POS; (2) our newly-proposed features: *C* POS + $next_1$ POS, $next_2$, path of $C \rightarrow$ root. Note that $prev_2$ and $next_2$ indicate the second previous word and the second next word of connective *C*, respectively.

3.1.3 Argument Extractor

After the relative position of Arg1 is classified as SS or PS in previous component, the argument extractor is to extract the spans of Arg1 and Arg2 for the identified discourse connectives. According to (Kong et al., 2014), Kong's constituent-based approach outperforms Lin's tree subtraction algorithm for the Explicit arguments extraction. However, Lin only focused on the SS case, and Kong treated the immediately preceding sentence as a special constituent for PS, which means that they just viewed the immediately preceding sentence as Arg1 and only extracted Arg2 for PS. So we only follow Kong's constituent-based approach to extract Arg1 and Arg2 for SS. However, for PS, we build two different extractors for Arg1 and Arg2 separately. Our intuition is that the two arguments have different syntactic and discourse properties and a unified model with the same feature set used for both may not have enough discriminating power.

SS Arguments Extractor: In the case of SS, we adopt (Kong et al., 2014)'s constituent-based approach without Joint Inference to extract Arg1 and Arg2.

For PS, we build two argument extractors for Arg1 and Arg2, respectively, as follows.

PS Arg1 Extractor: We consider the immediately previous sentence of connective *C* as the text span where Arg1 occurs and then build a extractor to label the Arg1 in it. Similar to Lin's Attribution span labeler, this extractor consists of two steps: splitting the sentence into clauses, and deciding, for each clause, whether it belongs to Arg1 or not. First we use nine punctuation symbols (...,.:;?!-~) to split the sentence into several parts and use the SBAR tag in its parse tree to split each part into clauses. Second, we build a classifier to decide each clause whether it belongs to Arg1 or not.

On the one hand, the attribution relation is annotated in PDTB, which expresses the "ownership" relationship between abstract objects and individuals or agents. However, the attribution annotation is excluded in CoNLL-2015 (Xue et al., 2015). Therefore we borrow several attribution features from (Lin et al., 2014) in order to distinguish the attribution-related span from others. On the other hand, according to the *minimality principle* of PDTB, the argument annotation includes the minimal span of text that is sufficient for the interpretation of the relation. Since connectives have very close relationship with discourse relation, we consider to adopt connective-related features to capture text span for relation. We choose the following features: (1) attribution-related features from (Lin et al., 2014): lemmatized verbs in *curr*, the first term of *curr*, the last term of *curr*, the last term of *prev* + the first term of *curr*, and (2) our proposed connective-related features: lowercased *C* string and *C* category (the syntactic category of the connective: subordinating, coordinating, or discourse adverbial), where *curr* and *prev* indicate the current and previous clause respectively and the corresponding category for the connective *C* is obtained from the list provided in (Knott, 1996).

PS Arg2 Extractor: The PS Arg2 Extractor is similar to the PS Arg1 Extractor. However, they differ as follows: (1) in the first step, we consider the sentence containing connective *C* as the text span where Arg2 occurs and besides the previous nine punctuation symbols, we also use the connective *C* to split the sentence; (2) we adopt different features to build classifier: lowercased verbs in *curr*, lemmatized verbs in *curr*, the first term of *curr*, the last term of *curr*, the last term of *prev*, the first term of *next*, the last term of *prev* + the first term of *curr*, the last term of *curr* + the first term of *next*, production rules extracted from *curr*, *curr* position (i.e., the position of *curr* in the sentence: start, middle or end), *C* string, lowercased *C* string, *C* position, *C* category, path of C's parent → root, compressed path of *C*'s parent → root.

3.1.4 Explicit Sense Classifier

From previous components, we have identified all discourse connectives and their arguments from the texts. Here, we move to decide what Explicit relation each of them conveys.

The features for this classifier consist of the following: (1) Lin's features: *C* string, *C* POS, $prev_1 + C$ (2) Pitler's features: *self-category*, *parent-category*, *left-sibling-category*, *right-sibling-category*, *C*-Syn interaction, Syn-Syn interaction. (3) our five newly proposed features: *parent-category linked context*, previous connective and its POS of *as* and previous connective and its POS of *when*. The first *parent-category linked context* feature is to provide more syntactic context information for the classification. The last four features are specially designed to disambiguate the relation senses of the connective *as* or *when*, since the two connectives often have ambiguity between Contingency.Cause.Reason and Temporal.Synchrony. As shown in Example 1, the previous connective of the discourse connective *as* is *But*, therefore the discourse connective *as* usually carries the Contingency.Cause.Reason sense rather than Temporal.Synchrony.

(1) *But the gains in Treasury bonds were pared* <u>as</u> **stocks staged a partial recovery.**
(Contingency.Cause.Reason – WSJ-1213)

3.2 Non-Explicit Parser

In this section, we discuss the identification of the Non-Explicit relations.

Since the Non-Explicit relations are only annotated for adjacent sentence pairs within paragraphs, we first collect all adjacent sentence pairs within each paragraph, but not identified in any Explicit relation. We assume the previous sentence as Arg1 and the next sentence as Arg2, and then identify the sense by the features extracted from (Arg1, Arg2). After that, we use Implicit Arg1 Extractor and Implicit Arg2 Extractor to label Arg1 and Arg2 for Non-EntRel relations in Non-Explicit, and for EntRel relations, we simply label the previous sentence as Arg1 and the next as Arg2.

Moreover, as shown in Figure 1, we use the Non-Explicit sense classifier again to identify the sense on the refined arguments (extracted arguments from Implicit Arg1&Arg2 Extractor) rather than the adjacent sentence pairs (i.e., previous sentence as Arg1, the next sentence as Arg2). Our expectation is that the overall parser performance might be improved if we extract features on refined argument spans rather than original argument spans.

3.2.1 Non-Explicit Sense Classifier

According to previous work, this component is the most difficult one in the discourse parser. And the features we adopted in this component are chosen from (Lin et al., 2009; Pitler et al., 2009; Rutherford and Xue, 2014), including: *production rules*, *dependency rules*, *first-last*, *first3*, *modality*, *verbs*,

Inquirer, *polarity*, *immediately preceding discourse connective of current sentence pair*, *Brown cluster pairs*. For the collection of *production rules*, *dependency rules*, and *Brown cluster pairs*, we used a frequency cutoff of 5 to remove infrequent features, and for Brown cluster, we choose 3,200 classes, as in (Rutherford and Xue, 2014).

3.2.2 Implicit Arg1 Extractor

The implicit Arg1 Extractor is performed to extract Arg1 for Non-EntRel relations in Non-Explicit, which is done similarly to the PS Arg1 Extractor. We first split the sentence into clauses and then decide each clause whether it belongs to Arg1 or not. The features extracted from the current and previous clauses (*curr* and *prev*) are: the first term of *curr*, the last term of *prev*, the cross product of the *prev* and *curr* production rules, the path of the first term of *curr* $\rightarrow$ the last term of *prev*, number of words of *curr*.

3.2.3 Implicit Arg2 Extractor

The implicit Arg2 Extractor is similar to that of Arg1, but different features are extracted from the current, previous, and next clauses (*curr*, *prev*, and *next*), including: lowercased verbs in *curr*, the first term of *curr*, the last term of *prev*, the last term of *prev* + the first term of *curr*, the last term of *curr* + the first term of *next*, *curr* position, the cross product of the *prev* and *curr* production rules, the cross product of the *curr* and *next* production rules, the path of the first term of *curr* $\rightarrow$ the last term of *prev*, number of words of *curr*.

4 Experiments on Training Data

To implement the 9 components described above, we compared two supervised machine learning algorithms, i.e., MaxEnt and Naive Bayes, implemented in MALLET toolkit[1]. For each component, we chose the algorithm with better performance. Specifically, we use Naive Bayes to build Non-Explicit Sense Classifier, and MaxEnt for the other 8 components.

We use PDTB Section 02-21 for training and Section 22 for development, which are provided by CoNLL-2015 with parse trees along with POS tags produced by the Berkeley Parser. And we participate in the closed tracks, that is, only two resources (i.e., Brown Clusters and MPQA Subjectivity Lexicon) are used in our discourse parser.

According to the requirement, a relation is considered to be correct if and only if: (1) the discourse connective is correctly detected (for explicit discourse relations); (2) the sense of a discourse relation is correctly predicted; (3) the text spans of the two arguments as well as their labels (Arg1 and Arg2) are correctly predicted. We use the official measure F_1 (harmonic mean of Precision and Recall) to evaluate performance.

4.1 Results of Explicit Parser

Table 1 reports the results of the explicit discourse parser on development data set of three components (i.e., Connective classifier, Arg1 position classifier and Explicit sense classifier) without error propagation (EP), where our new features are introduced. We find that the F_1 scores of all these classifiers are increased by adding our new features (+new).

Component	P&N and Lin			+ new		
	P	R	F_1 (%)	P	R	F_1 (%)
Connective Classifier	94.80	93.97	94.38	95.28	95.00	95.14
Arg1 Position Classifier	97.82	98.88	98.35	99.77	99.57	99.69
Explicit Sense Classifier	89.11	89.11	89.11	90.14	90.14	90.14

Table 1: Results for three components which add in our new features, no EP

To evaluate the performance of Explicit arguments extraction, we build the PS baseline by labeling the previous sentence of the connective as Arg1, and the text span between the connective and the beginning of the next sentence as Arg2. Table 2 summarizes the results of Explicit arguments extraction with exact matching and without error propagation, and the corresponding PS baseline is shown within parentheses. Note that we removed the leading or tailing punctuation from all text spans before evaluation. We see that the F_1 of PS is improved by a large margin for Arg1, Arg2 and Both by using two separate PS argument extractors, and the overall F_1 of Explicit arguments extraction is also increased by 2.51%.

4.2 Results of Non-Explicit Parser

Table 3 reports the results for Non-Explicit sense classification without error propagation, where we

[1] mallet.cs.umass.edu

	Arg1 F_1 (%)	Arg2 F_1 (%)	Both F_1 (%)
SS	70.56	88.54	64.72
PS	50.64(44.20)	75.10(66.09)	39.91(32.61)
All	64.15(61.93)	84.25(81.15)	56.61(54.10)

Table 2: Results for Explicit arguments extraction, where "All" indicates the arguments extraction for all the Explicit relations, and "Both" indicates Arg1 and Arg2 of a relation are both exactly matched, no EP

	P	R	F_1 (%)
EntRel sense	58.54	66.98	62.47
All Non-Explicit Senses	43.12	42.72	42.92

Table 3: Results for Non-Explicit sense classification, no EP

extract features on gold standard arguments of the Non-Explicit relations. The first row gives the result of the EntRel identification. Since we only extract arguments for Non-EntRel relations in Non-Explicit, the performance on EntRel identification is important, since it affects the performance of arguments extraction on Non-Explicit relations.

Table 4 reports the results for arguments extraction on Non-EntRel relations in Non-Explicit without error propagation, where the first row shows the result of the baseline system by labeling the previous sentence as Arg1 and the next sentence as Arg2, and the second row shows the result when using two Implicit extractors. As we expected, using two separate Implicit extractors achieves much better performance than the baseline. Table 5 reports the comparison results for the overall arguments extraction of parser with error propagation, where the first row indicates the performance when simply using the previous sentence as Arg1 and the next sentence as Arg2 for all Non-Explicit relations, and the second shows the results of using two Implicit argument extractors for Non-EntRel relations. We see that the performance of the arguments extraction increases, but not too much, due to the error propagation from the EntRel identification (P: 39.32%, R: 64.19%, F_1: 48.76%; EP).

Table 6 shows the overall results, where the first row is the overall performance of the parser when identify Non-Explicit sense on original arguments (i.e., adjacent sentence pairs), and the second row is the results on refined arguments. We find that the overall F_1 of the parser is improved 0.41% by extracting features on the refined arguments.

	Arg1 F_1	Arg2 F_1	Both F_1
w/o Impl extractors	61.80	69.92	48.56
with Impl extractors	70.02	77.42	55.85

Table 4: Results for using Implicit Arg1&Arg2 extractors on Non-EntRel relations in Non-Explicit, no EP

	Arg1 F_1	Arg2 F_1	Both F_1
w/o Impl extractors	66.06	77.06	56.31
with Impl extractors	66.97	77.21	57.21

Table 5: Results for overall argument extraction of the parser, EP

	P	R	F_1 (%)
on original arguments	37.18	37.67	37.43
on refined arguments	37.59	38.09	37.84

Table 6: Results of overall parser performance using Non-Explicit sense classifier on original and refined arguments

5 Results on Test Data Sets

The above described discourse parser system is evaluated on two test datasets provided by the shared task: (1) Section 23 in PDTB; (2) blind test set drawn from a similar source and domain in terms of F_1. The officially released results are shown in Table 7. Our parser ranks the first on both test datasets. Although the two test datasets are both from news wire domain and in PDTB style, there are difference between the two datasets. For example, not all discourse connectives in blind test dataset are listed in PDTB, e.g., "upon" is annotated as discourse connective in blind test dataset while it is not in PDTB.

We compare our discourse parser with Lin's on PDTB Section 23. We find that new features proposed in this work do help increase F_1 of Explicit connective classification by 0.54%. And for the Explicit arguments extraction, our parser achieves better performance as well. However, since the sense labels of Explicit and Non-Explicit relations in CoNLL-2015 differ from Lin's, i.e., Lin used partial sense labels of the second level (Type) by excluding several small categories while CoNLL-2015

	on PDTB Section 23						on blind test data set					
	our parser			Lin's parser			our parser			2nd rank parser		
	P	R	F_1 (%)	P	R	F_1 (%)	P	R	F_1 (%)	P	R	F_1 (%)
Explicit connective	94.83	93.49	**94.16**	-	-	93.62	93.48	90.29	**91.86**	92.57	87.41	89.92
Explicit Arg1 extraction	51.05	50.33	**50.68**	-	-	47.68	49.16	47.48	48.31	50.48	47.66	49.03
Explicit Arg2 extraction	77.89	76.79	**77.33**	-	-	70.27	75.61	73.02	**74.29**	72.76	68.71	70.68
Explicit Both extraction	45.54	44.90	**45.22**	-	-	40.37	42.09	40.65	**41.35**	40.76	38.49	39.59
Explicit only sense	35.52	34.69	34.93	-	-	-	29.69	26.24	**25.91**	33.15	24.81	25.22
Non-Explicit Arg1 extraction	64.83	69.50	67.08	-	-	-	58.66	63.25	**60.87**	39.47	47.93	43.29
Non-Explicit Arg2 extraction	66.02	70.78	68.32	-	-	-	71.88	77.49	**74.58**	51.58	62.63	56.57
Non-Explicit Both extraction	51.20	54.89	52.98	-	-	-	48.58	52.37	**50.41**	34.93	42.42	38.31
Non-Explicit only sense	53.18	10.45	9.06	-	-	-	44.74	8.64	**7.69**	37.08	7.83	6.81
All Arg1 extraction	59.20	61.03	60.10	-	-	-	55.12	56.58	**55.84**	44.61	48.64	46.54
All Arg2 extraction	71.43	73.64	72.52	-	-	-	73.49	75.43	**74.45**	60.02	65.43	62.60
All Both extraction	48.62	50.13	49.36	-	-	-	45.77	46.98	**46.37**	37.25	40.61	38.86
Sense (Expicit+Non-Explicit)	31.44	30.42	29.83	-	-	-	25.07	22.13	**21.82**	25.00	19.60	18.87
Overall Parser	29.27	30.08	29.72	-	-	20.64	23.69	24.32	**24.00**	20.94	22.83	21.84

Table 7: Results of our parser on PDTB Section 23 and the blind test dataset, Lin's parser on PDTB Section 23 and the 2nd rank parser on blind test dataset, "All" indicates all relations (Explicit and Non-Explicit relations), "-" indicates not available

used different sense labels (partial of the three sense levels with excluding and/or merging several small categories), the direct comparison on sense classification as well as the parser performance is not possible.

Table 7 also shows the results of our parser and the 2nd rank parser on blind test dataset, we see that our parser achieves better performance, especially on the arguments extraction.

6 Conclusion

In this work, we have implemented a refined discourse parser by adding new components and features based on Lin's system. Specifically, we (1) build two PS arguments extractors (i.e., PS Arg1 Extractor and PS Arg2 Extractor) to improve performance of Explicit arguments extraction, (2) propose new features for building three classifiers (i.e, Connective Classifier, Arg1 Position Classifier, Explicit Sense Classifier), (3) construct two Implicit arguments extractors (i.e., Implicit Arg1 Extractor and Implicit Arg2 Extractor) for Non-EntRel relations, and (4) perform Non-Explicit sense classification on refined arguments. Our system ranks the first on both test data sets, i.e. PDTB Section 23 and a blind test dataset.

Acknowledgements

This research is supported by grants from Science and Technology Commission of Shanghai Municipality under research grant no. (14DZ2260800 and 15ZR1410700) and Shanghai Collaborative Innovation Center of Trustworthy Software for Internet of Things (ZF1213).

References

Sucheta Ghosh, Richard Johansson, and Sara Tonelli. 2011. Shallow discourse parsing with conditional random fields. In *In Proceedings of the 5th International Joint Conference on Natural Language Processing (IJCNLP 2011*. Citeseer.

Alistair Knott. 1996. A data-driven methodology for motivating a set of coherence relations.

Fang Kong, Hwee Tou Ng, and Guodong Zhou. 2014. A constituent-based approach to argument labeling with joint inference in discourse parsing. In *Proceedings of the 2014 Conference on Empirical Methods in Natural Language Processing (EMNLP)*, pages 68–77, Doha, Qatar, October. Association for Computational Linguistics.

Man Lan, Yu Xu, Zheng-Yu Niu, et al. 2013. Leveraging synthetic discourse data via multi-task learning for implicit discourse relation recognition. In *ACL (1)*, pages 476–485. Citeseer.

Ziheng Lin, Min-Yen Kan, and Hwee Tou Ng. 2009. Recognizing implicit discourse relations in the Penn Discourse Treebank. In *Proceedings of the 2009 Conference on Empirical Methods in Natural Language Processing: Volume 1-Volume 1*, pages 343–351. Association for Computational Linguistics.

Ziheng Lin, Hwee Tou Ng, and Min-Yen Kan. 2014. A PDTB-styled end-to-end discourse parser. *Natural Language Engineering*, pages 1–34.

Emily Pitler and Ani Nenkova. 2009. Using syntax to disambiguate explicit discourse connectives in text. In *Proceedings of the ACL-IJCNLP 2009 Conference Short Papers*, pages 13–16. Association for Computational Linguistics.

Emily Pitler, Annie Louis, and Ani Nenkova. 2009. Automatic sense prediction for implicit discourse relations in text. In *Proceedings of the Joint Conference of the 47th Annual Meeting of the ACL and the 4th International Joint Conference on Natural Language Processing of the AFNLP: Volume 2-Volume 2*, pages 683–691. Association for Computational Linguistics.

Rashmi Prasad, Nikhil Dinesh, Alan Lee, Eleni Miltsakaki, Livio Robaldo, Aravind K Joshi, and Bonnie L Webber. 2008. The Penn Discourse TreeBank 2.0. In *LREC*. Citeseer.

Attapol T Rutherford and Nianwen Xue. 2014. Discovering implicit discourse relations through brown cluster pair representation and coreference patterns. *EACL 2014*, page 645.

Nianwen Xue, Hwee Tou Ng, Sameer Pradhan, Rashmi Prasad, Christopher Bryant, and Attapol Rutherford. 2015. The CoNLL-2015 Shared Task on Shallow Discourse Parsing. In *Proceedings of the Nineteenth Conference on Computational Natural Language Learning: Shared Task*, Beijing, China.

The UniTN Discourse Parser in CoNLL 2015 Shared Task: Token-level Sequence Labeling with Argument-specific Models

Evgeny A. Stepanov **Giuseppe Riccardi** **Ali Orkan Bayer**
Signals and Interactive Systems Lab
Department of Information Engineering and Computer Science
University of Trento, Trento, TN, Italy
{stepanov,riccardi,bayer}@disi.unitn.it

Abstract

Penn Discourse Treebank style discourse parsing is a composite task of identifying discourse relations (explicit or non-explicit), their connective and argument spans, and assigning a sense to these relations from the hierarchy of senses. In this paper we describe University of Trento parser submitted to CoNLL 2015 Shared Task on Shallow Discourse Parsing. The span detection tasks for explicit relations are cast as token-level sequence labeling. The argument span decisions are conditioned on relations' being intra- or inter-sentential. Non-explicit relation detection and sense assignment tasks are cast as classification. In the end-to-end closed-track evaluation, the parser ranked second with a global F-measure of 0.2184

1 Introduction

Discourse parsing is a challenging Natural Language Processing (NLP) task that has utility for many other NLP tasks such as summarization, opinion mining, etc. (Webber et al., 2011). With the release of Penn Discourse Treebank (PDTB) (Prasad et al., 2008), the researchers have developed discourse parsers for all (e.g. (Lin et al., 2014) or some (e.g. (Ghosh et al., 2011)) discourse relation types in the PDTB definition, or addressed particular discourse parsing subtasks (Pitler and Nenkova, 2009).

PDTB adopts non-hierarchical binary view on discourse relations: a discourse connective and its two arguments – *Argument 1* and *Argument 2*, which is syntactically attached to the connective. And, a relation is assigned particular sense from the sense hierarchy. It was identified that parsing *Explicit* discourse relations, that are signaled by a presence of a discourse connective (a closed class), is much easier task than detection and classification of *Implicit* discourse relations, where a discourse connective is implied, rather than lexically realized. Since Explicit and Implicit discourse relations in a document do not differ much in relative frequency, the low performance on one of the relation types limits the utility of discourse parsing for downstream applications.

In this paper we describe the University of Trento discourse parser for both explicit and non-explicit – implicit, alternatively lexicalized (AltLex), and entity (EntRel) relations – that was submitted to the CoNLL 2015 Shared Task on Shallow Discourse Parsing (Xue et al., 2015) and ranked 2nd. The parser makes use of token-level sequence labeling with Conditional Random Fields (Lafferty et al., 2001) for identification of connective and argument spans; and classification for identification of relation senses and argument configurations.

The parser architecture is described in Section 2. The features and individual model details are described in Sections 3 and 4, respectively. In Section 5 we describe official evaluation results. Section 6 discusses the lessons learned from the shared task and provides concluding remarks.

2 System Architecture

The discourse parser submitted for the CoNLL 2015 Shared Task is the extension of the parser described in (Stepanov and Riccardi, 2013; Stepanov and Riccardi, 2014). The overall architecture of the parser is depicted in Figure 1. The approach structures discourse parsing into a pipeline of several subtasks, mimicking the Penn Discourse Treebank (PDTB) (Prasad et al., 2008) annotation procedure as in (Lin et al., 2014).

The first step is *Discourse Connective Detection* (DCD) that identifies explicit discourse connectives and their spans. Then *Connective Sense Classification* (CSC) is used to classify these con-

Proceedings of the Nineteenth Conference on Computational Natural Language Learning: Shared Task, pages 25–31,
Beijing, China, July 26-31, 2015.

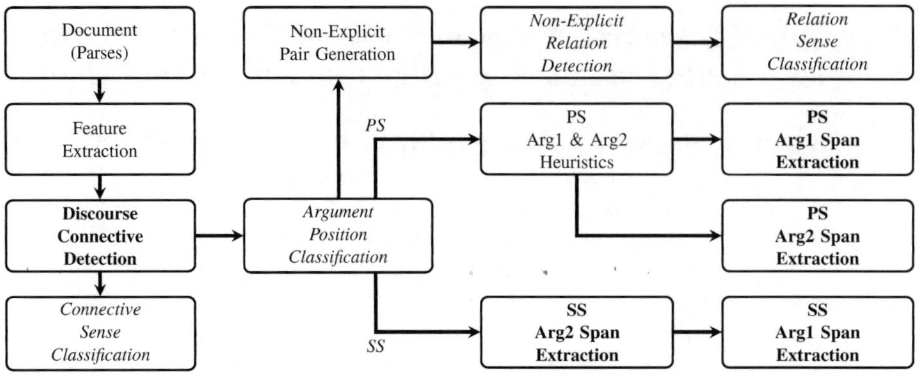

Figure 1: Discourse parser architecture. CRF modules are in **bold**; classification modules are in *italic*.

nectives into the PDTB hierarchy of senses; and *Argument Position Classification* (APC) to classify the connectives as requiring their *Argument 1* in the previous (PS) or the same sentence as *Argument 2* (i.e. classify relations as inter- and intra-sentential). With respect to the decision of the step an *Argument Span Extraction* (ASE) model is applied to label the spans of both arguments.

Separate *Argument Span Extraction* models are trained for each of the arguments of intra- and inter-sentential explicit discourse relations. Identification of *Argument 2* is much easier, since it is the argument syntactically attached to the discourse connective. Thus, for the intra-sentential (SS) relations, models are applied in a cascade such that the output of *Argument 2* span extraction in the input for *Argument 1* span extraction. For the inter-sentential (PS) relations, a sentence containing the connective is selected as *Argument 2*, and the sentence immediately preceding it as a candidate for *Argument 1*. Even though in 9% of all inter-sentential relations *Argument 1* is located in non-adjacent previous sentence (Prasad et al., 2008), this heuristic is widely used (Lin et al., 2014; Stepanov and Riccardi, 2013), and is known as Previous Sentence Heuristic.

In PDTB, the Non-Explicit discourse relations – Implicit, AltLex, and EntRel – are annotated for pairs of adjacent sentences except the pairs that were already annotated as explicit discourse relations (Prasad et al., 2007). Thus, in the *Non-Explicit Pair Generation* (NPG) step a list of adjacent sentence pairs is generated omitting the inter-sentential explicit relations identified in the APC step. In the *Non-Explicit Relation Detection* (NRD) step the candidate pairs are classified as holding a relation or not. The pairs identified as a relation are then classified into relation senses in the *Relation Sense Classification* (RSC) step.

Since the goal of *Discourse Connective Detection* and *Argument Span Extraction* tasks is to label the *spans* of a connective and its arguments, they are cast as token-level sequence labeling with CRFs using *CRF++* (Kudo, 2013). The *Non-Explicit Relation Detection* and *Sense* and *Argument Position* classification tasks are cast as supervised classification using AdaBoost algorithm (Freund and Schapire, 1997) implemented in *icsiboost* (Favre et al., 2007). In Section 3 we describe the features used for token-level sequence labeling and classification tasks; and in Section 4 models for each of the subtasks in more detail.

3 Features

Besides tokens, the PDTB corpus distributed to the participants contains Part-of-Speech tags, constituency and dependency parses. These resources are used to extract and generate both token-level and argument/relation-level features. Additionally, for argument/relation-level features Brown Clusters (Turian et al., 2010) are used.

3.1 Token-level Features

Discourse Connective Detection and *Argument Span Extraction* tasks of discourse parsing are cast as token-level sequence labeling with CRFs. The list of features used for the models is given in Table 1. Besides tokens and POS-tags, the rest of the features is described below.

Chunk-tag is the syntactic chunk prefixed with the information whether a token is at the beginning (B-), inside (I-) or outside (O) of the constituent (i.e. IOB format) (e.g. 'B-NP' indicates that a token is at the beginning of Noun Phrase

Feature	DCD	ASE: SS		ASE: PS	
		A1	*A2*	*A1*	*A2*
Token	Y	Y	Y	Y	Y
POS-tag	Y		Y	Y	Y
Chunk-tag	Y				
IOB-chain	Y	Y	Y	Y	Y
Dependency chain	Y		Y		
Connective Head	Y				
Connective Label		Y	Y		Y
Argument 2 Label		Y			

Table 1: Token-level features for Discourse Connective Detection (DCD) and Argument Span Extraction (ASE) for intra-sentential (SS) and inter-sentential (PS) explicit discourse relations.

chunk). The information is extracted from constituency parse trees using chunklink script (Buchholz, 2000).

IOB-chain is the path string of the syntactic tree nodes from the root node to the token, similar to Chunk-tag, it is prefixed with the IOB information. For example, the IOB-chain 'I-S/B-VP' indicates that a token is the first word of the verb phrase (B-VP) of the main clause (I-S).The feature is also extracted using the chunklink script (Buchholz, 2000).

Dependency chain is a feature inspired by *IOB-chain* and is the path string of the functions of the parents of a token, starting from root of a dependency parse. For example, the dependency chain 'root/nsubj/det' indicates that a token is a determiner of the subject of a sentence.

Connective Head is a binary feature that indicates whether a token is in the list of 100 PDTB discourse connectives. For example, all 'and' tokens will have this feature value '1'.

Connective Label and *Argument 2 Label* are the output labels of the *Discourse Connective Detection* and *Argument 2 Span Extraction* models respectively. The outputs are the IOB-tagged strings 'CONN' and 'ARG2'. Using these labels as features for Argument Span Extraction is useful for constraining the search space, since the *Connective*, *Argument 1* and *Argument 2* spans are not supposed to overlap.

Besides the features mentioned above, we have experimented with other token-level features: (1) morphological: lemma and inflection; (2) dependency: main verb of a sentence (i.e. root of the dependency parse) as a string and binary feature; (3) Connective Head as string. Even though previous work on discourse parsing (e.g. (Ghosh et al., 2011; Stepanov and Riccardi, 2013) found these features useful in token-level sequence labeling approach to *Argument Span Extraction* using gold parse trees, they were excluded from the submitted models since in greedy hill climbing their contributions were negative.

Using templates of CRF++ the token-level features are enriched with ngrams (2 & 3-grams) in the window of ± 2 tokens. That is, for each token there are 12 features per feature type: 5 unigrams, 4 bigrams and 3 trigrams. All features are conditioned on the output label independently of each other. Additionally, CRFs consider the previous token's output label as a feature.

3.2 Argument & Relation-level Features

In this section we describe features used for detecting non-explicit discourse relations and their sense classification. Since in these tasks the unit of classification is a relation rather than token, these features are extracted per argument of a relation and a relation as a whole.

Previous work on the topic makes use of wide range of features ranging from first and last tokens of arguments to a Cartesian product of all tokens in both arguments, which leads to a very sparse feature set. To reduce the sparseness in (Rutherford and Xue, 2014) the authors map the tokens to Brown Clusters (Turian et al., 2010) and improve the classification into top-level senses.

Inspired by the previous research, we have experimented with the following features that are extracted from both arguments:

1. Bag-of-Words;
2. Bag-of-Words prefixed with the argument ID (Arg1 or Arg2);
3. Cartesian product of all the tokens from both arguments;
4. Set of unique pairs from Cartesian product of Brown Clusters of all the tokens from both arguments (inspired by (Rutherford and Xue, 2014));
5. First, last, and first 3 words of each argument (from (Pitler et al., 2009; Rutherford and Xue, 2014));
6. Predicate, subject (both passive and active), direct and indirect objects, extracted from dependency parses (8 features);

7. Ternary features for pairs from 6 to indicate matches (1, 0) or NULL, if one of the arguments misses the feature (extension of 'similar subjects or main predicates' feature of (Rutherford and Xue, 2014)) (16 features);
8. Cartesian product of Brown Clusters of 6 (16 features);

These features are used for *Non-Explicit Discourse Relation Detection* and *Sense Classification* tasks, which are described in the next section.

4 Discourse Parsing Components

In this section we describe individual discourse parsing subtasks discussing features and models.

4.1 Discourse Connective Detection

Discourse Connective Detection is the first step in discourse parsing. The CRF model makes use of all the features in Table 3 (except Connective Label – its own output – and Argument 2 Label – the output of downstream component). Using just cased token features (i.e. 1, 2, 3-grams in the window of ± 2 tokens already has F-measure above 0.85. Adding other features gradually increases the performance on the development set to 0.9379. Other than the token itself, the feature that contributes the most to the performance is IOB-chain.

4.2 Connective Sense Classification

Connective Sense Classification takes the output of *Discourse Connective Detection* and classifies identified connectives into the hierarchy of PDTB senses. We have experimented with two approaches: (1) flat – directly classifying into full spectrum of senses including class, type and subtype (Prasad et al., 2008); and (2) hierarchical – first classifying into 4 top level senses (Comparison, Contingency, Expansion and Temporal) and then into the rest of the levels. For the purposes of the Shared Task partial senses (e.g. just class) were disallowed; thus, for the flat classification, instances having partial senses were removed from both training and development sets.

The flat classification into 14 senses using just cased token strings as bag-of-words yields the best performance and has accuracy of 0.8968 on the filtered development set using gold connective spans. The 4-way classification into top-level senses on a full development set using just connective tokens has accuracy of 0.9426. Adding POS-tags increases accuracy to 0.9456. Due to the error propagation, going to the second level of the hierarchy drops the performance slightly below the flat classification. None of the other features listed in Table 1 has a positive effect on classification. Adding argument spans lowered the performance as well.

4.3 Argument Position Classification

Argument Position Classification is an easy task, since explicit discourse connectives have a strong preference on the positions of its arguments, depending on whether they appear at the beginning or in the middle of a sentence. In the literature the task was reported as having a very high baseline (e.g. (Stepanov and Riccardi, 2013), 95% for whole PDTB). The features used for classification are cased connective token string (case here carries the information about connective's position in the sentence), POS-tags and IOB-chains. The accuracy on the development set given gold connective spans is 0.9868.

4.4 Argument Span Extraction

Argument Span Extraction models that make use of the Connective and Argument 2 Labels are trained on reference annotation. Even though, the performance of the upstream models (*Discourse Connective Detection* and *Argument Position Classification*) is relatively high compared to the *Argument Span Extraction* models, there is still error propagation.

For the *Argument Span Extraction* of explicit relations the search space is limited to a single sentence; thus, all multi sentence arguments are missed. This constraint has a little effect on *Argument 2* spans. However, since as a candidate for inter-sentential *Argument 1* we use only immediately preceding sentence, together with this constraint we miss 12% of relations. Thus, detection of *Argument 1* spans of inter-sentential relations is a hard task, additionally due to the fact that there is no other span (connective or Argument 2) to delimit it. Even though we have trained CRF models for the task, previous sentence heuristic was performing with insignificant difference. Thus, the heuristic was selected for the submitted version, and it was augmented with the removal of sentence initial and final punctuation. For *Argument 2* of inter-sentential relations performance of CRF models is acceptably high (≈ 0.80).

The span of *Argument 2* of intra-sentential relations is the easiest to detect, since it is syntactically attached to the connective; and performances are high (≈ 0.89 on the development set using the features in Table 1). Thus, its output is used as a feature for *Argument 1* extraction. Interesting fact is that POS-tags have a negative effect on the *Argument 1 Span Extraction*.

4.5 Non-Explicit Relation Detection

Based on the output of *Argument Position Classification* a set of adjacent sentence pairs is generated as candidates for non-explicit discourse relations: Implicit, AltLex, and EntRel. For training the classification models we have generated No-Relation pairs using reference annotation, excluding all the sentences involved in inter-sentential relations (some relations have multiple sentence arguments). Additionally, since arguments of non-explicit relations are stripped of leading and trailing punctuation, the No-Relation pairs were preprocessed. The task of detecting relations proved to be hard.

Similar to *Connective Sense Classification* we attempted (1) flat classification into all PDTB senses + No-Relation (i.e. merging the task with *Relation Sense Classification* described in Section 4.6) and (2) hierarchical – first detect the presence of a relation then classify it into the hierarchy of senses. For the hierarchical detection of Non-Explicit relations we tried (1) Relation vs. No-Relation classification and (2) classification into relation types (Implicit, AltLex, EntRel) + No-Relation. The model that has the highest F-measure for actual relations turned out to be binary Relation vs. No-Relation classification (0.6988). However, since in the testing mode we don't have access to argument span information the performance is expected to drop significantly. The most robust feature combination for the task is Cartesian product of Brown Clusters of all the tokens from both arguments and Cartesian product of Brown Clusters of predicate, subject and direct and indirect objects (4 and 8 from Section 3.2).

4.6 Relation Sense Classification

After a sentence pair is classified as a relation, it is further classified into the hierarchy of senses. The models are trained on all the features from Section 3.2, excluding prefixed Bag-of-Words and Cartesian product of all tokens. Relations are classified directly into 14 PDTB senses + EntRel.

The task is extremely hard, the classification accuracy is 0.3899 and the model misses infrequent senses. Table 2 lists the captured senses with their percentages in training data and F-measures on the development set. The distribution of senses has a direct effect on its F-measure.

Sense	%	F_1
Expansion.Conjunction	19.0	0.4247
Expansion.Restatement	14.4	0.3212
Contingency.Cause.Reason	12.2	0.2945
Comparison.Contrast	9.5	0.0980
Contingency.Cause.Result	8.6	0.0563
Expansion.Instantiation	6.5	0.1918
Temporal.Asynchronous.Precedence	2.7	0.1290
Less Frequent and Partial Senses	4.1	0.0000
EntRel	23.1	0.5730
All (micro-average)	–	0.3899

Table 2: F-measures of non-explicit relation sense classification per sense, ordered by frequency in the training set.

The performances reported so far are on a specific task without error propagation from the upstream tasks. In the next section we report official Shared Task evaluation results.

5 Official Evaluation Metrics and Results

The official evaluation of CoNLL 2015 Shared Task on Shallow Discourse Parsing is done on a per-discourse relation basis. A relation is considered to be predicted correctly if the parser correctly identifies (1) discourse connective span (head), (2) spans and labels of both arguments, and (3) sense of a relation. The predicted connective and arguments spans have to match the reference spans *exactly*. Consequently, to get a true positive for a relation the parser has to get true positive on all the subtasks.

The task organizers also provided the evaluation script that reported precision, recall and F-measures for *Discourse Connective Detection*, joint *Sense Classification* scores for explicit and non-explicit relations, and joint *Argument Span Extraction* score for explicit and non-explicit relations. For argument spans three scores were reported: *Argument 1* and *Argument 2* individually and jointly. For *Sense Classification* the script reported performance on each of the senses and their macro-average. Later, performances for explicit and non-explicit relations were split. The participants had to evaluate their systems on 3 data sets: (1) Development (WSJ Section 22), (2) Test (WSJ Section 23), and the blind test set annotated specifically for the Shared Task.

The performance of our parser on each of the

	Explicit			Non-Explicit			All Relations		
Task	**Dev**	**Test**	**Blind**	**Dev**	**Test**	**Blind**	**Dev**	**Test**	**Blind**
Connective	0.9219	0.9271	0.8992	–	–	–	0.9219	0.9271	0.8992
Arg1	0.5646	0.5008	0.4903	0.4586	0.4437	0.4329	0.5225	0.4775	0.4654
Arg2	0.7748	0.7616	0.7068	0.4912	0.4744	0.5657	0.6230	0.6068	0.6260
Arg1&2	0.5075	0.4460	0.3959	0.4000	0.3730	0.3831	0.4499	0.4065	0.3886
Sense	0.4573	0.3260	0.2522	0.0601	0.0678	0.0681	0.3121	0.2526	0.1887
Parser	0.4760	0.3956	0.2997	0.1577	0.1330	0.1577	0.3055	0.2536	0.2184

Table 3: Task-level and parser-level F-measures of the parser on the development, test, and blind test sets for explicit and non-explicit relations individually and jointly. The Sense values are macro-averages.

Team	**P**	**R**	**F1**
lan15	0.2369	0.2432	0.2400
stepanov15	0.2094	0.2283	0.2184
li15b	0.1981	0.1737	0.1851

Table 4: Parser-level precision (P), recall (R), and F-measures (F1) of the submitted system on the blind test set. UniTN system is in **bold**.

metrics (tasks) per evaluation set is reported individually and jointly for explicit and non-explicit relations in Table 3. From the results, it is clear that non-explicit *Relation Sense Classification* is the hardest task. The next hardest task is inter-sentential *Argument 1 Span Extraction*. According to the organizers, the development, test and blind test sets are coming from the same domain. However, we observe a gradual decline in performance from development to test and from test to the blind test sets for each of the tasks on explicit relations. For non-explicit relations, on the other hand, performances vary and in some cases the performance on the blind test set is the highest (*Argument 2* spans).

The parser ranked the second on the test and the blind test sets and the third on the development set. For the comparison we also report performances of the systems ranked the first and the third in Table 4. The global F-measure of our parser on the blind test set is 0.2184, which is 0.0219 points lower than the first ranked system and 0.0333 points higher than the next best system. Comparing the performance with all the participants, we have observed that our parser maintains higher recall across the subtasks.

6 Conclusion

In this paper we have presented University of Trento parser submitted to CoNLL 2015 Shared Task on Shallow Discourse Parsing. We have described the discourse parsing architecture and models for each of the subtasks. The subtasks are categorized into span detection and classification. The span detection tasks are for explicit relations – Discourse Relation Detection and Argument Span Extraction; they are cast as token-level sequence labeling using Conditional Random Fields and argument span decisions are conditioned on relations' being intra- or inter-sentential. Classification tasks – Connective Sense Classification, Argument Position Classification, Non-Explicit Relation Detection, and Non-Explicit Relation Sense Classification – employ AdaBoost algorithm.

Participation in the CoNLL 2015 Shared Task on Shallow Discourse Parsing gave the teams a unique opportunity to compare their discourse parsing approaches on the same training and testing splits and the same automatic features. Even though the ranking of submitted systems depends on performances of all the modules, we can conclude that token-level sequence labeling for *Argument Span Extraction* of explicit discourse relations is a viable approach.

Participation additionally allowed us to identify potential points of improvement for our parser. For example, even though Discourse Connective Detection as sequence labeling has an F-measure of 0.8992 on the blind test set, it ranks 4th. Since it is the first step in the pipeline, increasing the robustness of the model is essential.

Acknowledgments

The research leading to these results has received funding from the European Union – Seventh Framework Programme (FP7/2007-2013) under grant agreement No. 610916 – SENSEI.

References

Sabine Buchholz. 2000. chunklink.pl. http://ilk.uvt.nl/software/.

Benoit Favre, Dilek Hakkani-Tür, and Sebastien Cuendet. 2007. Icsiboost. https://github.com/benob/icsiboost/.

Yoav Freund and Robert E. Schapire. 1997. A decision-theoretic generalization of on-line learning and an application to boosting. *Journal of Computer and System Sciences*, 55(1):119–139, August.

Sucheta Ghosh, Richard Johansson, Giuseppe Riccardi, and Sara Tonelli. 2011. Shallow discourse parsing with conditional random fields. In *Proceedings of the 5th International Joint Conference on Natural Language Processing (IJCNLP 2011)*.

Taku Kudo. 2013. CRF++. http://taku910.github.io/crfpp/.

John Lafferty, Andrew McCallum, and Fernando C. N. Pereira. 2001. Conditional random fields: Probabilistic models for segmenting and labeling sequence data. In *Proceedings of 18th International Conference on Machine Learning*, pages 282–289.

Ziheng Lin, Hwee Tou Ng, and Min-Yen Kan. 2014. A PDTB-styled end-to-end discourse parser. *Natural Language Engineering*, 20:151 – 184.

Emily Pitler and Ani Nenkova. 2009. Using syntax to disambiguate explicit discourse connectives in text. In *Proceedings of the ACL-IJCNLP Conference*, pages 13–16.

Emily Pitler, Annie Louis, and Ani Nenkova. 2009. Automatic sense prediction for implicit discourse relations in text. In *Proceedings of the 47th Annual Meeting of the ACL and the 4th IJCNLP of the AFNLP*, pages 683–691.

Rashmi Prasad, Eleni Miltsakaki, Nikhil Dinesh, Alan Lee, Aravind Joshi, Livio Robaldo, and Bonnie L Webber. 2007. The Penn Discourse Treebank 2.0 annotation manual.

Rashmi Prasad, Nikhil Dinesh, Alan Lee, Eleni Miltsakaki, Livio Robaldo, Aravind Joshi, and Bonnie Webber. 2008. The Penn Discourse Treebank 2.0. In *Proceedings of the 6th International Conference on Language Resources and Evaluation (LREC 2008)*.

Attapol T. Rutherford and Nianwen Xue. 2014. Discovering implicit discourse relations through Brown Cluster pair representation and coreference patterns. In *Proceedings of the 14th Conference of the European Chapter of the Association for Computational Linguistics (EACL 2014)*.

Evgeny A. Stepanov and Giuseppe Riccardi. 2013. Comparative evaluation of argument extraction algorithms in discourse relation parsing. In *Proceedings of the 13th International Conference on Parsing Technologies (IWPT 2013)*, pages 36–44, Nara, Japan, November.

Evgeny A. Stepanov and Giuseppe Riccardi. 2014. Towards cross-domain PDTB-style discourse parsing. In *EACL Workshops - Proceedings of the Louhi 2014: The Fifth International Workshop on Health Text Mining and Information Analysis*, pages 30–37, Gothenburg, Sweden, April. ACL.

Joseph Turian, Lev Ratinov, and Yoshua Bengio. 2010. Word representations: A simple and general method for semisupervised learning. In *In ACL*, pages 384–394.

Bonnie L. Webber, Markus Egg, and Valia Kordoni. 2011. Discourse structure and language technology. *Natural Language Engineering*, pages 1–54.

Nianwen Xue, Hwee Tou Ng, Sameer Pradhan, Rashmi Prasad, Christopher Bryant, and Attapol Rutherford. 2015. The CoNLL-2015 Shared Task on Shallow Discourse Parsing. In *Proceedings of the Nineteenth Conference on Computational Natural Language Learning: Shared Task*.

The SoNLP-DP System in the CoNLL-2015 shared Task

Fang Kong Sheng Li Guodong Zhou
School of Computer Science and Technology, Soochow University, China
Gangjiang Road 333#, Suzhou, Jiangsu of China 215006
kongfang@suda.edu.cn qcl6355@gmail.com gdzhou@suda.edu.cn

Abstract

This paper describes the submitted discourse parsing system of the natural language group of Soochow University (SoNLP-DP) to the CoNLL 2015 shared task. Our System classifies discourse relations into explicit and non-explicit relations and uses a pipeline platform to conduct every subtask to form an end-to-end shallow discourse parser in the Penn Discourse Treebank (PDTB). Our system is evaluated on the CoNLL-2015 Shared Task closed track and achieves the 18.51% in F1-measure on the official blind test set.

1 Introduction

Discourse parsing determines the internal structure of a text via identifying the discourse relations between its text units and plays an important role in natural language understanding that benefits a wide range of downstream natural language applications, such as coherence modeling (Barzilay and Lapata, 2005; Lin et al., 2011), text summarization (Lin et al., 2012), and statistical machine translation (Meyer and Webber, 2013).

As the largest discourse corpus, the Penn Discourse TreeBank (PDTB) corpus (Prasad et al., 2008) adds a layer of discourse annotations on the top of the Penn TreeBank (PTB) corpus (Marcus et al., 1993) and has been attracting more and more attention recently (Elwell and Baldridge, 2008; Pitler and Nenkova, 2009; Prasad et al., 2010; Ghosh et al., 2011; Kong et al., 2014; Lin et al., 2014). Different from another famous discourse corpus, the Rhetorical Structure Theory(RST) Treebank corpus(Carlson et al., 2001), the PDTB focuses on shallow discourse relations either lexically grounded in explicit discourse connectives or associated with sentential adjacency. This theory-neutral way makes no commitment to any kind of higher-level discourse structure and can work jointly with high-level topic and functional structuring (Webber et al., 2012) or hierarchial structuring (Asher and Lascarides, 2003).

Although much research work has been conducted for certain subtasks since the release of the PDTB corpus, there is still little work on constructing an end-to-end shallow discourse parser. The CoNLL 2015 shared task (Xue et al., 2015) evaluates end-to-end shallow discourse parsing systems for determining and classifying both explicit and non-explicit discourse relations. A participant system needs to (1)locate all explicit (e.g., "because", "however", "and".) discourse connectives in the text, (2)identify the spans of text that serve as the two arguments for each discourse connective, and (3) predict the sense of the discourse relations (e.g., "Cause", "Condition", "Contrast").

In this paper, we describe the system submission from the NLP group of Soochow university (SoNLP-DP). Our shallow discourse parser consists of multiple components in a pipeline architecture, including a connective classifier, argument labeler, explicit classifier, non-explicit classifier. Our system is evaluated on the CoNLL-2015 Shared Task closed track and achieves the 18.51% in F1-measure on the official blind test set.

The remainder of this paper is organized as follows. Section 2 presents our shallow discourse parsing system. The experimental results are described in Section 3. Section 4 concludes the paper.

2 System Architecture

In this section, after a quick overview of our system, we describe the details involved in implementing the end-to-end shallow discourse parser.

2.1 System Overview

A typical text consists of sentences glued together in a systematic way to form a coherent discourse.

Proceedings of the Nineteenth Conference on Computational Natural Language Learning: Shared Task, pages 32–36,
Beijing, China, July 26-31, 2015.

Referring to the PDTB, shallow discourse parsing focus on shallow discourse relations either lexically grounded in explicit discourse connectives or associated with sentential adjacency. Different from full discourse parsing, shallow discourse parsing transforms a piece of text into a set of discourse relations between two adjacent or non-adjacent discourse units, instead of connecting the relations hierarchically to one another to form a connected structure in the form of tree or graph.

Specifically, given a piece of text, the end-to-end shallow discourse parser returns a set of discourse relations in the form of a discourse connective (explicit or implicit) taking two arguments (clauses or sentences) with a discourse sense. That is, a complete end-to-end shallow discourse parser includes:

- connective identification, which identifies all connective candidates and labels them as whether they function as discourse connectives or not,
- argument labeling, which identifies the spans of text that serve as the two arguments for each discourse connective,
- explicit sense classification, which predicts the sense of the explicit discourse relations after achieving the connective and its arguments,
- non-explicit sense classification, for all adjacent sentence pairs within each paragraph without explicit discourse relations, which classify the given pair into EntRel, NoRel, or one of the Implicit/AltLex relation senses.

Figure 1 shows the components and the relations among them. Different from the traditional approach (i.e., Lin et al. (2014)), considering the interaction between argument labeler and explicit sense classifier, co-occurrence relation between explicit and non-explicit discourse relations in a text, our system does not employ a complete sequential pipeline framework.

2.2 Connective Identification

Our connective identifier works in two steps. First, the connective candidates are extracted from the given text referring to the PDTB. There are 100 types of discourse connectives defined in the PDTB. Then every connective candidate is checked whether it functions as a discourse connective.

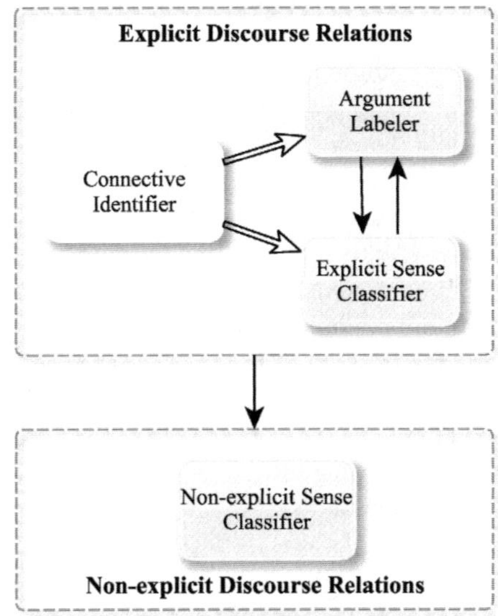

Figure 1: Framework of our end-to-end shallow discourse parser

Pitler and Nenkova (2009) showed that syntactic features extracted from constituent parse trees are very useful in disambiguating discourse connectives. Followed their work, Lin et al. (2014) found that a connective's context and part-of-speech (POS) are also helpful. Motivated by their work, we get a set of effective features, includes:

- Lexical: connective itself, POS of the connective, connective with its previous word, connective with its next word, the location of the connective in the sentence, i.e., start, middle and end of the sentence.
- Syntactic: the highest node in the parse tree that covers only the connective words (dominate node), the context of the dominate node [1], whether the right sibling contains a VP, the path from the parent node of the connective to the root of the parse tree.

Besides, we observed that the syntactic class of the connective[2] and connective modifier (such as

[1]We use POS combination of the parent, left sibling and right sibling of the dominate node to represent the context. When no parent or siblings, it is marked NULL.

[2]All the connectives are classified into four well-defined syntactic classes: subordinating conjunctions, coordinating conjunctions, prepositional phrases and adverbs.

apparently, in large part, etc.) give a very strong indication of its discourse usage. So we introduce both as two additional features.

2.3 Argument Labeling

The argument labeler needs to label the Arg1 and Arg2 spans for every connective determined by connective identifier. Following the work of Kong et al. (2014), we employ the constituent-based approach to argument labeling by first extracting the constituents from a parse tree are casted as argument candidates, then determining the role of every constituent as part of Arg1, Arg2, or NULL, and finally, merging all the constituents for Arg1 and Arg2 to obtain the Arg1 and Arg2 text spans respectively.

Specifically, similar to semantic role labeling (SRL), we use a simple algorithm to prune out those constituents that are clearly not arguments to the connective in question. The pruning algorithm works recursively in preprocessing, starting from the target connective node, i.e. the lowest node dominating the connective. First, all the siblings of the connective node are collected as candidates. Then we move on to the parent of the connective node and collect its siblings. This progress goes on until we reach the root of the parse tree.

After extracting the argument candidates, a multi-category classifier is employed to determine the role of every argument candidate (i.e., Arg1, Arg2, or NULL) with features reflecting the properties of the connective, the candidate constituent and relationship between them. Features include,

- Connective related features: connective itself, its syntactic category, its sense class.[3]
- Number of left/right siblings of the connective.
- The context of the constituent. We use POS combination of the constituent, its parent, left sibling and right sibling to represent the context. When there is no parent or siblings, it is marked NULL.
- The path from the parent node of the connective to the node of the constituent.
- The position of the constituent relative to the connective: left, right, or previous.

[3]In training stage, we extract the gold sense class from the annotated corpus. And in testing stage, the sense classification will be employed to get the automatic sense.

2.4 Explicit sense classification

After a discourse connective and its two arguments are identified, the sense classifier is proved to decide the sense that the relation conveys.

Although the same connective may carry different semantics under different contexts, only a few connectives are ambiguous (Pitler and Nenkova, 2009). Following the work of Lin et al. (2014), we introduce three features to train a sense classifier: the connective itself, its POS and the previous word of the connective.

Besides, since we observed that various relative positions (i.e., Arg1 precedes Arg2, Arg2 precedes Arg1, Arg2 is embedded within Arg1, or Arg1 is embedded within Arg2) are helpful for sense classification, we includes the relative position as an additional feature.

2.5 Non-explicit sense Classification

Referring to the PDTB, the non-explicit relations[4] are annotated for all adjacent sentence pairs within paragraphs. So non-explicit sense classification only considers the sense of every adjacent sentence pair within a paragraph without explicit discourse relations.

Our non-explicit sense classifier includes seven traditional features:

Verbs: Following the work of Pitler et al. (2009), we extract the pairs of verbs from the given adjacent sentence pair (i.e., Arg1 and Arg2). Besides that, the number of verb pairs which have the same highest VerbNet verb class (Kipper et al., 2006) is included as a feature. the average length of verb phrases in each argument, and the POS of main verbs are also included.

Polarity: This set of features record the number of *positive*, *negated positive*, *negative* and *neutral* words in both arguments and their cross-product. The polarity of every word in arguments is derived from Multi-perspective Question Answering Opinion Corpus(MPQA) (Wilson et al., 2005). Intuitively, polarity features would help recognize Comparison relations.

Modality: We include a set of features to record the presence or absence of specific modal words (i.e., can, may, will, shall, must, need) in Arg1 and Arg2, and their cross-product. The intuition

[4]The PDTB provides annotation for Implicit relations, AltLex relations, entity transition (EntRel), and otherwise no relation (NoRel), which are lumped together as Non-Explicit relations.

behind this feature set is that the Contingency relations seem to have more modal words.

Production rules: According to Lin et al. (2009), the syntactic structure of one argument may constrain the relation type and the syntactic structure of the other argument. Three features are introduced to denote the presence of syntactic productions in Arg1, Arg2 or both. Here, these production rules are extracted from the training data and the rules with frequency less than 5 are ignored.

Dependency rules: Similar with Production rules, three features denoting the presence of dependency productions in Arg1, Arg2 or both are also introduced in our system.

Fisrt/Last and First 3 words: This set of features include the first and last words of Arg1, the first and last words of Arg2, the pair of the first words of Arg1 and Arg2, the pair of the last words as features, and the first three words of each argument.

Brown cluster pairs: We include the Cartesian product of the Brown cluster values of the words in Arg1 and Arg2. In our system, we simply take 100 Brown clusters provided by CoNLL shared task.

Besides, we introduce two features which describe the automatic determined connective list contained by Arg1 and Arg2, respectively, to capture the co-occurrence relationship between non-explicit and explicit discourse relations.

3 Experimentation

We train our system on the corpora provided in the CoNLL-2015 Shared Task and evaluate our system on the CoNLL-2015 Shared Task closed track. All our classifiers are trained using the OpenNLP maximum entropy package[5] with the default parameters (i.e. without smoothing and with 100 iterations). We firstly report the official score on the CoNLL-2015 shared task on development, test and blind test sets. Then, the supplementary results provided by the shared task organizes are reported.

In Table 1, we present the official results of our system performances on the CoNLL-2015 development, test and blind test sets, respectively. From the results, we can find that,

- For Connective identification, our system achieved satisfactory results.

[5]http://maxent.sourceforge.net/

	Development	Test	Blind Test
Arg1&2	43.12	37.01	33.23
Arg1	57.28	52.45	46.28
Arg2	67.72	63.57	61.70
Connective	94.22	94.77	91.62
Sense	17.80	18.38	16.93
Parser	26.32	20.64	18.51

Table 1: the official F1 score of our system.

- For argument labeling, the performance of Arg2 is better than Arg1 and the performance gaps are more than 10% in F1-measure. And the combined results of Arg1 and Arg2 extractor reduced so much in comparison with the performance of Arg1 or Arg2.
- For sense classification, there is a lot of room to improve.
- For the overall parser performance, obviously, a lot of work is needed for end-to-end discourse parsing before practical application.

		Arg1&2	Arg1	Arg2	Sense	Parser
Dev	Exp	34.67	38.67	74.37	20.18	29.78
	nonExp	49.94	62.13	62.37	7.37	23.54
Test	Exp	30.21	34.02	74.48	20.59	25.30
	nonExp	42.38	57.71	54.95	6.77	16.97
Blind	Exp	30.42	36.43	73.04	17.36	22.95
	nonExp	35.87	49.87	51.07	5.24	14.35

Table 2: the supplementary F1 score of our system.

In Table 2, we reported the supplementary results provided by the shared task organizes on the development, test and blind test sets. These additional experiments investigate the performance of our shallow discourse parsing for explicit and non-explicit relations separately. From the results, we can find that the sense classification for both explicit and non-explicit discourse relations are the biggest obstacles to the overall performance of discourse parsing.

4 Conclusion

We have presented the SoNLP-DP system from the NLP group of Soochow university that participated in the CoNLL-2015 shared task. Our system is evaluated on the CoNLL-2015 Shared Task closed track and achieves the 18.51% in F1-measure on the official blind test set.

Acknowledgements

This research is supported by Key project 61333018 and 61331011 under the National Natural Science Foundation of China, Project 6127320 and 61472264 under the National Natural Science Foundation of China.

References

Nicholas Asher and Alex Lascarides. 2003. *Logics of Conversation*. Cambridge Unversity Press.

Regina Barzilay and Mirella Lapata. 2005. Modeling local coherence: An entity-based approach. In *Proceedings of the 43rd Annual Meeting of the Association for Computational Linguistics*.

Lynn Carlson, Daniel Marcu, and Mary Ellen Okurowski. 2001. Building a discourse-tagged corpus in the framework of rhetorical structure theory. In *Proceedings of Second SIGdial Workshop on Discourse and Dialogue*.

Robert Elwell and Jason Baldridge. 2008. Discourse connective argument identification with connective specific rankers. In *Second IEEE International Conference on Semantic Computing*.

Sucheta Ghosh, Richard Johansson, Giuseppe Riccardi, and Sara Tonelli. 2011. Shallow discourse parsing with conditional random fields. In *Proceedings of the 5th International Joint Conference on Natural Language Processing*.

Karin Kipper, Anna Korhonen, Neville Ryant, and Martha Palmer. 2006. Extending verbnet with novel verb classes. In *Fifth Internal Conference on Language Resources and Evaluation*.

Fang Kong, Hwee Tou Ng, and Guodong Zhou. 2014. A constituent-based approach to argument labeling with joint inference in discourse parsing. In *Proceedings of the 2014 Conference on Empirical Methods in Natural Language Processing*.

Ziheng Lin, Min-Yen Kan, and Hwee Tou Ng. 2009. Recognizing implicit discourse relations in the Penn Discourse Treebank. In *Proceedings of the 2009 Conference on Empirical Methods in Natural Language Processing*.

Ziheng Lin, Hwee Tou Ng, and Min-Yen Kan. 2011. Automatically evaluating text coherence using discourse relations. In *Proceedings of the 49th Annual Meeting of the Association for Computational Linguistics*.

Ziheng Lin, Chang Liu, Hwee Tou Ng, and Min-Yen Kan. 2012. Combining coherence models and machine translation evaluation metrics for summarization evaluation. In *Proceedings of the 50th Annual Meeting of the Association for Computational Linguistics*.

Ziheng Lin, Hwee Tou Ng, and Min-Yen Kan. 2014. A PDTB-styled end-to-end discourse parser. *Natural Language Engineering*, 20(2):151–184.

Mitchell P. Marcus, Beatrice Santorini, and Mary Ann Marcinkiewicz. 1993. Building a large annotated corpus of English: The Penn Treebank. *Computational Linguistics*, 19(2):313–330.

Thomas Meyer and Bonnie Webber. 2013. Implicitation of discourse connectives in (machine) translation. In *Proceedings of the Workshop on Discourse in Machine Translation*.

Emily Pitler and Ani Nenkova. 2009. Using syntax to disambiguate explicit discourse connectives in text. In *Proceedings of the ACL-IJCNLP 2009 Conference Short Papers*.

Rashmi Prasad, Nikhil Dinesh, Alan Lee, Eleni Miltsakaki, Livio Robaldo, Aravind Joshi, and Bonnie Webber. 2008. The Penn Discourse TreeBank 2.0. In *Proceedings of the LREC 2008 Conference*.

Rashmi Prasad, Aravind Joshi, and Bonnie Webber. 2010. Exploiting scope for shallow discourse parsing. In *Proceedings of the Seventh International Conference on Language Resources and Evaluation*.

Bonnie Webber, Marcus Egg, and Valia Kordoni. 2012. Discourse structure and language technology. *Natural Language Engineering*, 18(4):437–490, 10.

Theresa Wilson, Janyce Wiebe, and Paul Hoffmann. 2005. Recognizing contextual polarity in phrase-level sentiment analysis. In *Proceedings of Human Language Technology Conference and Conference on Empirical Methods in Natural Language Processing*.

Nianwen Xue, Hwee Tou Ng, Sameer Pradhan, Rashmi Prasad, Christopher Bryant, and Attapol Rutherford. 2015. The conll-2015 shared task on shallow discourse parsing. In *Proceedings of the Nineteenth Conference on Computational Natural Language Learning: Shared Task*.

Shallow Discourse Parsing Using Constituent Parsing Tree*

Changge Chen[1,2], **Peilu Wang**[1,2], **Hai Zhao**[1,2†]
[1]Department of Computer Science and Engineering,
Shanghai Jiao Tong University, Shanghai 200240, China
[2]Key Laboratory of Shanghai Education Commission
for Intelligent Interaction and Cognitive Engineering,
Shanghai Jiao Tong University, Shanghai 200240, China
{changge.chen.cc,plwang1990}@gmail.com, zhaohai@cs.sjtu.edu.cn

Abstract

This paper describes our system in the closed track of the shared task of CoNLL-2015. We formulize the discourse parsing work into a series of classification subtasks. The official evaluation shows that the proposed framework can give competitive results and we give a few discussions over latent improvement as well.

1 System Overview

We design our shallow discourse parser as a sequential pipeline to mimic the annotation procedure as the Penn Discourse Treebank (we will use PDTB instead in the rest of this paper) annotator (Lin et al., 2014). Figure 1 gives the pipeline of the system. The system can be roughly split into two parts: the explicit and the non-explicit. The first part consists of three steps, which sequentially are Explicit Classifier, Explicit Argument Labeler, and Explicit Sense Classifier. While the non-explicit part consists of Filter, Non-explicit and Non-explicit Sense Classifiers. Non-explicit relations include *'Implicit'*, *'AltLex'*, *'EntRel'*, but not *'NoRel'*.

We adopt an adapted maximum entropy model as the classification algorithm for every steps. Our system only exploits resources provided by the organizer.

*This work of C. Chen, P. Wang, and H. Zhao was supported in part by the National Natural Science Foundation of China under Grants 60903119, 61170114, and 61272248, the National Basic Research Program of China under Grant 2013CB329401, the Science and Technology Commission of Shanghai Municipality under Grant 13511500200, the European Union Seventh Framework Program under Grant 247619, the Cai Yuanpei Program (CSC fund 201304490199, 201304490171, and the art and science interdiscipline funds of Shanghai Jiao Tong University (a study on mobilization mechanism and alerting threshold setting for online community, and media image and psychology evaluation: a computational intelligence approach under Grant 14X190040031(14JCRZ04).

†Corresponding author

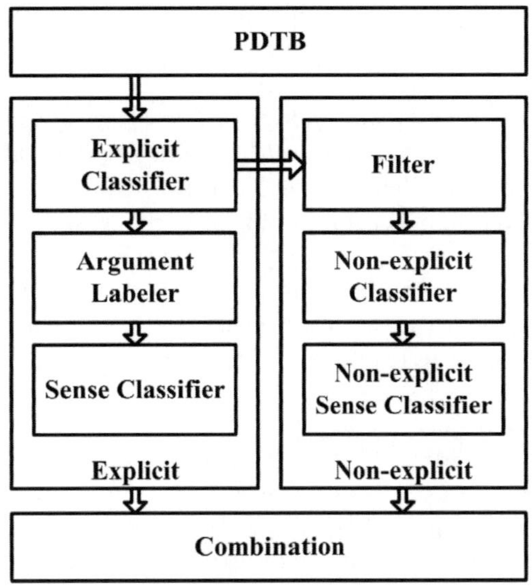

Figure 1: Pipeline of the system

Explicit connectives in train set	14722
Level-order Scan	13911

Table 1: Performance of level-order scan

We first give a brief introduction over each step of the entire system as the following. After the Explicit Classifier detects explicit connectives, the Explicit Argument Labeler then prunes and classifies the *'Arg1'* and *'Arg2'* of the detected connective. Then, Explicit Sense Classifier integrates results of previous two steps when trying to distinguish different senses. The second part of the system starts with filtering out obvious false cases. Then the Non-explicit classifier classifies the non-relations into three classes, i.e., *'Implicit'*, *'AltLex'*, *'EntRel'*. Finally, the Non-explicit Sense classifier determines the sense of the non-explicit relation. In the last two steps, we take the *'EntRel'* as a sense of implicit relation, which we will explain later.

Proceedings of the Nineteenth Conference on Computational Natural Language Learning: Shared Task, pages 37–41,
Beijing, China, July 26-31, 2015. ©2014 Association for Computational Linguistics

Tag	P	R	F
Arg1	0.7748	0.7544	0.7645
Arg2	0.8102	0.9658	0.8812
NULL	0.9922	0.9781	0.9851

Table 2: Performance of Argument Labler

2 System Modules

2.1 Explicit Part

In this part, our parser extracts the explicit relations. An explicit example is given below.

He added that "having just one firm do this isn't going to mean a hill of beans. But **if this prompts others to consider the same thing, then it may become much more important**.

'Arg1' is shown in italic, and *'Arg2'* is shown in bold. The discourse connective is underlined and the sense of this explicit relation is *'Comparison.Concession'*.

2.1.1 Explicit Classifier

There are 100 explicit connectives in PDTB annotation (Prasad et al., 2008). However, some connectives, e.g., *'and'*, do not express a discourse relation. We use a level-order traverse to scan every node in the constituent parse tree to select the connective candidates. This method gives us a high recall in the train set as shown in Table 1.

Seven features are considered (Pitler and Nenkova, 2009):

a) Self Category The highest dominated node which covers the connective.

b) Parent Caterogy The category of the parent of the self category.

c) Left Sibling Category The syntactic category of immediate left sibling of the self-category. It would be *'NONE'* if the connective is the leftmost node.

d) Right Sibling Category The immediate right sibling of the self category. It also would be assigned *'NONE'* if the self-category has been the rightmost node.

e) VP Existence We set a binary feature to indicate whether the right sibling contains a VP.

f) Connective In addition to those features proposed by Pilter and Nenvoda, we introduce connective feature. The potential connective itself would be a strong sign of its function. A few of discourse connectives that are deterministic. For example, *'in addition'* will always be *'Expansion.Conjunction'*.

Maximum Entropy classifier has shown good performance in various previous works (Wang et al., 2014; Jia et al., 2013; Zhao and Kit, 2008). Based on these features, we trained a Maximum Entropy classifier. In order to check the performance of the classifier only, we evaluate the classifier on connective candidates that selected by a level-order traverse. This gives 93.87% accuracy and 90.1% F1 score on dev set.

2.1.2 Explicit Argument Labeler

With all explicit connectives detected, we exploit a constituent-based approach to perform argument labeling (Kong et al., 2014). Along the path from the connective node to the root node in the constituent parse tree, all the siblings of every node on the path are selected as candidates for *'Arg1'* and *'Arg2'*. For these candidates, we compare them with PDTB to label them as *'Arg1'*, *'Arg2'*, or *'NULL'*. However, this argument prune strategy focuses on intra sentence. In addition, Kong et al. unified the intra- and inter-sentence cases by treating the immediate preceding sentence as a special constituent. Based on our empirical results, the inter-sentences only contribute to the augment candidate Arg1. Kong et al. also reported a very high recalls (80-90%) on *'Arg1'* and *'Arg2'* extraction, though our re-implementation only receive recalls 37.5% and 51.3% of the *'Arg1'* and *'Arg2'*, respectively. And about 87.75% of all the pruning out constituents are labeled as *'NULL'*. Similar to treating the immediate preceding sentence as *'Arg1'* candidate, we take the remaining part of the sentence that is adjacent to the connective as *'Arg2'* candidate. This approach gives a boost in *'Arg2'* recall, as high as 93.1%.

We extract features from constituent parser tree (Zhao and Kit, 2008; Zhao et al., 2009). The extracted features can be divided into two parts. The first part captures information about the connective itself:

a) Con-str Case-sensitive string of the given connective.

b) Con-Lstr The lowercase string of the connective.

c) Con-iLSib Number of left sibling of the connective.

d) Con-iRSib Number of right sibling of the connective.

The second part consists of features from the

syntactic constituent:
e) NT-Ctx Context of the constituent. We use POS combination of the constituent, its parent, left sibling and right sibling to represent the context.
f) Con-NT-Path The path from the parent of the connective to the node of the constituent.
g) Con-NT-Position The positive of the constituent relative to the connective: left, right, or previous.

After the parser categories all the candidates constituent into *'Arg1'*, *'Arg2'*, and *'NULL'*, Kong et al. adopted a Linear Integer Programming to impose constraints that the number of *'Arg1'* and **'Arg2'** should no less than one, The extracted arguments should not overlap with the connective. Our experiments also show that some constraints are useless. For example, constraint that the pruned out candidates should not overlap with the connective. The pruning algorithm considers the siblings of the node along the path, there is no chance that the pruned out candidate would overlap with the connective node.

Without considering the error propagated by the pruning process, the argument labeler gives results as Table 2.

2.1.3 Explicit Sense Classifier

In this part we only take a naive approach that take the most frequent sense of the detected explicit connective. A better approach needs to build a sense classifier with syntactic features of the connective such as POS, and position and length of arguments.

2.2 Non-Explicit Part

This part is based on the result of explicit part. We assume that Explicit and Non-explicit relations cannot exist in the same sentence simultaneously. So we take out sentences which have been labeled as Explicit in the first part. Then, we take all the adjacent sentences left in the article as candidate implicit relations. There are 13,155 implicit relations given in the train set.

2.2.1 Filter

Apart form filtering out the explicit connective, we also discard sentences between two paragraphs. After these two filtering steps we get 8,728 non-explicit relations.

2.2.2 Non-explicit Classifier

At first glance, we should build a classifier that can distinguish the relations *'Implicit'*, *'AltLex'*, and *'EntRel'*. We give the distribution of each relations in the train set in Table 3.

	Implicit	AltLex	EntRel
#	13,155	524	4,133
%	73.85	2.94	23.2

Table 3: Distribution of Non-Explicit Relations in train set

Sense	#	%
*Ent Rel	4,133	23.2
*Expn..Conj.	3,321	18.64
*Expn..Rest.	2,543	14.28
*Cont. Cause. Reason	2,135	11.99
*Comp..Cont.	1,646	9.24
*Cont..Cause.Result	1,519	8.53
* Expn..Inst.	1,165	6.54
*Temp..Asyn..Prec.	460	2.58
*Comp..Conc.	197	1.11
*Temp..Sync.	169	0.95
Comparison	145	0.81
*Temp..Asyn..Suc.	143	0.8
*Expn..Alt..Chosen alt.	142	0.8
Expn.	75	0.42
*Expn.Alt.	11	0.06
*Cont.Cond.	4	0.02
*Expn..Exc.	2	0.01
Cont..Cause	1	0.00
Temp.	1	0.00
Cont.	1	0.00

Table 4: Distribution of Non-explicit Senses in train set.*

We can see the *'AltLex'* only covers about 2.94%, which is relatively negligible comparing with *'Implicit'*(73.85%) and *'EntRel'*(23.2%). So we decide to focus only on the latter two relations, and the classifier only works on these two relations. Instead of building a single classifier, we set all the non-explicit relations as *'Implicit'* here, and view *'EntRel'* as a sense of implicit relation.

2.2.3 Non-explicit Sense Classifier

The distribution of all senses in the train set is given in Table 4. The current shared task only asks

*Abbreviations: Expansionz(Expn.), Conjunction(Conj.), Restatement(Rest.), Contingency(Cont.), Instantiation(Inst.), Temporal(Temp.), Asynchronous(Asyn.), Precedence(Prec.), Comparison(Comp.),Concession(Conc.), Synchrony(Sync.), Asynchronous(Asyn.), Succession(Suc.), alternative(alt.), Condition(Cond.), Exception(Exc.)

	Blind	Test	Dev
Explicit Conn. F	0.8168	0.7867	0.8609
Explicit Conn. P	0.8117	0.7784	0.8528
Explicit Conn. R	0.8219	0.7952	0.8691
Arg1 Arg2 Ext. F	0.047	0.0457	0.0681
Arg1 Arg2 Ext. P	0.0453	0.0424	0.0643
Arg1 Arg2 Ext. R	0.0488	0.0495	0.0724
Arg1 Ext. F	0.0629	0.0657	0.0845
Arg1 Ext. P	0.0607	0.061	0.0798
Arg1 Ext. R	0.0653	0.0712	0.0898
Arg2 Ext. F	0.2182	0.2166	0.264
Arg2 Ext. P	0.2104	0.2011	0.2492
Arg2 Ext. R	0.2266	0.2347	0.2806
Parser F	0.0358	0.0443	0.0655
Parser P	0.0346	0.0411	0.0618
Parser R	0.0372	0.048	0.0696

Table 5: Detailed Results

us to detect 15 senses, which are marked by star. We can see that senses below the double line account less than 1%. Based on this observation, we decide only consider those significant sense.

What's more, we can see that the most frequent sense is *'EntRel'*. This leads to our another strategy: At first we set all the candidate non-explicit senses as *'Implicit'* and view *'EntRel'* as a sense. Then when the Non-explicit Sense Classifier labels the sense as *'EntRel'*, the Non-explicit Sense Classifier re-labels the type of corresponding relation as *'EntRel'*.

Previous studies attempt to predict the missing connective of implicit relations (Zhou et al., 2010; Pitler et al., 2009) . It has been shown that connective is very predictive for the sense of the relation (Kong et al., 2014). Consequently, we can get the intuition that features for predicting the missing connective are also useful for predicting the implicit sense. Thus we use word-pair features to train our Non-explicit Sense Classifier:

b) Arg1Last The last word of *'Arg1'*.
a) Arg1First The first word of *'Arg1'*.
c) Arg2First The first word of *'Arg2'*.
d) Arg2Last The last word of *'Arg2'*.
e) FirstS Arg1First + Arg2First.
f) LastS Arg1Last + Arg2Last.
g) Arg1First3 The first three words of *'Arg1'*.
h) Arg1Last3 The last three words of *'Arg2'*.
i) Arg2First3 The first three words of *'Arg2'*.

3 Evaluation

A comprehensive evaluation towards our parser has been given in Table 5. We can see that the first step of our parser, i.e., Explicit Classifier, does a moderate job. However, our work to extract the *'Arg1'* and *'Arg2'* cannot be regarded as success. Since our parser is in a sequential mode, all steps after that receive negative impacts.

4 Conclusion and Future Work

In this paper, a sequential system is proposed to do shallow discourse parsing. We demonstrate that the whole task can be worked out by a pipeline consists of several subtasks.

In future, we will tune our Argument Labeler in order to gain a better result in the explicit part .

References

Zhongye Jia, Peilu Wang, and Hai Zhao. 2013. Grammatical error correction as multiclass classification with single model. pages 74–81, Sofia, Bulgaria, August.

Fang Kong, Hwee Tou Ng, and Guodong Zhou. 2014. A constituent-based approach to argument labeling with joint inference in discourse parsing. In *Proceedings of the 2014 Conference on Empirical Methods in Natural Language Processing*, pages 68–77, Doha, Qatar, October.

Ziheng Lin, Hwee Tou Ng, and Min-Yen Kan. 2014. A PDTB-styled end-to-end discourse parser. *Natural Language Engineering*, 20:151–184, April.

Emily Pitler and Ani Nenkova. 2009. Using syntax to disambiguate explicit discourse connectives in text. In *Proceedings of the Joint Conference of the 47th Annual Meeting of the ACL and the 4th International Joint Conference on Natural Language Processing of the AFNLP*, pages 13–16, Suntec, Singapore, August.

Emily Pitler, Annie Louis, and Ani Nenkova. 2009. Automatic sense prediction for implicit discourse relations in text. In *Proceedings of the Joint Conference of the 47th Annual Meeting of the ACL and the 4th International Joint Conference on Natural Language Processing of the AFNLP*, pages 683–691, Suntec, Singapore, August.

Rashmi Prasad, Dinesh Nikhil, Alan Lee, Eleni Miltsakaki, Livio Robaldo, Aravind K Joshi, and Bonnie L Webber. 2008. The Penn discourse treebank 2.0. In *The International Conference on Language Resources and Evaluation*, Marrakech, Morocco, May.

Peilu Wang, Zhongye Jia, and Hai Zhao. 2014. Grammatical error detection and correction using a single maximum entropy model. pages 74–82, Baltimore, Maryland, USA, July.

Hai Zhao and Chunyu Kit. 2008. Parsing syntactic and semantic dependencies with two single-stage maximum entropy models. In *Proceedings of the Twelfth Conference on Computational Natural Language Learning*, pages 203–207, Manchester, August.

Hai Zhao, Wenliang Chen, Jun'ichi Kazama, Kiyotaka Uchimoto, and Kentaro Torisawa. 2009. Multilingual dependency learning: Exploiting rich features for tagging syntactic and semantic dependencies. In *Proceedings of the Thirteenth Conference on Computational Natural Language Learning: Shared Task*, pages 61–66, Boulder, Colorado, June.

Zhi-Min Zhou, Yu Xu, Zheng-Yu Niu, Man Lan, Jian Su, and Chew Lim Tan. 2010. Predicting discourse connectives for implicit discourse relation recognition. In *Proceedings of the 23rd International Conference on Computational Linguistics*, pages 1507–1514, Beijing, China, August.

A Minimalist Approach to Shallow Discourse Parsing and Implicit Relation Recognition

Christian Chiarcos and **Niko Schenk**
Applied Computational Linguistics Lab
Goethe University Frankfurt am Main
{chiarcos,n.schenk}@em.uni-frankfurt.de

Abstract

We describe a minimalist approach to shallow discourse parsing in the context of the CoNLL 2015 Shared Task.[1] Our parser integrates a rule-based component for argument identification and data-driven models for the classification of explicit and implicit relations. We place special emphasis on the evaluation of implicit sense labeling, we present different feature sets and show that (i) word embeddings are competitive with traditional word-level features, and (ii) that they can be used to considerably reduce the total number of features. Despite its simplicity, our parser is competitive with other systems in terms of sense recognition and thus provides a solid ground for further refinement.

1 Introduction

Comprehending sentences and other textual units requires capabilities beyond capturing the lexical semantics of their components. Contextual information is needed, i.e., a semantically coherent representation of the logical structure of a text—be it written or spoken discourse, unidirectional or bidirectional communication, etc. Different formalisms have been proposed to model these assumptions in frameworks of coherence relations and discourse structure (Mann and Thompson, 1988; Lascarides and Asher, 1993; Webber, 2004). In a more applied NLP context, the goal of *shallow discourse parsing* (SDP) is to automatically detect relevant discourse units and to label the relations that hold between them. Unlike *deep discourse parsing*, a stringent logical formalization or the establishment of a global data structure, say, a tree, is not required.

With the release of the Penn Discourse Treebank (Prasad et al., 2008, PDTB), annotated training data for SDP has become available and, as a consequence, the field has considerably attracted researchers from the NLP and IR community. Informally, the PDTB annotation scheme describes a discourse unit as a syntactically motivated character span in the text, and augments with relations pointing from argument 2 (*Arg2*, prototypically, a discourse unit associated with an explicit discourse marker) to its antecedent, i.e., the discourse unit *Arg1*. Relations are labeled with a relation type (its *sense*) and the associated discourse marker (either as found in the text or as inferred by the annotator). PDTB distinguishes *explicit* and *implicit* relations depending on whether such a connector or cue phrase (e.g., *because*) is present, or not.[2] As an illustration, consider the following example from the PDTB:

> **Arg1**: *Solo woodwind players have to be creative if they want to work a lot*
> **Connector**: *because*
> **Arg2**: *their repertoire and audience appeal are limited*

In this explicit relation, Arg1 and Arg2 are directly connected by the cue word; the relation type is *Contingency.Cause.Reason*—one out of roughly 20 three-level senses marking the relation sense between any given argument pair in the PDTB.

We participate in the CoNLL 2015 Shared Task (Xue et al., 2015) with a minimalist end-to-end shallow discourse parser developed from scratch. It was, however, originally not specifically developed for this purpose, but created in preparation of more elaborate experiments on implicit intersentential relations in discourse, an aspect not explicitly addressed by the evaluation of the Shared Task.

[1] `http://www.cs.brandeis.edu/~clp/conll15st/index.html`

[2] The set of relation types is completed by alternative lexicalization (*AltLex*, discourse marker rephrased), entity relation (*EntRel*, i.e., anaphoric coherence), resp. the absence of any relation (*NoRel*).

Proceedings of the Nineteenth Conference on Computational Natural Language Learning: Shared Task, pages 42–49,
Beijing, China, July 26-31, 2015.

The remainder of the paper describes the architecture and functionality of our system: A rule-based component identifies explicit and implicit argument-pairs and two statistical, data-driven models classify senses. Our system suffers from the surface-based definition of argument spans and their evaluation as string ranges, but with respect to sense disambiguation (in particular, in terms of precision), it is competitive with other systems in the task. Inspired by the diversity of different approaches to handle the more challenging—and more interesting—non-explicit relations, our description focuses on inferring implicit senses and benefits from abstracting from traditional surface-based features in favor of distributional representations of the argument spans.

2 Related Work

At the moment, few full-fledged end-to-end discourse parsers exist, but they use different theories of discourse, e.g., PDTB (Lin et al., 2010), or RST (duVerle and Prendinger, 2009; Feng and Hirst, 2012). Most of the literature on automated discourse analysis has focused on specialized subtasks:

Argument identification is approached by, e.g., Ghosh et al. (2012) on the word and inter-sentential level, using a CRF-based approach including local and global features. Kong et al. (2014) tackle argument span detection on the constituent-level with features for subtrees and special constraints.

Explicit relation classification Classifying the senses of explicit relations is rather straightforward, given the cue phrase. Pitler and Nenkova (2009) introduce a refinement using syntactic features to disambiguate explicit connectives which increases performance close to a human baseline.

Implicit relation classification In the early attempt by Marcu and Echihabi (2002), implicit relation classification was grounded on synthetic training data (relation patterns with explicit cue phrases removed) and a Naive Bayes model trained on word-pair features. Aggregation over such word-pairs was described by Biran and McKeown (2013), while Park and Cardie (2012) optimized feature sets through feature selection, preprocessing and special binning techniques.

Out of these, implicit relation classification remains the most problematic subtask, and attracted

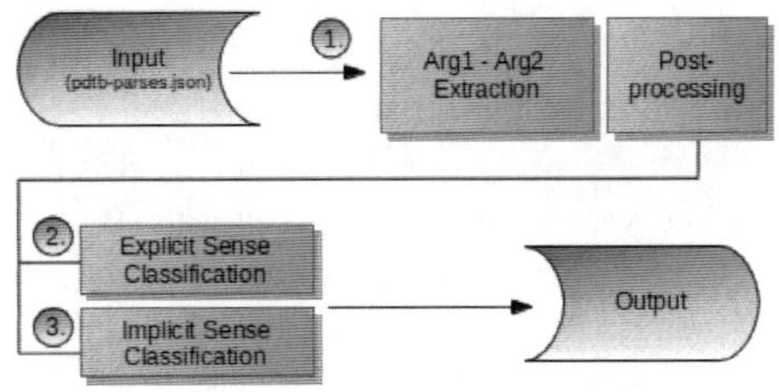

Figure 1: Our three-component SDP pipeline.

considerable interest: Pitler et al. (2009) present an extensive evaluation of mostly linguistically motivated features for implicit sense labeling in a 4-way classification experiment. Useful indicators, among others, are verb information, polarity labels and the first and last three words of an argument. Lin et al. (2009) refine their work by introducing contextual and dependency information from the argument pairs and show that syntactic phrase-structure features help in level-2 relation type classifications. Moreover, Zhou et al. (2010) use a language model to "predict" explicit connectives from implicit relations. Our approach is most similar to the one by Rutherford and Xue (2014), who successfully integrate distributional representations to substitute word-pair features.

3 Approach

Our SDP system participates in the *closed track* of the Shared Task.[3] Its components are illustrated in Figure 1. Input is tokenized text in the provided JSON format including meta information about parts-of-speech and sentence boundaries.

3.1 Argument Identification

The SDP pipeline processes the documents sentence by sentence. Due to the strict time constraints of the Shared Task, we have set up a rule-based detector for both Arg1 and Arg2 spans as follows:

- Extract an *explicit* Arg1–Arg2 pair, where Arg2 is a complete sentence starting with an explicit connective.[4] The previous sentence serves as Arg1.

[3] `http://www.cs.brandeis.edu/~clp/conll15st/dataset.html`

[4] An exhaustive list of explicit cue words was obtained from the training section of the PDTB, ranging from unigrams to 7-grams.

- Refining step 1, we extract sentence-internal *explicit* Arg1–Arg2 pairs by applying the pattern `BOS-Arg1-cue word-punctuation-Arg2-EOS`.[5] Note that we require a punctuation symbol between both arguments to prevent the template from extracting, e.g., coordinated NPs such as *chairman and chief executive*.

- We take special care of *explicit* temporal Arg1–Arg2 relations and extract patterns of the form `BOS-cue word-Arg2-comma-Arg1-EOS`. Cue words are, e.g., *while*, *although*, *unless*.

- More complicated *explicit* patterns split the second argument into two parts by the cue word as with *however* in: *Argument identification is tough. Writing patterns, however, is easy.*

- Finally, we extract all relations between adjacent, complete sentences as Arg1 and Arg2 spans as *implicit*, iff Arg1–Arg2 is not already an explicit relation and Arg1–Arg2 does not cross a paragraph boundary.

- EntRel and AltLex relations are beyond the scope of our current parser as both taken together make up only 14.3% of all relations in the training section of the PDTB.

Post processing A rule-based *post-processor* is applied on top of the previous component. Its purpose is to fix token lists for argument spans according to the guidelines of the Shared Task as no partial credit is given for non-exact matches. For example, a leading or trailing punctuation, quote or attribution spans must not be part of any of the arguments.

This rule-based model had specifically to be developed for the Shared Task; it replaced a more elaborate argument identifier based on structured representations rather than character spans to represent the arguments of discourse relations.

3.2 Labeling Explicit Senses

Given two argument spans and an explicit connective, we aim to predict the correct relation type (sense). To this end, we trained a simple statistical model[6] in a supervised setting on all explicit relations whose only feature is the cue word itself. An exhaustive list of cue words (features) was obtained from the training section of the PDTB data. Moreover, we restricted the set of labels to those eight senses that appear only frequently enough, i.e. we excluded those whose proportion is less than 5% of all explicit senses in the training section.

3.3 Labeling Implicit Senses

A third component handles the classification of *implicit senses* for any implicit Arg1–Arg2 pair. Similar to the previous subtask, we restrict the label set (here to six senses). We trained various models only on implicit relations. Inspired by the previous literature on implicit sense classification, we experimented with different surface-based word-pair feature sets for Arg1 and Arg2, as well as more abstract representations for the word forms, such as embeddings and word vectors:[7]

1. Word-pair (WP) token features of Arg1 and Arg2: (i) normal-case (N) as encountered in the text and (ii) after lower-case normalization (l), both with frequency thresholds.

2. Similar to (1.) but using word stems (Porter, 1980) instead.

3. Similar to (1.) but using a Brown cluster 3200 representation (Turian et al., 2010) for each word form if it exists. Otherwise, we use the word form as feature.

A subsequent experiment is concerned with finding a more compact representation of both Arg1 and Arg2 spans: For each argument pair, we computed two real-valued vectors (600 features in total), in which each argument is represented by a 300-dimensional feature vector. These were obtained by summing over all skip-gram neural word embeddings (Mikolov et al., 2013) present in each argument weighted by the respective number of elements (embeddings) found in each argument. The normalization is necessary to handle sentences of different lengths.

[5] `BOS` and `EOS` mark the beginning and the end of sentence, respectively.

[6] In all our experiments, we made use of the JAVA implementation of *libsvm* (Chang and Lin, 2011) with linear kernel and default parameters.

[7] A word-pair is defined as the cross product of any combination of words in both Arg1 and Arg2. Punctuation symbols were removed before processing. All features are treated as boolean if present (true) or absent (false).

Testing the effect of both Brown clusters and neural word embeddings, a final experiment combines them into one feature set for each implicit argument pair.

4 Evaluation

4.1 Argument Identification

In the overall task (based on the blind test set), our system is ranked at position 13 – rather poorly compared to 17 submitted systems in total (including a baseline). This is due to the imperfect argument identification, and in particular due to the erroneous recognition of explicit cue phrases. The system suffers from low overall recall of the identified explicit argument spans, including the connective.[8] A simple error analysis reveals that patterns in which cue phrases do not directly start the second argument are hard to identify by our rule-based system. Moreover, punctuation symbols pose problems to the system as well (cf. our discussion in Section 4.3). A separate evaluation shows that post-processing argument pairs improves F-score by 2%.

Despite these obvious drawbacks, we would like to draw special attention to our statistical components for sense classification: for the argument pairs which were correctly recognized, our system is ranked at position 4 for sense precision, even outperforming the best three systems. We will elaborate more on these models in the next subsection.

4.2 Explicit and Implicit Senses

The classification of explicit senses with only the connector word as single feature reaches an accuracy of 80.48% using the PDTB training–development split. This is still below state-of-the art (94% in Pitler and Nenkova, 2009)[9]—yet satisfying for our lightweight system with its original emphasis on implicit relations.

Table 1 shows the results for implicit sense classification (472 instances in total) using different feature sets.[10] First, models trained on any of the feature sets significantly outperform the majority class baseline (25.4%, *Expansion.Conjunction*).[11] Applying lower-case normalization to the input tends to improve classifier performance, but using a frequency threshold on the minimum number of occurrences of a feature does not: This is an interesting observation and not in line with the previous literature on implicit sense classification; Lin et al. (2009), for example, use a frequency cutoff of 5 for feature selection. Also, stemming as another type of normalization seems not to be useful either and yields slightly lower accuracies.

Noticeably, substituting surface-level word-pair features by the Brown Cluster 3200 embeddings yields a better performance. The difference is, however, not statistically significant.[12] More important, however, may be the positive side effect of a smaller feature space (≈1.4 million) which is reduced by 23%.

We expect the skip-gram neural word embeddings (word vectors) to perform even better than Brown clusters: They are comparable in their contextual features but preserve the topology of the original feature space. Indeed, these are competitive with the low-frequency word-pair features and even significantly better than the configurations l_3, l_4, l_5. Their greatest benefit can be seen in the overall number of real-valued features per instance (which is only 600 in our setting). Finally, a combination of Brown clusters and skip-gram embeddings yields the best results for the classification of implicit senses. This gain over using the embeddings alone may possibly be attributed to non-linearities in the feature space which may be partially captured in the Brown clusters, but not with embeddings in a SVM.[13] We report detailed scores for this best-performing classifier in Table 2.

4.3 Discussion & Open Issues

4.3.1 Argument Span Identification

Exact argument identification is a crucial preprocessing step for any SDP pipeline. Our shallow

[8] Ranks for expl. Arg1-Arg2 prec., recall, F_1: 12, 10, 11. Ranks for expl. connective prec., recall, F_1: 15, 16, 15.

[9] Note, however, that this is 4-way sense classification.

[10] We also tested a broad band-width of sentiment and phrase-structure features, but with the resulting accuracies not outperforming the current experiments, these are omitted for reasons of brevity.

[11] In all experiments, we applied the χ^2 test statistic to assess significance.

[12] We have tested the other Brown cluster representations provided, as well, but 100, 320 and 1000 cluster sets yielded lower accuracies.

[13] All results reported above were obtained with linear kernels. These experiments have also been conducted with RBF and polynomial kernels, whose performance was not reported here, as it did not yield an improvement. However, truly non-linear models would be possible with multi-layered neural networks. While this may yield better results for word embeddings as features, such an experiment is left for future research.

	N_0/l_0	N_1/l_1	N_2/l_2	N_3/l_3	N_4/l_4	N_5/l_5
WP / Tokens	36.65/38.14	36.23/34.53	33.68/32.84	32.84/33.05	31.57/32.63	30.08/32.63
WP / Stems	– /36.23	– /33.89	– /32.84	– /31.99	– /33.05	– /30.72
WP / Brown Cluster 3200	36.86/38.77	35.38/35.17	33.90/36.07	35.38/34.11	34.96/33.47	32.63/33.89
Word Vectors	36.23/37.28					
WP / Brown Cluster + Word Vectors	37.28/**39.41**					

Table 1: Accuracies for 6-way implicit sense labeling and different feature sets when tokens are treated in normal-case (N) or after lower-case preprocessing (l). Subscripts indicate frequency thresholds for feature selection (0 means no threshold applied). Majority class baseline: 25.4%.

	Prec	Rec	F_1
Expansion.Conjunction	43.09	67.50	52.59
Expansion.Restatement	32.68	49.50	39.37
Comparison.Contrast	42.85	18.29	25.64
Contingency.Cause.Reason	41.26	35.61	38.23
Contingency.Cause.Result	40.00	16.32	23.18
Expansion.Instantiation	46.15	12.76	20.00

Table 2: Detailed classification scores for the best-performing classifier combining Brown Cluster 3200 and skip-gram embeddings.

discourse parser suffers from low overall recall of the correctly recognized (explicit) spans, which we see as the main source of poor performance in the task evaluation.

Even though a system description may not be the right place for a general discussion about the appropriate representation of how arguments of discourse relations are to be defined and represented, we would like to point out that we see a potential issue in the rather strict evaluation of exact matches within the Shared Task (which does not allow for partial matches). Likewise problematic is an arguable definition of gold spans for Arg1 and Arg2 in the provided training data. As an illustration consider the following example:[14]

Gold:
Arg1: *At any rate India needs the sugar*
Arg2: *it will be in sooner or later to buy it*

Our System Output:
Arg1: *At any rate, she added, "India needs the sugar*
Arg2: *it will be in sooner or later to buy it.*

At least on a general basis, both argument spans are correctly identified by our system. The only difference is that punctuation symbols and attribution spans (*she added*) are not present in the gold data. Note, however, that a rule-based removal of such patterns is far from trivial, as syntactic patterns are complex and the PDTB gold data reveals many inconsistencies, especially regarding leading and trailing punctuation symbols. In this particular example, our system is capable of

(i) identifying the correct explicit connective (*so*), and

(ii) classifying its correct sense (*Contingency.Cause.Result*).

Nevertheless, it is not given any credit, as the system's token lists do not match the gold data. Very much related to the span identification problem sketched above is the detection of discontinuous argument spans and cases in which our system adds a subordinate clause to the argument, which is not present in the gold data. We believe that—in line with the annotation guidelines of the PDTB—these are relevant factors to consider when implementing a SDP, but that it should not affect the overall evaluation in such a strict and rigid manner. We would therefore encourage future evaluations to

- *either* employ additional metrics permitting partial matches, e.g., using sliding-window metrics such as Pevzner and Hearst (2002),
- *or* to ground argument definitions in psycholinguistically more plausible models of propositions, cf. Lascarides and Asher (1993) or Kintsch (1998), resp.—their more operationalizable approximation in terms of, say, frame semantics as previously annotated for the PDTB data in the context of PropBank

[14]Document ID: `wsj_2265`, Relation ID: 36896.

and NomBank (Palmer et al., 2005; Meyers et al., 2004).

The latter idea may be challenging, as it involves efficient handling of multi-layer annotations for different major annotation projects, yet, experiments in this direction have successfully been conducted (Pustejovsky et al., 2005). This integrative direction of research has been the original focus of our system.

4.3.2 Frequency Cutoffs for Word-Pair Feature Selection

Our experiments indicate that frequency cutoffs to select word-pair features for implicit relation recognition do not seem to improve classifier performance. While some previous approaches (most notably Lin et al., 2009) incorporate cutoffs in their experiments, others do not. But if a frequency filter is applied, the specific value for the threshold is usually not motivated.

We see a possible explanation for the negative impact of cutoffs in the extremely sparse feature space: Many word-pair features which are present in the training section of the PDTB are not found in the development set and vice versa, and with frequency cutoffs applied, sparsity even grows further. Closely related to our observation are earlier findings that using even a small stop word list has adverse effects on performance, which seems implausible at first sight (Blair-Goldensohn et al., 2007).

Biran and McKeown (2013) address this issue in closer detail by replacing the sparse lexical word-pair features by more dense, aggregated score features. Based on their experiments, the authors argue that the most powerful features are mainly function words. Yet, their lack of semantic content whatsoever still calls for an explanation why they are useful in distinguishing the different types of implicit relations—except through overfitting the data.

As a side experiment, we performed 10-fold cross validation on the PDTB, and again trained implicit relations by varying the cutoff. The results are in line with our experiments reported in Table 1 showing the same trend, which reinforces the aforementioned sparsity issue.

Overall, we believe that more aggregated types of features have advantages over sparse features and that they are better in representing the underlying semantic relationship between argument pairs. We elaborate on this in our final subsection.

4.3.3 Abstracting from Surface-Level Features

Our experiments for implicit relation classification have shown that is is beneficial to abstract from surface-level (token) features for two reasons:

(i) word embeddings seem to express a more general, semantic representation of the underlying relationship between two arguments in the discourse and

(ii) the number of features involved in a classification can be significantly reduced which has a positive effect on the computational side.

Future research should be concerned with a closer inspection of how combinations of word embeddings can be used to increase classification results, especially when no explicit connectives are available. Instead of vector addition, as applied in our setting, we think that traditional vector-based similarity measures comparing both arguments spans seem to be highly promising in approaching their underlying semantic relationship.

5 Conclusion

In the context of the CoNLL 2015 Shared Task, we have described a minimalist approach to shallow discourse parsing with an emphasis on implicit relation recognition.

Our system combines task-specific adaptations, i.e., rule-based discourse unit identification via templates, with data-driven models to infer senses of (esp. implicit) discourse relations.

We described the system architecture and experiments conducted on implicit sense labeling. In this context, we motivated the need to model the relationship between arguments in a more abstract way using distributional representations instead of surface-based features. Our experiments are in line with previous work (most notably by Rutherford and Xue, 2014), while having shown that more abstract representations are at least equally powerful in predicting the correct senses and, also, that sparsity issues can be overcome. A slight improvement in performance has yielded a combination of distributional profiles for argument spans (Brown clusters and skip-gram neural word embeddings) which is promising and should be addressed in closer detail in future work.

References

Or Biran and Kathleen McKeown. 2013. Aggregated Word Pair Features for Implicit Discourse Relation Disambiguation. In *Proceedings of the 51st Annual Meeting of the Association for Computational Linguistics, ACL 2013, 4-9 August 2013, Sofia, Bulgaria, Volume 2: Short Papers*, pages 69–73.

Sasha Blair-Goldensohn, Kathleen McKeown, and Owen Rambow. 2007. Building and Refining Rhetorical-Semantic Relation Models. In Candace L. Sidner, Tanja Schultz, Matthew Stone, and ChengXiang Zhai, editors, *HLT-NAACL*, pages 428–435. The Association for Computational Linguistics.

Chih-Chung Chang and Chih-Jen Lin. 2011. LIBSVM: A library for support vector machines. *ACM Transactions on Intelligent Systems and Technology*, 2:27:1–27:27. Software available at `http://www.csie.ntu.edu.tw/~cjlin/libsvm`.

David A. duVerle and Helmut Prendinger. 2009. A Novel Discourse Parser Based on Support Vector Machine Classification. In *Proceedings of the Joint Conference of the 47th Annual Meeting of the ACL and the 4th International Joint Conference on Natural Language Processing of the AFNLP: Volume 2 - Volume 2*, ACL '09, pages 665–673, Stroudsburg, PA, USA. Association for Computational Linguistics.

Vanessa Wei Feng and Graeme Hirst. 2012. Text-level Discourse Parsing with Rich Linguistic Features. In *Proceedings of the 50th Annual Meeting of the Association for Computational Linguistics: Long Papers - Volume 1*, ACL '12, pages 60–68, Stroudsburg, PA, USA. Association for Computational Linguistics.

Sucheta Ghosh, Giuseppe Riccardi, and Richard Johansson. 2012. Global Features for Shallow Discourse Parsing. In *Proceedings of the 13th Annual Meeting of the Special Interest Group on Discourse and Dialogue (SIGDIAL)*, pages 150–159.

Walter Kintsch. 1998. *Comprehension: A Paradigm for Cognition*. Cambridge University Press, Cambridge.

Fang Kong, Tou Hwee Ng, and Guodong Zhou. 2014. A Constituent-Based Approach to Argument Labeling with Joint Inference in Discourse Parsing. In *Proceedings of the 2014 Conference on Empirical Methods in Natural Language Processing (EMNLP)*, pages 68–77. Association for Computational Linguistics.

Alex Lascarides and Nicholas Asher. 1993. Temporal Interpretation, Discourse Relations and Commonsense entailment. *Linguistics and Philosophy*, 16(5):437–493.

Ziheng Lin, Min-Yen Kan, and Hwee Tou Ng. 2009. Recognizing Implicit Discourse Relations in the Penn Discourse Treebank. In *Proceedings of the 2009 Conference on Empirical Methods in Natural Language Processing: Volume 1 - Volume 1*, EMNLP '09, pages 343–351, Stroudsburg, PA, USA. Association for Computational Linguistics.

Ziheng Lin, Hwee Tou Ng, and Min-Yen Kan. 2010. A PDTB-Styled End-to-End Discourse Parser. *CoRR*, abs/1011.0835.

William C. Mann and Sandra A. Thompson. 1988. Rhetorical structure theory: Toward a functional theory of text organization. *Text*, 8(3):243–281.

Daniel Marcu and Abdessamad Echihabi. 2002. An Unsupervised Approach to Recognizing Discourse Relations. In *Proceedings of the 40th Annual Meeting on Association for Computational Linguistics*, ACL '02, pages 368–375, Stroudsburg, PA, USA. Association for Computational Linguistics.

Adam Meyers, Ruth Reeves, Catherine Macleod, Rachel Szekely, Veronika Zielinska, Brian Young, and Ralph Grishman. 2004. Annotating Noun Argument Structure for NomBank. In *Proceedings of the Fourth International Conference on Language Resources and Evaluation (LREC'04)*. European Language Resources Association (ELRA).

Tomas Mikolov, Kai Chen, Greg Corrado, and Jeffrey Dean. 2013. Efficient Estimation of Word Representations in Vector Space. *CoRR*, abs/1301.3781.

Martha Palmer, Daniel Gildea, and Paul Kingsbury. 2005. The Proposition Bank: An Annotated Corpus of Semantic Roles. *Comput. Linguist.*, 31(1):71–106, March.

Joonsuk Park and Claire Cardie. 2012. Improving Implicit Discourse Relation Recognition Through Feature Set Optimization. In *Proceedings of the 13th Annual Meeting of the Special Interest Group on Discourse and Dialogue*, page 108–112, Seoul, South Korea, July. Association for Computational Linguistics, Association for Computational Linguistics.

Lev Pevzner and Marti A Hearst. 2002. A critique and improvement of an evaluation metric for text segmentation. *Computational Linguistics*, 28(1):19–36.

Emily Pitler and Ani Nenkova. 2009. Using Syntax to Disambiguate Explicit Discourse Connectives in Text. In *ACL 2009, Proceedings of the 47th Annual Meeting of the Association for Computational Linguistics and the 4th International Joint Conference on Natural Language Processing of the AFNLP, 2-7 August 2009, Singapore, Short Papers*, pages 13–16.

Emily Pitler, Annie Louis, and Ani Nenkova. 2009. Automatic Sense Prediction for Implicit Discourse Relations in Text. In *Proceedings of the Joint Conference of the 47th Annual Meeting of the ACL and the 4th International Joint Conference on Natural Language Processing of the AFNLP: Volume 2 - Volume 2*, ACL '09, pages 683–691, Stroudsburg, PA, USA. Association for Computational Linguistics.

M.F. Porter. 1980. An algorithm for suffix stripping. *Program*, 14(3):130–137.

Rashmi Prasad, Nikhil Dinesh, Alan Lee, Eleni Miltsakaki, Livio Robaldo, Aravind Joshi, and Bonnie Webber. 2008. The Penn Discourse TreeBank 2.0. In *In Proceedings of LREC*.

James Pustejovsky, Adam Meyers, Martha Palmer, and Massimo Poesio, 2005. *Proceedings of the Workshop on Frontiers in Corpus Annotations II: Pie in the Sky*, chapter Merging PropBank, NomBank, TimeBank, Penn Discourse Treebank and Coreference, pages 5–12. Association for Computational Linguistics.

Attapol Rutherford and Nianwen Xue. 2014. Discovering Implicit Discourse Relations Through Brown Cluster Pair Representation and Coreference Patterns. In *Proceedings of the 14th Conference of the European Chapter of the Association for Computational Linguistics*, pages 645–654. Association for Computational Linguistics.

Joseph Turian, Lev-Arie Ratinov, and Yoshua Bengio. 2010. Word Representations: A Simple and General Method for Semi-Supervised Learning. In *Proceedings of the 48th Annual Meeting of the Association for Computational Linguistics*, pages 384–394, Uppsala, Sweden, July. Association for Computational Linguistics.

Bonnie L. Webber. 2004. D-LTAG: extending lexicalized TAG to discourse. *Cognitive Science*, 28(5):751–779.

Nianwen Xue, Hwee Tou Ng, Sameer Pradhan, Rashmi Prasad, Christopher Bryant, and Attapol Rutherford. 2015. The CoNLL-2015 Shared Task on Shallow Discourse Parsing. In *Proceedings of the Nineteenth Conference on Computational Natural Language Learning: Shared Task*, Beijing, China.

Zhi-Min Zhou, Yu Xu, Zheng-Yu Niu, Man Lan, Jian Su, and Chew Lim Tan. 2010. Predicting Discourse Connectives for Implicit Discourse Relation Recognition. In *Proceedings of the 23rd International Conference on Computational Linguistics: Posters*, COLING '10, pages 1507–1514, Stroudsburg, PA, USA. Association for Computational Linguistics.

A Hybrid Discourse Relation Parser in CoNLL 2015

Sobha Lalitha Devi., Sindhuja Gopalan., Lakshmi S., Pattabhi RK Rao., Vijay Sundar Ram R., and Malarkodi C.S.
AU-KBC Research Centre
MIT Campus of Anna University
Chromepet, Chennai, India
sobha@au-kbc.org

Abstract

The work presented here describes our participation in CoNLL 2015 shared task in the closed track. Here we have used a hybrid approach, where Machine Learning (ML) technique and linguistic rules are used to identify the discourse relations. We have developed this system with a view that it consistently works across all domains and all types of text corpus. We have obtained encouraging results. The performance on blind test data and test data were similar.

1 Introduction

This paper describes our system, used in CoNLL-2015 shared task "Shallow Discourse Parsing". The goal of this task is to parse a piece of text into a set of discourse relations that exist between two adjacent or non-adjacent discourse units. Discourse relations are the coherence relations between two sentences that can be realized explicitly or implicitly in a text. Discourse connectives play a role in signaling the relations in a discourse. They connect two discourse units, which may be a sentence, clause or multiple sentences. These units are called arguments. Hence a discourse relation includes the connective and its arguments. The relations can be intra sentential or inter sentential i.e. it can occur within a sentence or across sentences.

Penn Discourse Tree Bank (PDTB) is used as the shared task data set for training and development. For the testing the shared task organizers have provided a blind set data, which is not from PDTB. PDTB is a richly annotated resource for discourse relations and their arguments. To develop PDTB, 1 million words Wall Street Journal is used as a corpus. It is annotated with five types of relations, Explicit, Implicit, EntRel, AltLex and NoRel. Discourse relations in PDTB are broadly classified into two types based on how the relations are realized in the text. When the relation is realized explicitly by a lexical item that belongs to syntactically well defined classes, those connectives are classified as "Explicit connectives". If a relation exists between adjacent sentences in the absence of explicit markers, "Implicit relation" can be inferred.

The main objective of the work presented here is to develop a system for identifying different types of discourse relations automatically. We have followed a hybrid approach, where we first use Machine Learning (ML) technique to identify the discourse relations and then enhance the results using a rule based approach. In the following sections, we give a detailed description of our system.

2 Explicit Relation Identification

Discourse relation is realized by Explicit connectives between two discourse units. The discourse units can be a clause, sentence or multiple sentences. The units they connect are referred as argument 1 and argument 2. Explicit connectives mainly belong to three syntactic classes, which include Subordinating conjunction, Coordinating conjunction and Discourse adverbials. PDTB provides sense classification for Explicit, Implicit and AltLex relations. Discourse connectives are broadly classified into four classes based on science.

a) Expansion b) Contingency c) Temporal, d). Comparison.

In order to refine the sense classification further, each class is defined with further types and subtypes. In this paper, we present a hybrid system for automatic identification of connectives and their arguments from parse text, developed using graph based machine learning technique CRFs and linguistic rules.

Proceedings of the Nineteenth Conference on Computational Natural Language Learning: Shared Task, pages 50–55,
Beijing, China, July 26-31, 2015.

CRFs is a finite state model with un-normalized transition probability. It solves label bias problem efficiently. It has a single exponential model for joint probability of the entire sequence of labels when an observation sequence is given (Lafferty et al, 2001). The true power of graphical models lies in their ability to model many variables that are independent of each other (Sutton et al, 2011). For our work we have used the CRF++, which is a simple and customizable tool (Kudo, 2005).

The identification of explicit relations includes two subtasks, 1. Connective identification and classification 2. Argument identification and extraction. The discourse relations occur as inter-sentential or intra-sentential in a text. First, our system identifies whether a connective exist as discourse connective in the context. Consider the below example,

Example [1]

Morgan Stanley and Kidder Peabody, the two biggest program trading firms, staunchly defend their strategies.

In Example [1], the lexical item "and" is not a discourse connective but acts as conjunction joining two nouns Morgan Stanley and Kidder Peabody. Hence it is important to identify whether the connective acts as discourse connective or not in a context.

After identifying the discourse connective, the system predicts its sense. One connective can have multiple senses.

Example [2]

Several big securities firms backed off from program trading a few months after the 1987 crash . But most of them, led by Morgan Stanley & Co., moved back in earlier this year. ("But" Sense: Comparison.Contrast)

Example [3]

Just the thing for the Vivaldi-at-brunch set, the yuppie audience that has embraced New Age as its very own easy listening. But you can't dismiss Mr. Stoltzman's music or his motives as merely commercial and lightweight. ("But" Sense: Comparison.Concession)

In above Examples [2] & [3], "But" acts as an inter sentential connective. Although "But" in the above examples is syntactically similar, it has a different sense.

In these examples "But" acts as comparitive connective, but vary in its type. In the CoNLL version of PDTB data "but" with the sense "Comparison.Contrast" occurred in 70.48% cases. In some cases, the sense for a connective may vary even at class level.

After identifying and predicting the sense of a connective, the span of arguments they connect needs to be identified. It is not necessary that the relation should occur between adjacent sentences. It may span across sentences. However, PDTB follows a minimality principle for annotating the arguments. The minimal information required to complete the interpretation of the arguments is annotated.

2.1 System description

Motivated by the work of Lin et al (2009), we have designed our system as a pipeline, where the relations are identified in sequential order. First, the system identifies and predicts the discourse connectives and their sense. Then, using the identified connectives argument 1 and argument 2 spans are identified and extracted. Then, the system examines all sentence pairs. The pair that is not identified in explicit relation is then classified into Implicit, Entrel or Altlex relation by the system.

2.2 System description Connective Identification and Sense Prediction

In the task of connective identification, the system is first trained to identify the connectives syntactically i.e. to identify whether the connective functions as a discourse connective or not. Then, the connectives are classified based on its sense. We have extracted the word and other syntactic features such as POS, chunk and Clausal information from PDTB parse text. In the task of identifying the discourse connectives, the system is trained using lexico-syntactic features like Word, Parts-of-speech (POS), Chunk, Combination of word, POS and chunk and Clause in a window size of 3. The lexicon itself acts as a good feature to identify the discourse connectives. POS, chunk and clausal information help in disambiguating the connectives.

Example [4]

after IN B-PP Temporal.Asynchronous.Succession
interviewing VBG B-VP o

Generally, "after" exists as connective and also as preposition or adverbs in a corpus. But when "after" is followed by a gerund, it acts as discourse connective. The POS for a gerund is "VBG" and hence plays an important role in discourse connective identification. The clausal information also helps in identifying a lexical unit as discourse connective because when a discourse connective exists in a sentence, then it will be mostly succeeded or preceded by a clause. In addition to these features, we have used dictionary inside the CRFs. We have developed the dictionary based on connectives that are not ambiguous. After identifying the connectives, we analysed the errors generated by the system. We found the system has tagged the connectives that are not discourse connectives. Hence it resulted in false positives.

Example[5]
Our offer is to buy any and all shares tentered at $18 a share.

In the above example "and" is not a discourse connective, but the system tagged wrongly discourse connective.

Example [6]
A spokesman for Dow Jones said he hadn't seen the group's filing, but added, ``obviously Dow Jones disagrees with their conclusions.

In the above example the connective "but" was not identified by the system. Hence, we used post processing rules to improve the connective identification.

Once the discourse connectives are identified, the system predicts the sense of the connectives. Using the above mentioned lexico-syntactic features and connectives, we developed individual models for each type of sense. In the case of sense identification, connective itself is a good feature, as only few connectives are ambiguous. To solve the ambiguity in the case of sense classification, the preceding and succeeding POS and words were useful to some extent. Using these models, senses of connectives are identified separately. Then we merged the output based on the confidence scores.

Error analysis on sense classification showed that the sense is wrongly predicted by the system. Consider the below example [7], where "until" is predicted as "Contingency.Condition" by the system, but the sense of the connective "until" is "Temporal.Asynchronous.Precedence"

Example [7]
He's an ex-hurler who's one of the leading gurus of the fashionable delivery, which looks like a fastball until it dives beneath the lunging bat.

Heuristic based post processing rules were used to correct and improve the sense prediction.

2.3 Argument identification

In the next phase, the system is trained to identify the arguments and their text spans. We have followed the method used by Menaka et al (2011) for identification of causal relations from Tamil data. In their work, instead of identifying the whole argument, the boundaries of the arguments were identified. Similarly, we created individual model for each boundary, i.e. for Argument 1 start, Argument 1 end, Argument 2 start and Argument 2 end. The connective tagged input is given for argument extraction. For argument identification we have developed separate models for inter and intra sentential relation. Each connective is processed separately and is given as input to inter sentential and intra sentential models. We have used the following features for identifying the argument boundaries.

a. Word , POS, Chunk
b. Combination of word, POS, Chunk
c. Clausal boundaries
d. Sentence boundaries
e. Connective.

We have used connectives as features, as the argument 2 start and argument 1 end are syntactically associated with the connective in most of the cases. Hence, when the connective is identified, the position of Argument 2 start and Argument 1 end boundary can be located. In most of the cases the Argument 1 start is present at the initial position of a sentence or clause and Argument 2 end at the final position of a sentence or clause. In the case of inter sentential relation, the previous sentence to the connective acts as Argument 1. Here, the sentence final position acts as Argument 1 end. Therefore, sentence and clausal boundaries are used as features for argument identification in our work. After identifying the argument boundaries separately, we merged the output from four language models. In order to improve the system's performance for argument extraction further, we used linguistic and heuristic rules. In the following paragraph, we describe some of the linguistic and heuristic rules.

Rules Description

Example [8]
At Shearson Lehman, executives created potential new commercials Friday night and throughout the weekend, then had to regroup yesterday afternoon.

In the above example Argument 2 end was not marked by the system. In such case we used heuristic rule to identify the Argument 2 end boundary.

Example [9]
The agency has already spent roughly $ 19 biollion selling 34 insolvent S&Ls, and it is likely to sell or merge 600 by the time the bailout concludes.

The above Example [9] is a simple discourse relation that exists in the corpus. Using simple linguistic rules, such relations can be identified. In this case, when punctuation mark "," (comma) is followed by a connective; the span above comma is marked as Argument 1 and the span below connective is marked as Argument 2.

3 Non-Explicit Relation Identification

In the task of Non-Explicit relation identification, we identify the sentences which can possibly have implicit relations, AltLex and EntRel relations. And then the sense of the Implicit connective and AltLex is identified. The identification of implicit relation between a pair of sentences is done using a machine learning technique, CRFs. From the input data we look for sentences without Explicit connectives and form pair of sentences by considering its previous sentence. Features extracted from this pair of sentences are given to the CRFs engine to identify the presence of implicit relation. We use the following features:

i. **Presence of common words:** The count of commonly occurring words in the argument 1 and argument 2 is taken. Here we remove the stop words.
ii. **Difference in the polarity:** The average polarity of each sentence is calculated. First each word is marked with its polarity score as obtained from the MPQA polarity lexicon provided by the task organizers. The average score of each sentence in the pair is calculated by aggregating the individual word scores. If the polarities are same in both sentences, then the feature is given the value of 0:0, if sentence 1 has positive score and sentence two has negative score, then feature is given a value of 1:-1, else vice-versa.
iii. Commonality of the words in the initial and terminal positions of the sentences
iv. Presence of common brown cluster IDs
v. Presence of common bigrams and trigrams

The output obtained from the machine learning engine is given the secondary engine. In the secondary engine, we check the coreference between the pair of sentence using anaphora resolution system. Those pair of sentences which have common coreference mentions we consider this pair of sentences to have implicit relations.

We have used an in-house developed anaphora resolution system (Sobha, 2011), which uses salience measure based approach.

Thus we identify the sentence pairs which have the implicit relations in them. The next task is to identify the sense of the Implicit connective between this pair of sentences. For the purpose of identifying the sense (i.e., sense classification), we first identify or learn common patterns from the Implicit and Explicit sense annotated training data. And these patterns are given as features to the CRFs machine learning, which would finally mark the sense of the implicit relation. In the previous reported works we observe that most of the sense classification was restricted to four top level senses i.e., Expansion, Contingency, Comparison and Temporal, whereas in our present work we need to identify the senses to finer granularity levels; such as "Expansion.Alternative.Chosen alternative", "Contingency.Cause.Result". Thus, this leads to the 14 different senses.

The common patterns in the Explicit and Implicit training data are learned based on the two factors Polarity scores and the verb clusters obtained from the VerbNet. The patterns are formed by considering two factors from argument 1 and argument 2 and a tuple is formed. This tuple consists <Verb_class of argument 1, Polarity of argument 1, Verb_class of argument 2, Polarity of argument 2, Associated sense> The number of common patterns learned from the Explicit and Implicit annotated training data is observed to be 535 unique patterns. And it has been observed in the data that also majority of these patterns is majorly associated with the senses "Expansion.Conjunction" (48.03%), "Expansion.Restatement" (17.19%), "Comparison.Contrast" (15.14%).

When we used these learned patterns on the development data to identify the similarities of the patterns, we obtained only a similarity of 35% of the patterns. This showed that sense classification in implicit relations is very much subjective and depends on the semantics of the arguments argument 1 and argument 2. But in this work we have restricted ourselves with syntactic features and patterns as described earlier for developing a CRFs machine learning system for sense classification. The other syntactic features used are Part-of-speech (POS tags), First-Last-First three words of the arguments, bigrams and trigrams of POS tags, count of common brown cluster IDs. The features of First-last-first three words, count of common brown clusters, polarity score are used as described in (Pitler et al., 2009; Lin et al., 2009; Louis et al., 2010; Zhou et al., 2010). For the pair of sentences for which the sense has been identified, the first sentence is tagged as Argument 1 and the second sentence is tagged as Argument 2.

4 Results

In the table 1, we show the results obtained for our system for Explicit and Non-Explicit relations and overall.

We can observe from the results identifying implicit relation has been a harder task.

In the argument identification sub task we observe that identification of argument boundaries which are farther from the connective had been tough. Since the PDTB follows the principle of minimality, identifying the minimal span by system was not possible in 30% of the cases. This was due to the fact that we were only using syntactic features for learning. Since argument 2 was syntactically bound to the connective in most of the cases, the system could learn the argument 2 span better than the argument 1 span.

The system failed to identify correct Argument 1 span in cases where coordinating conjunction is the connective and Argument 1 span crosses more than two clauses or sentences. Especially for the connectives "and" and "or" identifying Argument 1 span has been ambiguous.

In this work we have restricted or assumed that in inter-sentential connective Argument 1 and Argument 2 spans are within the current and previous sentences and does not cross $(n-1)^{th}$ sentence. Though in reality, there are more than 5% cases which have an argument span of more than n and $(n-1)^{th}$ sentence. This assumption was made because more than 90% of the connectives which are inter sentential have a span of only two sentences and was also computationally simple.

5 Conclusion

This paper describes our participation in CoNLL 2015 shared task of Shallow discourse parsing. We have developed an automatic system which identifies different discourse relations along with their senses. Our main objective was to develop a system which works consistently across any given corpus or text. And we find that our system has performed consistently with same performance metrics for both PDTB test section and blind test set provided by the task organizers. We have obtained an overall F1 score for the discourse parser as 0.1502, precision of 0.159 and recall of 0.1423. The scores are encouraging.

	Blind Test Data			**PDTB Test Data**			**Development Data**		
Details	**F1**	**Precision**	**Recall**	**F1**	**Precision**	**Recall**	**F1**	**Precision**	**Recall**
All Arg 1 Argument 2 extraction	0.3317	0.3512	0.3143	0.3126	0.3176	0.3079	0.439	0.4407	0.4373
All Argument 1 extraction	0.3998	0.4233	0.3788	0.3807	0.3867	0.3749	0.5173	0.5193	0.5153
All Argument 2 extraction	0.5447	0.5767	0.5161	0.4624	0.4697	0.4554	0.59	0.5923	0.5877
All Explicit connective	0.8449	0.9232	0.7788	0.8644	0.9436	0.7974	0.928	0.9804	0.8809
All Sense	0.1232	0.1357	0.1253	0.132	0.2579	0.1284	0.213	0.4087	0.203
All Parser	**0.1502**	**0.159**	**0.1423**	**0.1461**	**0.1484**	**0.1439**	**0.2635**	**0.2646**	**0.2625**
CoNLL Baseline – All Parser	**0.0386**	**0.0376**	**0.0397**	**0.0306**	**0.0285**	**0.033**	-	-	-
Explicit only Arg 1 Argument 2 extraction	0.3473	0.3795	0.3201	0.3077	0.3359	0.2839	0.5469	0.5777	0.5191
Explicit only Argument 1 extraction	0.4449	0.4861	0.4101	0.3664	0.4	0.338	0.629	0.6645	0.5971
Explicit only Argument 2 extraction	0.642	0.7015	0.5917	0.4968	0.5423	0.4583	0.7591	0.802	0.7206
Explicit only Explicit connective	0.8449	0.9232	0.7788	0.8644	0.9436	0.7974	0.928	0.9804	0.8809
Explicit only Sense	0.2175	0.2639	0.2028	0.1924	0.347	0.1779	0.3745	0.5425	0.3494
Explicit only Parser	**0.2673**	**0.2921**	**0.2464**	**0.2678**	**0.2923**	**0.247**	**0.4911**	**0.5188**	**0.4662**
CoNLL Baseline – Explicit only Parser	**0.0**	**1.0**	**0.0**	**0.0**	**1.0**	**0.0**	-	-	-
Non-Explicit only Arg 1 Argument 2 extraction	0.3191	0.3295	0.3093	0.3166	0.3045	0.3297	0.3503	0.3378	0.3638
Non-Explicit only Argument 1 extraction	0.357	0.3687	0.3461	0.3828	0.3682	0.3986	0.4089	0.3943	0.4246
Non-Explicit only Argument 2	0.466	0.4812	0.4518	0.4329	0.4164	0.4508	0.4683	0.4349	0.4683

extraction									
Non-Explicit only Sense	0.0393	0.2081	0.043	0.0301	0.1015	0.0334	0.0643	0.2122	0.0647
Non-Explicit only Parser	**0.0553**	**0.0571**	**0.0536**	**0.0482**	**0.0464**	**0.0502**	**0.0764**	**0.0737**	**0.0794**
CoNLL Baseline – Non-Explicit only Parser	**0.0498**	**0.0376**	**0.0735**	**0.0393**	**0.0285**	**0.063**	-	-	-

Table 1. System Results for Blind Test Data, PDTB Test Data and Development data – This shows the results for all three different types of text corpora. Also, this shows the results for Explicit and Non Explicit relations separately.

Reference

Lafferty, J., McCallum, A., Pereira, F. 2001. *Conditional Random Fields:Probabilistic Models for Segmenting and Labeling Sequence Data*. In International Conference on Machine Learning., pages.1-8.

Ziheng Lin, Min-Yen Kan, and Hwee Tou Ng. 2009. *Recognizing implicit discourse relations in the Penn discourse treebank*. In EMNLP, pages 343–351.

Annie Louis, Aravind K. Joshi, Rashmi Prasad, and Ani Nenkova. 2010. *Using entity features to classify implicit discourse relations*. In SIGDIAL Conference, pages 59–62.

Menaka S., Pattabhi RK Rao., Sobha Lalitha Devi. 2011.*Automatic Identification of Cause-Effect Relations in Tamil Using CRFs*, In A. Gelbukh (ed), Springer LNCS Vol. 6608/2011 pp 316-327

Emily Pitler, Mridhula Raghupathy, Hena Mehta, Ani Nenkovak, Alan Lee, and Aravind K. Joshi. 2008. *Easily identifiable discourse relations*. In COLING (Posters), pages 87–90

Rashmi Prasad, Nikhil Dinesh, Alan Lee, Eleni Miltsakaki, Livio Robaldo, Aravind Joshi, Bonnie Webber. 2008. *The Penn Discourse TreeBank 2.0.* In Proceedings of LREC, 2008.

Sobha Lalitha Devi, Vijay Sundar Ram., Pattabhi RK Rao. 2011. *Resolution of Pronominal Anaphors using Linear and Tree CRFs.* In Proceedings of 8th DAARC, Faro, Portugal.

Charles Sutton and Andrew McCallum. 2011. *An Introduction to Conditional Random Fields*. Foundations and Trends in Machine Learning, Vol. 4(4), pages 267–373.

Ben Wellner, Lisa Ferro, Warren R. Greiff, and Lynette Hirschman. 2006. *Reading comprehension tests for computer-based understanding evaluation.* Natural Language Engineering, 12(4):305–334.

Zhi-Min Zhou, Yu Xu, Zheng-Yu Niu, Man Lan, Jian Su, and Chew Lim Tan. 2010. *Predicting discourse connectives for implicit discourse relation recognition*. In COLING (Posters), pages 1507–1514.

Kudo T. 2005. CRF++, an open source toolkit for CRF, http://crfpp.sourceforge.net

The CLaC Discourse Parser at CoNLL-2015

Majid Laali **Elnaz Davoodi** **Leila Kosseim**
Department of Computer Science and Software Engineering,
Concordia University, Montreal, Quebec, Canada
{m_laali, e_davoo, kosseim}@encs.concordia.ca

Abstract

This paper describes our submission (*kosseim15*) to the CoNLL-2015 shared task on shallow discourse parsing. We used the UIMA framework to develop our parser and used ClearTK to add machine learning functionality to the UIMA framework. Overall, our parser achieves a result of 17.3 F_1 on the identification of discourse relations on the blind CoNLL-2015 test set, ranking in sixth place.

1 Introduction

Today, discourse parsers typically consist of several independent components that address the following problems:

1. *Discourse Connective Classification*: The concern of this problem is the identification of discourse usage of discourse connectives within a text.

2. *Argument Labeling*: This problem focuses on labeling the text spans of the two discourse arguments, namely ARG1 and ARG2.

3. *Explicit Sense Classification*: This problem can be reduced to the sense disambiguation of the discourse connective in an explicit discourse relation.

4. *Non-Explicit Sense Classification*: The target of this problem is the identification of implicit discourse relations between two consecutive sentences.

To illustrate these tasks, consider Example (1):

(1) *We would stop index arbitrage* when **the market is under stress.**[1]

The task of *Discourse Connective Classification* is to determine if the marker *"when"* is used to mark a discourse relation or not. *Argument Labeling* should segment the two arguments ARG1 and ARG2 (in this example, ARG1 *is italicized* while **ARG2 is bolded**). Finally, *Explicit Sense Classification* should identify which discourse relation is signaled by *"when"* - in this case CONTINGENCY.CONDITION.

In this paper, we report on the development and results of our discourse parser for the CoNLL 2015 shared task. Our parser, named *CLaC Discourse Parser*, was built from scratch and took about 3 person-month to code. The focus of the CLaC Discourse Parser is the treatment of explicit discourse relations (i.e. problem 1 to 3 above).

2 Architecture of the CLaC Discourse Parser

We developed our parser based on the UIMA framework (Ferrucci and Lally, 2004) and we used ClearTK (Bethard et al., 2014) to add machine learning functionality to the UIMA framework. The parser was written in Java and its source code is distributed under the BSD license[2].

Figure 1 shows the architecture of the CLaC Discourse Parser. Motivated by Lin et al. (2014), the architecture of the CLaC Discourse Parser is a pipeline that consists in five components: *CoNLL Syntax Reader*, *Discourse Connective Annotator*, *Argument Labeler*, *Discourse Sense Annotator* and *CoNLL JSON Exporter*. Due to lack of time, we did not implement a *Non-Explicit Classification* in our pipeline and only focused on explicit discourse relations.

The *CoNLL Syntax Reader* and the *CoNLL JSON Exporter* were added to the CLaC Discourse Parser in order for the input and the output of the parser to be compatible with the CoNLL

[1] The example is taken from the CoNLL 2015 trial dataset.

[2] All the source codes can be downloaded from https://github.com/mjlaali/CLaCDiscourseParser.git

Proceedings of the Nineteenth Conference on Computational Natural Language Learning: Shared Task, pages 56–60,
Beijing, China, July 26-31, 2015.

Figure 1: Components of the CLaC Discourse Parser

2015 Shared Task specifications. The *CoNLL Syntax Reader* parses syntactic information (i.e. POS tags, constituent parse trees and dependency parses). CoNLL organisers and adds this syntactic information to the documents in the UIMA framework. To create a stand-alone parser, the *CoNLL Syntax Reader* can be easily replaced with the `cleartk-berkeleyparser` component in the CLaC discourse Parser pipeline. This component is a wrapper around the Berkeley syntactic parser (Petrov and Klein, 2007) and distributed with ClearTK. The Berkeley syntactic parser was actually used in the CoNLL shared task to parse texts and generate the syntactic information.

The *CoNLL JSON Exporter* reads the output discourse relations annotated in the UIMA documents and generates a JSON file in the format required for the CoNLL shared task. We will discuss the other components in details in the next sections.

2.1 Discourse Connective Annotator

To annotate discourse connectives, the *Discourse Connective Annotator* first searches the input texts for terms that match a pre-defined list of discourse connectives. This list of discourse connectives was built solely from the CoNLL training dataset of around 30K explicit discourse relations and contains 100 discourse connectives. Each match of discourse connective is then checked to see if it occurs in discourse usage or not.

Inspired by (Pitler et al., 2009), we built a binary classifier with six local syntactic and lexicalized features of discourse connectives to classify discourse connectives as discourse usage or non-discourse usage. These features are listed in Table 1 in the row labeled *Connective Features*.

2.2 Argument Labeler

When ARG1 and ARG2 appear in the same sentence, we can exploit the syntactic tree to label boundaries of the discourse arguments. Motivated by (Lin et al., 2014), we first classify each constituent in the parse tree into to three categories: part of ARG1, part of ARG2 or NON (i.e. is not part of any discourse argument). Then, all constituents which were tagged as part of ARG1 or as part of ARG2 are merged to obtain the actual boundaries of ARG1 and ARG2.

Previous studies have shown that learning an argument labeler classifier when all syntactic constituents are considered suffers from many instances being labeled as NON (Kong et al., 2014). In order to avoid this, we used the approach proposed by Kong et al. (2014) to prune constituents with a NON label. This approach uses only the nodes in the path from the discourse connective (or *SelfCat* see Table 1) to the root of the sentence (*Connective-Root path nodes*) to limit the number of the candidate constituents. More formally, only constituents that are directly connected to one of the *Connective-Root path nodes* are considered for the classification.

For example, consider the parse tree of Example (1) shown in Figure 2. The path from the discourse connective *"when"* to the root of the sentence contains these nodes: {WRB, WHADVP, SBAR, VP_2, VP_1, S_1}. Therefore, we only consider {S_2, NP_2, VB, MD, NP_1} for obtaining discourse arguments.

If the classifier does not classify any constituent as a part of ARG1, we assume that the ARG1 is not in the same sentence as ARG2. In such a scenario, we consider the whole text of the previous sentence as ARG1.

In the current implementation, we made the assumption that discourse connectives cannot be multiword expressions. Therefore, the Argument Labeler cannot identify the arguments of parallel discourse connectives (e.g. *either..or*, *on one hand..on the other hand*, etc.)

We used a sub-set of 9 features proposed by Kong et al. (2014) for the Argument Labeler classifier. The complete list of features is listed in Table 1.

2.3 Discourse Sense Annotator

Although some discourse connectives can signal different discourse relations, the naïve approach that labels each discourse connective with its most

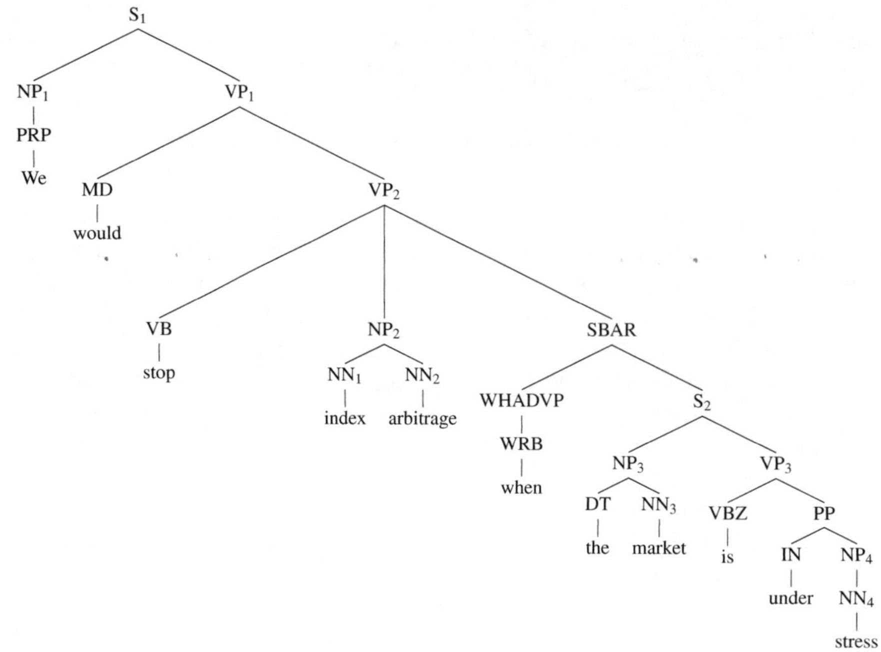

Figure 2: The Parse Tree Provided by CoNLL 2015 for Example (1)

Category	Description	Example
Connective Features	1. The discourse connective text in lowercase.	*when*
	2. The categorization of the case of the connective: *all lowercase*, *all uppercase* and *initial uppercase*	all lowercase
	3. The highest node in the parse tree that covers the connective words but nothing more	WRB
	4. The parent of *SelfCat*	WHADVP
	5. The left sibling of *SelfCat*	null
	6. The right sibling of *SelfCat*	S
Syntactic Node Features	7. The path from the node to the *SelfCat* node in the parser tree	$S \uparrow SBAR \downarrow WHADVP$
	8. The context of the node in the parse tree. The context of a node is defined by its label the label of its parent, the label of left and right sibling in the parse tree.	S-SBAR-WHADVP-null
	9. The position of the node relative to the *SelfCat* node: *left* or *right*	left

Table 1: Features Used in the CLaC Discourse Parser

frequent relation performs rather well. According to Pitler et al. (2009), such an approach can achieve an accuracy of 85.86%. Due to lack of time, we implemented this naïve approach for the Discourse Sense Annotator, using the 100 connectives mined from the dataset (see Section 2.1) and their most frequent relation as mined from the CoNLL training dataset.

3 Experiments and Results

As explained in Section 2, the CLaC Discourse Parser contains two main classifiers, one for the *Discourse Connective Annotator* and one for the *Argument Labeler*. We used the off-the-shelf implementation of the C4.5 decision tree classifier (Quinlan, 1993) available in WEKA (Hall et al., 2009) for the two classifiers and trained them us-

	Discourse Connective Classifier	Argument Labeler	Discourse Parsing (explicit only)	Discourse Parsing (explicit and implicit)
Best Result	91.86%	41.35%	30.58%	24.00%
CLaC Parser	**90.19%**	**36.60%**	**27.32%**	**17.38%**
Average	74.20%	23.89%	18.28%	13.25%
Standard deviation	23.24%	13.01%	9.93%	6.41%

Table 2: Summary of the Results of the CLaC Discourse Parser in the CoNLL 2015 Shared Task.

ing the CoNLL training dataset.

Although the CLaC discourse parser only considers explicit discourse relations (which only accounts for about half of the relations), the parser ranked 6th among the 17 submitted discourse parsers. The overall F_1 score of the parser and the individual performance of the *Discourse Connective Classifier* and the *Argument Labeler* in the blind CoNLL test data are shown in Table 2. As Table 2 shows, the performance of the parser is consistently above the average. In addition, the performance of the *Discourse Connective Classifier* is very close to the best result.

Note that all numbers presented in Table 2 were obtained when errors propagate through the pipeline. That is to say, if a discourse connective is not correctly identified by the *Discourse Connective Classifier* for example, the arguments of this discourse connective will not be identified. Thus, the recall of the *Argument Labeler* will be affected.

The CoNLL 2015 results of the submitted parsers show that the identification of ARG1 is more difficult than ARG2. In line with this, the CLaC Discourse Parser performed better on the identification of ARG2 (with the F_1 score of 69.18%) than ARG1 (with the F_1 score of 45.18%). Table 3 provides a summary of the results for the identification of Arg1 and Arg2. An important source of errors in the identification of ARG1 is that *attribute spans* are contained within ARG1. For example in (2), the CLaC Discourse Parser incorrectly includes the text "*But the RTC also requires "working" capital*" within ARG1.

	Arg1	Arg2
Best Result	49.68%	74.29%
CLaC Parser	**45.18%**	**69.18%**
Average	30.77%	50.91%
Std. deviation	15.31%	20.58%

Table 3: Results of the Identification of ARG1 and ARG2.

(2) But the RTC also requires "working" capital *to maintain the bad assets of thrifts that are sold* until **the assets can be sold separately**.[3]

With regards to the identification of ARG2, we observed that subordinate and coordinate clauses are an important source of errors. For example in (3), the subordinate clause "*before we can move forward*" is erroneously included in the ARG2 span when the CLaC Discourse Parser parses the text. The cause of such errors are usually rooted in an incorrect syntax parse tree that was fed to the parser. For instance in (3), the text "*we have collected on those assets before we can move forward*" was incorrectly parsed as a single clause covered by an S node with the subordinate "*before we can move forward*" as a child of this S node. However, in the correct parse tree the subordinate clause should be a sibling of the S node.

(3) *We would have to wait* until **we have collected on those assets** before we can move forward.[3]

4 Conclusion

In this paper, we described the CLaC Discourse Parser which was developed from scratch for the CoNLL 2015 shared task. This 3 person-month effort focused on the task of the *Discourse Connective Classification* and *Argument Labeler*. We used a naïve approach for sense labelling and consider only explicit relations. Yet, the parser achieves an overall F_1 measure of 17.38%, ranking in 6th place out of the 17 parsers submitted to the CoNLL 2015 shared task.

5 Acknowledgement

The authors would like to thank the CoNLL 2015 organisers and the anonymous reviewers. This

[3]The example is taken from the CoNLL 2015 development dataset.

work was financially supported by NSERC.

References

[Bethard et al.2014] Steven Bethard, Philip Ogren, and Lee Becker. 2014. ClearTK 2.0: Design patterns for machine learning in UIMA. LREC.

[Ferrucci and Lally2004] David Ferrucci and Adam Lally. 2004. UIMA: An architectural approach to unstructured information processing in the corporate research environment. *Natural Language Engineering*, 10(3-4):327–348.

[Hall et al.2009] Mark Hall, Eibe Frank, Geoffrey Holmes, Bernhard Pfahringer, Peter Reutemann, and Ian H. Witten. 2009. The WEKA data mining software: An update. *ACM SIGKDD explorations newsletter*, 11(1):10–18.

[Kong et al.2014] Fang Kong, Hwee Tou Ng, and Guodong Zhou. 2014. A Constituent-Based Approach to Argument Labeling with Joint Inference in Discourse Parsing. In *Proceedings of the 2014 Conference on Empirical Methods in Natural Language Processing (EMNLP)*, pages 68–77, Doha, Qatar, October.

[Lin et al.2014] Ziheng Lin, Hwee Tou Ng, and Min-Yen Kan. 2014. A PDTB-styled end-to-end discourse parser. *Natural Language Engineering*, 20(02):151–184.

[Petrov and Klein2007] Slav Petrov and Dan Klein. 2007. Improved Inference for Unlexicalized Parsing. In *Proceedings of NAACL HLT 2007*, page 404–411, Rochester, NY, April.

[Pitler et al.2009] Emily Pitler, Annie Louis, and Ani Nenkova. 2009. Automatic sense prediction for implicit discourse relations in text. In *Proceedings of the 47th Annual Meeting of the ACL and the 4th IJCNLP of the AFNLP*, page 683–691, Suntec, Singapore, August.

[Quinlan1993] J. Ross Quinlan. 1993. *C4.5: Programs for Machine Learning*. Morgan Kaufmann Publishers Inc., San Francisco, CA, USA.

Shallow Discourse Parsing with Syntactic and (a Few) Semantic Features

Shubham Mukherjee, Abhishek Tiwari, Mohit Gupta and Anil Kumar Singh
Department of Computer Science and Engineering
Indian Institute of Technology (BHU), Varanasi, India
{shubham.mukherjee.cse11,abhishek.ktiwari.cse11,
mohit.gupta.cse11,aksingh.cse}@iitbhu.ac.in

Abstract

Discourse parsing is a challenging task and is crucial for discourse analysis. In this paper, we focus on labelling argument spans of discourse connectives and sense identification in the CoNLL-2015 shared task setting. We have used syntactic features and have also tried a few semantic features. We employ a pipeline of classifiers, where the best features and parameters were selected for each individual classifier, based on experimental evaluation. We could only get results somewhat better than of the baseline on the overall task, but the results over some of the sub-tasks are encouraging. Our initial efforts at using semantic features do not seem to help.

1 Introduction

Different natural language constructs are dependent on each other to form a coherent discourse. Extraction of discourse relations is a challenging task. Interest in discourse parsing has increased after the release of the Penn Discourse TreeBank (PDTB) (Miltsakaki et al., 2004). Shallow discourse parsing involves classifying connectives, relation classification and labelling argument spans, the last of which is considerably harder.

Previously, an end-to-end model by Lin et al. (2014) was developed which used only syntactic features from parse trees and improved the discourse parser performance. In our paper, we have constructed an analogous pipeline of classifiers which extracts the shallow discourse information based on the PDTB based annotation scheme. However, since discourse relations directly affect the semantic understanding of the text, the use of semantic features can prove useful if explored. We tried to use a few such features, though without much success. Implicit relations were handled using a heuristic-based baseline parser.

2 Resources and Corpus

For our purposes, we needed syntactic parse trees for the extraction of syntactic features, for which we used the PDTB corpus. These features were used for training each classifier stage of the pipeline.

The PDTB is the first large-scale corpus including a million words taken from the Wall Street Journal (Miltsakaki et al., 2004) and is based on the observation that no discourse relations in any language have been identified with more than two arguments. It uses the connective as the predicate, and the two text spans as the predicate's argument. Specifically, the span syntactically attached to the connective is Arg1 and the second span is Arg2.

The relative position of the Arg1 and Arg2 can appear in any order, at any distance to each other, although the position of Arg2 is fixed once the connective is identified in case of explicit relations. There are distribution statistics from (Miltsakaki et al., 2004) which will prove beneficial in our algorithm. For example, in explicit relations, Arg1 precedes Arg2 39.51% of times and lies in the same sentence 60.38% of the times. Even when Arg1 precedes Arg2, 79.9% of cases are with adjacent sentences. Also, almost all (96.8%) of the implicit cases are where Arg1 precedes Arg2.

For our experiments, we required syntactic features derived from parse trees, along with semantic features. Tokenisation was based on the gold standard PTB tree structure. The parsed trees, which were provided by CoNLL-2015 shared task organisers, were created by the Berkeley parser and were provided in the *json* format.

We did not use any other resources.

Proceedings of the Nineteenth Conference on Computational Natural Language Learning: Shared Task, pages 61–65,
Beijing, China, July 26-31, 2015.

3 Related Work

Argument labelling can be done by locating parts within an argument, or by labelling the entire span, the latter being the preferred method. Explicit connective classification is usually done beforehand. (Pitler and Nenkova, 2009) achieved an F-Score of 94.19% which was extended by (Lin et al., 2014) to get an F-score of 95.36%.

Various approaches have been used for argument span labelling. (Ghosh et al., 2014) used a linear tagging approach based on Conditional Random Fields. (Lin et al., 2014), however, used a completely different approach using argument node classification within the syntax tree. Our approach resembles the architecture used by (Lin et al., 2014), with the addition of a few semantic features. Surprisingly, semantic features have not been tried for this task.

A hybrid approach was explored by (Kong et al., 2014) taking advantages of both the linear tagging and sub-tree extraction by using a constituent based approach. In contrast, we employ the idea of integrating additional heuristic and semantic features at different points in the pipeline.

For non-explicit relations, (Lin et al., 2009) have used word-pair features, which was the Cartesian product of all words from Arg1 and Arg2. Simple heuristic-based approaches have also shown reasonably high accuracy (Xue et al., 2015).

4 An Overview of Our Approach

Similar to the Lin et. al. (2014) model, we employed use a pipeline of classifiers, namely Explicit Connective Classifier, Argument Position Classifier, Argument Identifier and Sense Classifier. We used a seperate but linked parser for non-explicit cases. Given only the raw text of the sentence(s) and their parse trees, we attempt to determine:

1. Whether the sentence(s) have discourse relation present. And if so, the location of the connective in case of explicit relations.

2. The Argument span of the two arguments in terms of token numbers.

3. The sense of the discourse relation.

For this purpose, we employed a modular approach, building classifiers for each stage of the process. Each module effectively performs a classification task.

Each classifier was trained individually with the inclusion of heuristics and a variety of features. Evaluation after each modification enabled selection of better parameters for that particular module. In particular, the methodology used for connective matching and usage of the uncovered sets is explained in sections 5.1 and 8, respectively. We also explored the use of semantic features at each stage.

5 Explicit Connective Classification

Explicit connective classification involves two steps: (a) matching all the occurrences of the connective and (b) disambiguating them as discourse vs. non-discourse. We have used the set of 99 connective heads from the PDTB Annotation Manual[1] (2007) to match the connectives and then classified them based on the features extracted from the connective.

5.1 Connective Matching

The PDTB Annotation Manual gives an exhaustive list of 99 connective heads, based on which we generated rules for extracting occurrences of each of the connectives (such as *and*, *or*, *therefore* etc.). As a prepossessing step in the training dataset, the entire connective span was first mapped to the connective heads using a mapper script for cases like "either... or" and "if... then", which had to be treated separately by considering the entire segment as a whole. This method ensures that all connectives are identified exhaustively and the training process improves.

5.2 Features Used

(Lin et al., 2014) used an extension of the syntactic features used by (Pitler and Nenkova, 2009), which resulted in a higher F-score of 95.36%. They were extracted after generating appropriate graphical representation of the parse tree[2]. We employed the same features, along with a few semantic features (see section 7).

[1] `http://www.seas.upenn.edu/~pdtb/PDTBAPI/pdtb-annotation-manual.pdf`

[2] Python NLTK library was used for all syntax features in every module.

6 Argument Identification with Additional Heuristics

Argument identification is directly dependent on the relative position of the arguments as shown by (Lin et al., 2014). For Arg1 occurring before Arg2 (the PS class), a baseline parser with the assumption of adjacent sentences was used. This is motivated by the fact that 79.9% of cases within the PS class lie in this category. Extension of the same logic was used for non-explicit discourse relations as described in section 8. Where both arguments occur in the same sentence (the SS class) (Lin et al., 2014) used node classification with syntactic parse tree. In our system, we used additional heuristics observed from manual observations of incorrect cases.

After applying the implementation, we manually observed each case in the training set where there was a mismatch between the expected and predicted results. Observations showed that the Arg1 node tends to appear towards the root of the sentence encompassing the entire sentence. And the Arg2 node often tends to appear towards the leaf nodes.

Although in some cases the Arg1 node may indeed be the root of the syntax tree, but those cases were infrequent. Hence, after altering the algorithm to specifically avoid any of the above mentioned scenarios, the results showed marginal but noticeable improvement in both arg1 and arg2 performance. F-Score of the Arg1 node detection improved by 2.14% and the corresponding score for the Arg2 node improved by 0.1%.

7 Use of Semantic Features

All the related work referred to in this paper only used syntactic features for every classifier. Intuitively speaking, there seems to be a good case for using semantic features, in addition to syntactic features. However, the extraction of semantic features from raw text is comparatively hard.

Many semantic features also tend to be inconsistent or sparse. Features detected in one sentence may be completely absent in a large majority of sentences, leading to ineffective features.

7.1 The Boxer Tool

The C&C tool Boxer (Bos, 2014), developed by Johan Bos, is a toolkit for creating the semantic representation of sentences, developed by Johan Bos. Boxer is capable of extracting features from the majority of sentences, although it has some limitations. Boxer works by chunking the sentence into blocks or 'boxes' and then subsequently identifying semantic relations between them. The Boxer tool also marks the tokens of specific semantic roles such as agent, patient etc. We only used the features which were more commonly occurring. These were: the POS tag of the agent's token, the theme's token and the patient's token. We used the POS tags instead of the tokens themselves because tags are more general whereas tokens become too specific (with lower frequencies). Based on results and on more reflection we realize that this choice was not well motivated.

7.2 Application of Features

As mentioned in section 4, we tried the integration of semantic features at each feasible point in the pipeline and tested the results. Since labelling of Arg1 and Arg2 nodes is done through node-wise feature extraction, semantic features, which are extracted from a sentence as a whole, could not be easily integrated. Semantic features were included in two classifier stages: (a) the argument position classifier and (b) the sense classifier. This was the best combination we could get for semantic features. However, the integration of these additional features did not improve the overall performance. Instead, there was a 1.1% decrease in the overall parser F1 score. The inability of the semantic features to improve the classifier performance can be attributed to the fact that the particular features used had high correlation with syntactic features.

8 Non-explicit Identification

We have used a simple heuristic-based baseline parser as done by Lin et al. (2014) for implicit connectives. The parser is based on the adjacent sentence argument assumption mentioned in section 6. This is motivated by the fact that non-explicit relation also have a majority of cases in this category, akin to the PS case for explicit relations.

We used sets to mark the sentences in the same sentence category for explicit relations as covered. The rest of the sentences were marked as uncovered. Distinction between explicit and non-explicit cases were made while marking the sentences. The argument spans were then marked taking a pair of sentences as arguments, the sentence occurring earlier being Arg1. The explicit relation

Classifier	Precision	Recall	F1 Score	Type of Classifier
Connective Classifier	91.76%	91.70%	91.73%	Maximum-Entropy
Argument Position	98.79%	97.11%	97.94%	Maximum-Entropy
Argument Position + Semantic Features	97.61%	93.18%	95.34%	Naive-Bayesian
Argument Extraction (Arg1 + Arg2)	21.89%	34.47%	26.78%	Maximum-Entropy
Sense	29.95%	6.33%	5.95%	Maximum-Entropy
Sense + Semantic Features	27.81%	5.39%	4.68%	Naive-Bayesian

Table 1: Individual Classifier Analysis

	Dev Set			
Parameter	**Without Semantic Features**	**With Semantic Features**	**Blind Set**	**Test Set**
Arg 1 Arg2 extraction f1	26.78%	26.78%	21.71%	22.52%
Arg 1 Arg2 extraction precision	21.89%	21.89%	18.14%	18.19%
Arg 1 Arg2 extraction recall	34.46%	34.37%	27.05%	29.55%
Arg1 extraction f1	36.25%	36.25%	32.2%	32.7%
Arg1 extraction precision	29.63%	29.63%	26.9%	26.41%
Arg1 extraction recall	46.66%	46.66%	40.12%	42.91%
Arg2 extraction f1	49.82%	49.81%	48.87%	44.68%
Arg2 extraction precision	40.73%	40.73%	40.82%	36.1%
Arg2 extraction recall	64.14%	64.14%	60.88%	58.64%
Explicit connective f1	93.55%	93.55%	89.3%	93.06%
Explicit connective precision	95.41%	95.41%	91.67%	93.93%
Explicit connective recall	91.76%	91.76%	87.05%	92.2%
Sense f1	5.95%	4.68%	6.44%	7.17%
Sense precision	29.95%	27.81%	14.87%	25.67%
Sense recall	6.33%	5.39%	7.16%	8.05%
Overall Precision	7.21%	6.32%	6.38%	5.78%
Overall Recall	11.35%	9.96%	9.51%	9.39%
Overall F1	8.82%	7.74%	7.64%	7.15%

Table 2: Overall Parser Performance for Explicit Connectives

sentences among these were then sense classified, along with the PS category explicit sentences.

9 Explicit Sense Classification

Sense classification is the final step in our model. (Lin et al., 2014) reported an F-Score of 86.77% using connective-based features over the PDTB corpus. The integration of semantic features was done as described in section 7. This degraded the F-Score by 1.3%. Thus, the use of (the few) semantic features with high correlation to syntactic features decreases the performance.

10 Evaluation

The pipeline architecture which was used had several classifiers, each of which was evaluated individually on two kinds of training models: (a) the Naive-Bayesian classifier and (b) the Maximum Entropy classifier. For each of the individual classifiers, training and test sets were divided in a 4:1 ratio with a 5-fold cross-validation.

Table 1 presents the individual classifier results. Each phase was tested on the Naive-Bayesian and the Maximum Entropy classifiers. The better one for each sub-task is displayed. It should be noted that sense classification was computed only when both Arg1 and Arg2 spans exactly matched. Sense classification with incorrect argument spans would not be a useful statistical measure.

The overall parser performance was also measured when the complete end-to-end pipeline was implemented for sentences, accompanied by their corresponding syntactic parse trees and feature representations. Table 2 presents the overall best performance on the blind set after multiple trials on a sufficiently large subset of the PDTB corpus. It further compares performance of the overall system with semantic features included vis-a-vis without them. The overall parser performance is only somewhat better (nearly double) than those of the baseline, but the sense classification recall, sense precision and Arg1 extraction precision are bringing down the overall F1 score, as the performance on other sub-tasks is relatively much better. We are investigating the cause for this.

11 Conclusion

We used an end-to-end shallow discourse parser, which is an extension of the work described in (Lin et al., 2014), with the addition of some heuristics and a few semantic features obtained from the Boxer tool. The core idea is using syntactic and semantic features for classification and labelling. However, we were not able to get better results with the semantic features that we tried. We plan to explore more sophisticated semantic features. While our overall performance was relatively low, we did get good results for some of the sub-tasks. We will try to include more results in the final version of the paper.

References

Johan Bos. 2014. Open-domain semantic parsing with boxer. In *Proceedings of the 20th Nordic Conference of Computational Linguistics*, pages 301–304.

Sucheta Ghosh, Richard Johansson, Giuseppe Riccardi, and Sara Tonelli. 2014. Shallow discourse parsing with conditional random fields. In *Proceedings of the 5th International Joint Conference on Natural Language Processing.*

Fang Kong, Hwee Tou Ng, and Guodong Zhou. 2014. A constituent-based approach to argument labeling with joint inference in discourse parsing. In *Proceedings of the 2014 Conference on Empirical Methods in Natural Language Processing (EMNLP).*

Ziheng Lin, Min-Yen Kan, and Hwee Tou Ng. 2009. Recognizing implicit discourse relations in the penn discourse treebank. In *Proceedings of the 2009 Conference on Empirical Methods in Natural Language Processing.*

Ziheng Lin, Hwee Tou Ng, and Min-Yen Kan. 2014. A pdtb-styled end-to-end discourse parser. *Natural Language Engineering, Cambridge Univ Press.*

Leni Miltsakaki, Rashmi Prasad, Aravind Joshi, and Bonnie Webber. 2004. The penn discourse treebank. In *Proceedings of the Fourth International Conference on Language Resources and Evaluation.*

Emily Pitler and Ani Nenkova. 2009. Using syntax to disambiguate explicit discourse connectives in text. In *Proceedings of the ACL-IJCNLP 2009 Conference Short Papers.*

Nianwen Xue, Hwee Tou Ng, Sameer Pradhan, Rashmi Prasad, Christopher Bryant, and Attapol Rutherford. 2015. The conll-2015 shared task on shallow discourse parsing. In *Proceedings of the Nineteenth Conference on Computational Natural Language Learning: Shared Task.*

JAIST: A two-phase machine learning approach for identifying discourse relations in newswire texts

Nguyen Truong Son
University of Science, VNU
Ho Chi Minh City
Viet Nam
ntson@fit.hcmus.edu.vn

Ho Bao Quoc
University of Science, VNU
Ho Chi Minh City
Viet Nam
hbquoc@fit.hcmus.edu.vn

Nguyen Le Minh
Japan Advanced Institute of
Science and Technology
Ishikawa, 923-1292
Japan
nguyenml@jaist.ac.jp

Abstract

In this paper, we present a machine learning approach for identifying shallow discourse relations in news wire text. Our approach has 2 phases. The arguments detection phase will identify arguments and explicit connectives by using the Conditional Random Fields (CRFs) learning algorithm with a set of features such as words, parts of speech (POS) and features extracted from the parsing tree of sentences. The second phase, the sense classification phase, will classify arguments and explicit connectives into one of fifteen types of senses by using the SMO classifier with a simple feature set. The performance of system was evaluated three different data sets given by the CoNLL 2015 Shared Task. The parser of our system was ranked 4 of 16 participating systems on F-measure when evaluating on the blind data set (strict matching).

1 Introduction

The shallow discourse parsing task given by the CoNLL 2015 Shared Task proposed by Xue et al. (2015) aims to extract discourse relations in newswire texts. Each discourse relation is a set of four: two arguments, connective words and senses. However, the connective words may not be available in case of implicit discourses. Identifying discourse relations is clearly an important part of natural language understanding that benefits a wide range of natural language applications. A number of applications of discourse information have been proposed for recent years. For example, in the task of identifying paraphrase texts, Bach et al. (2014) has used discourse information to compute the similarity score between two sentences or Somasundaran et al. (2009) has used discourse relations to improve the performance of the opinion polarity classification task.

In the past, this task is solved at different levels. Lin et al. (2009) have used supervised learning method to build a maximum entropy classifier to identify implicit relations. Ghosh et al. (2011, 2012) have used CRFs with a set of local and global features to recognize arguments of discourses from texts. However, in contrast to the CoNLL 2015 SDP Shared Task, Ghosh et al. (2011, 2012) just considered explicit relations with explicit connectives have been provided.

Our team approach for this shared task composes two phases. In the first phase, we use CRFs and a set of features such as words, POS and pattern features based on parsing tree of sentences to build models for recognizing arguments and connective words. In the second phase, we use the SMO algorithm, an optimization of SVM, to build a classifier to predict the senses of discourse relations.

The remainder of this paper is structured as follows: Section 2 describes the details of the proposed system for solving the task of identifying shallow discourse relations given by CoNLL 2015 Shared Task. We also describe the experimental results and some analysis in Section 3. Finally, Section 4 presents our conclusions and future works.

2 System description

Our parser system is divided into 2 phases. Firstly, documents without discourse information will be passed through the argument detection phase to recognize components of discourse relations such as both of arguments and explicit connectives if it is possible. Secondly, the sense classification phase will identify the sense of discourse relation by using a SVM classifier then format

Proceedings of the Nineteenth Conference on Computational Natural Language Learning: Shared Task, pages 66–70,
Beijing, China, July 26-31, 2015.

the results according to the expected output of evaluate system.

2.1 Phase 1: detection of arguments

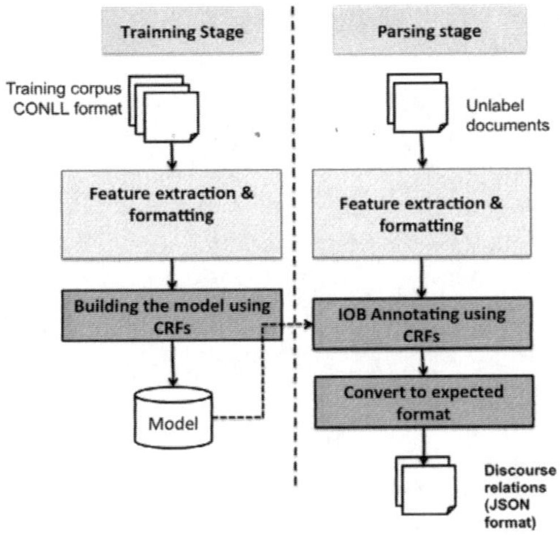

Figure 1. Workflow of the arguments detection phase

The workflow of the first phase consists of two stages. In the training stage, we use machine-learning algorithms to build models, which will be used to identify boundaries of components in the parsing stage. In order to learn models by using machine learning (ML) algorithms, we use some popular features in such as words, parts of speech. Besides, we extract a set of pattern features based on the parsing tree of sentences.

According to our analysis of discourse relations, two arguments of each discourse relation may be appeared at different positions: in the same sentence, in two consecutive sentences or in far apart sentences. Based on the statistic of discourse relations in the training dataset, we see that the number of discourse relations which two arguments located in the same sentence or two consecutive sentences is in a large quantity (92.5%). Therefore, our system focus on identifying these kinds of discourse relations by building two models: one for recognizing discourse relations in the same sentence (**SS**) and another model for recognizing discourse relations in two consecutive sentences (**2CS**).

To build learning models using ML algorithms, we need to extract the features from the data set for the input of the ML algorithm. Each type of discourse relation (SS-type or 2CS-type) has some common features and some reserved features. Table 1 describes all features that are used for machine learning approaches in our experiments.

Table 1. List of all features using for identifying arguments and connectives

#	**Feature description**
Common features for both SS-type and 2CS-type	
A	Word
B	POS
C	Stem
D	Belongs to connective list
E	Brown cluster
F	Noun phrase / verb phrase
G	CLAUSES_from_S
*Pattern features of **SS** discourse relations*	
H	S_CC_S
I	SBAR_CC_SBAR
K	SBAR_IN_S
Pattern features of 2CS discourse relations	
L	1st sentence: RIGHTMOST_S 2nd sentence: S_begin_with_CC
M	1st sentence: RIGHTMOST_S 2nd sentence: NP_ADVP_VP
N	1st sentence: RIGHTMOST_S 2nd sentence: S_begin_with_ADVP
O	1st sentence: RIGHTMOST_S 2nd sentence: S_begin_with_PP

After all required features are extracted, the training data and these extracted features will be formatted as the input format of the machine learning algorithm tool in which words of discourse relations are marked labels using IOB notations. We use CRF++ (Taku Kudo, 2005), an implementation of the Conditional Random Fields (John Lafferty et al, 2001) to train models from the training data sets.

After models are built, they were used to predict the discourse labels of new documents (in the parsing stage) then the result will be converted into expected format.

Section 2.1.1 and 2.1.2 will describe the details of all features we used in our experiments.

2.1.1 Common features:

- *Popular language features* (**A-C**): including words, their parts of speeches and their stems.
- *Connective features (**D**)*: The features show whether or not the words belong to a predefined connective list. Predefined connective lists are constructed from connective words in the training data set. Then we use these lists to extract this feature for building the model.
- *Brown clusters features (**E**)*: Brown clusters, introduced and prepared by Turian (2010), were successfully applied in some

named entity recognition tasks. In Brown clusters, the semantic similarities of words in the same cluster are higher than of words in different clusters. We use the Brown cluster index of words as a feature for the ML process.

- *Noun phrases, verb phrases and clauses* features ***(F, G)***: all words of a noun phrase, verb phrase or clauses are often located entirely in arguments. Moreover, the beginning of arguments is often the same with the beginning of noun phrases, verb phrases or clauses. We extract noun phrases, verb phrases and clause based on the syntactic parse tree of sentences.

2.1.2 Pattern based features based on syntactic parse trees

Our analysis on the training corpus shows that the syntactic information based on the syntactic parse trees is very important for identify discourse relations. According to our analysis, sentences that express discourse relations are usually follow some special syntax. Therefore, if we can extract features based on these special syntaxes, the system will recognize arguments of discourse relations more exactly.

Due to the linguist characteristic of discourses in sentences, each kind of discourse relations (SS-type or 2CS-type) has different pattern feature sets. Below are patterns based on syntactic parse trees we have used to extract features for each of type:

Pattern features for SS-type discourses recognition (H, I, K): We have three patterns that help to recognize boundaries of arguments of SS-type discourse relations. These patterns are based on the syntactic characteristic of discourse expressions using prepositions or conjunctions such as *and, but, if, although, …* For example, the pattern S_CC_S (**feature H**) and SBAR_CC_SBAR (**feature I**) indicate S nodes of which child nodes matched with the pattern *S(.*)CC(.*)S(.*)* or *SBAR(.*)CC(.*)SBAR(.*)*. In this case, related S-nodes or SBAR-nodes may be the arguments of a discourse relation. Figure 2 shows an example of sentences which matches with pattern S_CC_S. In this example, the matched left S node and the right S node are arguments of a discourse relation in the training data set. Another pattern is SBAR_IN_S (Feature **K**). This pattern matched with sentences of which SBAR node has an IN node ("if", "although", "before", "after", "though") follow by an S node. If a sentence match with this pattern, the S node is often the first arguments and the rest is often the second argument of a discourse relation. Figure 3 shows an example of sentences matched with the pattern SBAR_IN_S.

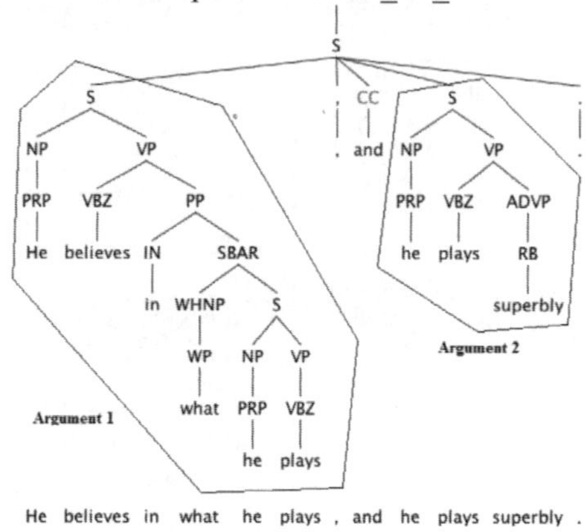

Figure 2. The matching of a discourse relation with the pattern *S_CC_S*

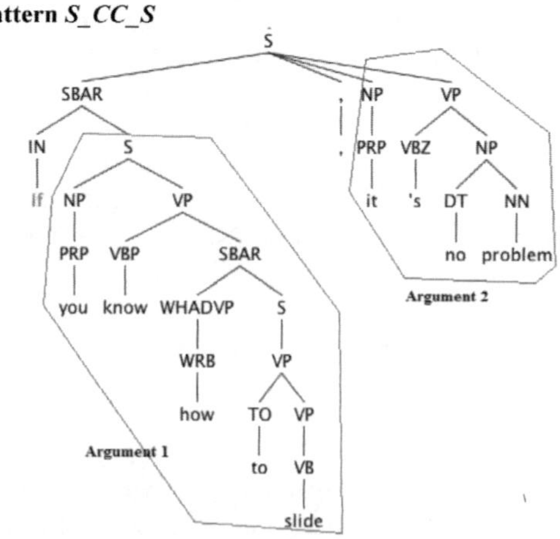

Figure 3. The matching of a discourse relation with the IN_SBAR pattern

Pattern features for 2CS-type discourses recognition (L, M, N, O): When arguments of discourse relations are not located in the same sentence the task is more difficult. To build the model for identifying 2CS discourses, we will extract pattern-based features of each pair of sentences in the training data set based on parsing tree of sentences. Our analysis on the training corpus shows that if a pair of sentence in which the second sentence begins with *a conjunction, an adverb, and a preposition* (e.g. *"for example", "by comparison"* and so on) or *a noun phrase followed by an adverb (e.g., "also")*, the right most clauses of first sentence and the left most sentence in the second sentence may be arguments of a discourse relation. We use patterns from L-O to extract these features.

2.2 Phase 2: Sense classification

After arguments and explicit connectives of discourses are identified, we need to identify the sense of these discourses. These discourses without sense information are passed through a classifier with a model trained in the training stage to identify the correct senses of discourse relations.

This model used in the above step are built by using the Sequential Minimal Optimization algorithm (SMO), a fast algorithm for training support vector machines (John Platt, 1998), with some simple features such as: connective words; type of discourses (SS or 2CS); does the first character of connective words capital or not? The workflow of sense classification phase is shown in Figure 4.

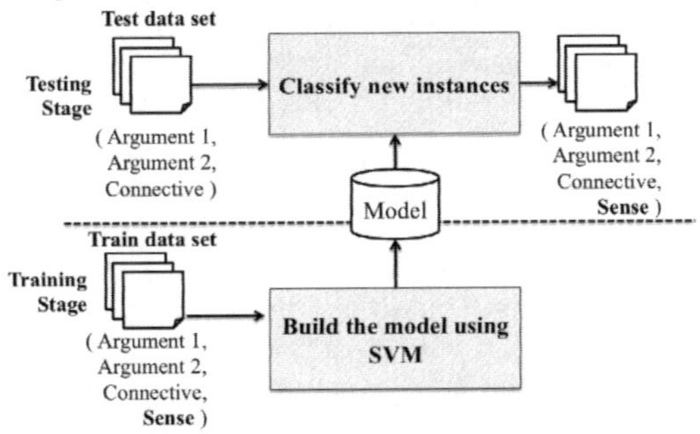

Figure 4. Workflow of the sense classification phase

We use LIBSVM (Chang and Lin. 2011) – a library that implemented SMO algorithm to build the model and classify discourses into the senses category. The trained model for sense classification task achieves an F-score of 79.8% (Precision=80.9%, R=81.6%) when evaluate using cross validation 10-fold method.

One limitation of our sense classification step is that it just takes into account discourses with explicit connectives, so the sense recognition of non-implicit discourses still has not been solved yet.

3 Experimental results

Table 2 shows the evaluation result of our system on the three data sets provided by the CONLL Shared task 2015, the rank column is the rank of our system when compare with other participating systems. In general, this task is a difficult task, so the result is not as high as our expectation. Moreover, due to the usage of special syntactic patterns extracted from parse trees, the precision scores of our system is higher than other teams. However, these patterns just cover several special cases, so the recall score of our system is low.

Table 2. The evaluation result of our system on the blind, test and dev data sets

	BLIND data set		**TEST** data set		**DEV** data set	
	score	**rank**	**score**	**rank**	**score**	**rank**
Arg 1 Arg2 extraction (%)						
F1	32.11	7	35.43	7	40.07	8
P	42.72	3	52.98	**1**	58.92	**1**
R	25.72	11	26.61	12	30.36	12
Arg1 extraction (%)						
F1	40.99	6	42.43	7	46.60	8
P	54.53	3	63.45	**1**	**68.51**	**1**
R	32.84	12	31.87	12	35.31	12
Arg2 extraction (%)						
F1	48.53	9	47.99	7	48.99	11
P	64.56	6	71.77	2	72.03	4
R	38.88	12	36.05	13	37.12	13
Explicit connective (%)						
F1	61.66	12	63.89	15	65.53	14
P	88.55	10	91.87	8	91.56	10
R	47.30	13	48.97	16	51.03	16
Overall parser performance (%)						
F1	18.28	**4**	20.25	8	26.10	5
P	24.31	**2**	30.29	2	38.38	1
R	14.64	**6**	15.21	10	19.78	8
Sense (%)						
F1	15.61	6	13.61	8	19.93	5
P	40.55	1	49.34	1	63.15	1
R	12.44	8	10.73	12	15.01	9

The comparison of the evaluation result between explicit discourses and non-explicit discourses are shown in Table 3. With the help of special patterns based on explicit connectives and parse trees, the result of explicit discourses recognition is higher than the result of non-explicit discourses recognition for both of precision and recall scores.

Table 3. Comparison result between explicit discourses and non-explicit discourses

	BLIND set			**TEST data set**		
	ALL	Explicit	Non-Exp.	ALL	Explicit	Non-Exp.
Arg 1 Arg2 extraction (%)						
F1	32.11	34.23	30.44	35.43	38.16	32.44
P	42.72	49.16	38.28	52.98	54.88	50.41
R	25.72	26.26	25.27	26.61	29.25	23.92
Arg1 extraction (%)						
F1	40.99	44.08	36.9	42.43	43.82	38.85
P	54.53	63.3	46.4	63.45	63.01	60.37
R	32.84	33.81	30.63	31.87	33.59	28.64
Arg2 extraction (%)						
F1	48.53	51.35	46.13	47.99	56.25	38.85
P	64.56	73.74	58	71.77	80.89	60.37
R	38.88	39.39	38.28	36.05	43.12	28.64
Explicit connective (%)						
F1	61.66	61.66	0	63.89	63.89	0
P	88.55	88.55	0	91.87	91.87	0
R	47.3	47.3	0	48.97	48.97	0

Overall parser performance						
F1	18.28	27.2	11.25	20.25	33.22	8.01
P	24.31	39.06	14.15	30.29	47.76	12.45
R	14.64	20.86	9.34	15.21	25.46	5.91
Sense (%)						
F1	15.61	22.89	1.61	13.61	19.14	1.23
P	40.55	42.58	84.51	49.34	48.43	86.6
R	12.44	17.88	2.54	10.73	14.66	1.97

The feature set based on the syntactic parse tree is very important for our system. Table 4 shows the comparison between two different feature set on the development data set. The **FULL** feature set consists of all feature including lexical, part of speeches, and pattern features based on syntactic parse trees and so on. However, in the **SHORT** feature set, we remove all pattern features based on syntactic parse trees to evaluate the importance of these features. The result, which just considered discourse relations in the same sentences, showed that there is a significant improvement when we use the **FULL** feature set instead of the **SHORT** feature set.

Table 4. The comparison between FULL and SHORT feature set

	FULL	SHORT
Arg 1 Arg2 extraction		
F1	0.505	0.315
P	0.684	0.559
R	0.401	0.219
Arg1 extraction		
F1	0.567	0.382
P	0.766	0.677
R	0.449	0.266
Arg2 extraction		
F1	0.612	0.433
P	0.827	0.769
R	0.485	0.302

FULL	SHORT
Explicit connective	
0.670	0.512
0.886	0.885
0.539	0.360
Overall parser	
0.452	0.270
0.612	0.479
0.359	0.188
Sense	
0.232	0.159
0.665	0.612
0.184	0.109

4 Conclusion

Our approach to the Shallow Discourse Parsing at CONLL 2015 Shared task was to create a 2-phase system that identifies discourse relations in newswire text. Results show that our approach achieves the high precision of all systems and was ranked 4th in terms of F1-measure when strict matching is used.

In the future we would like to improve the recall of our approach by exploring the use of a wider range of features.

References

N. Xue, H.T. Ng, S. Pradhan, R. Prasad, C. Bryant, A. Rutherford. 2015. *The CoNLL-2015 Shared Task on Shallow Discourse Parsing*. In Proceedings of the Nineteenth Conference on Computational Natural Language Learning: Shared Task. Beijing, China.

N.X. Bach, N.L. Minh, and A. Shimazu. 2014. Exploiting discourse information to identify paraphrases. *Expert Systems with Applications*, 41(6):2832–2841, May.

J. Lafferty, A. McCallum, and F.C.N Pereira. 2001. Conditional random fields: Probabilistic models for segmenting and labeling sequence data.

S. Ghosh, R. Johansson, and S. Tonelli. 2011. Shallow discourse parsing with conditional random fields. In *In Proceedings of the 5th International Joint Conference on Natural Language Processing (IJCNLP 2011*. Citeseer.

S. Ghosh, G. Riccardi, and R. Johansson. 2012. Global features for shallow discourse parsing. In *Proceedings of the 13th Annual Meeting of the Special Interest Group on Discourse and Dialogue*, pages 150–159. Association for Computational Linguistics.

T. Kudo. 2005. CRF++: Yet another CRF toolkit. *Software available at http://crfpp. sourceforge. net*.

J. Platt. 1998. Sequential minimal optimization: A fast algorithm for training support vector machines.

C.C. Chang and C.J. Lin. 2011. LIBSVM: a library for support vector machines. *ACM Transactions on Intelligent Systems and Technology (TIST)*, 2(3):27.

S. Somasundaran, G. Namata, J. Wiebe, and L. Getoor. 2009. Supervised and unsupervised methods in employing discourse relations for improving opinion polarity classification. In *Proceedings of the 2009 Conference on Empirical Methods in Natural Language Processing*, pages 170–179.

Z. Lin, M.Y. Kan, and H.T. Ng. 2009. Recognizing implicit discourse relations in the Penn Discourse Treebank. In *Proceedings of the 2009 Conference on Empirical Methods in Natural Language Processing: Volume 1-Volume 1*, pages 343–351.

J. Turian, L. Ratinov, and Y. Bengio. 2010. Word representations: a simple and general method for semi-supervised learning. In *Proceedings of the 48th annual meeting of the association for computational linguistics*, pages 384–394.

The DCU Discourse Parser: A Sense Classification Task

Tsuyoshi Okita, Longyue Wang, Qun Liu
Dublin City University, ADAPT Centre
Glasnevin, Dublin 9, Ireland
{tokita,lwang,qliu}@computing.dcu.ie

Abstract

This paper describes the discourse parsing system developed at Dublin City University for participation in the CoNLL 2015 shared task. We participated in two tasks: a connective and argument identification task and a sense classification task. This paper focuses on the latter task and especially the sense classification for implicit connectives.

1 Introduction

This paper describes the discourse parsing system developed at Dublin City University for participation in the CoNLL 2015 shared task (Xue et al., 2015). We participated in two tasks: a connective and argument identification task and a sense classification task. This paper focuses on the latter task.

We divide the whole process into two stages: the first stage concerns an identification of triples $(Arg1, Conn, Arg2)$ and pairs $(Arg1, Arg2)$ while the second stage concerns a sense classification of the identified individual triples and pairs. The first phase of the identification of connective and arguments are described in (Wang et al., 2015), which bases on the framework of (Lin et al., 2009) and is also presented in this shared task as a different paper. Hence, we omit the detailed description of the first stage (See (Wang et al., 2015) for identification of connectives and arguments). This paper focuses on the second stage which concerns sense classification.

2 Sense Classification

We use off-the-shelf classifiers with four kinds of features: relational phrase embedding, production, word-pair and heuristic features. Among them, we test the method which incorporates relational phrase embedding features for $Arg1$ and $Arg2$ for discourse parsing. Production features are proposed in (Lin et al., 2014) and word-pair features are reported in (Lin et al., 2014; Rutherford and Xue, 2015). Heuristic features, which is specific for explicit sense classification, are described in (Lin et al., 2014).

	Rel phrase (2.1)	Prod (2.2)	Word pair (2.3)	Heuristic feat (2.4)
Implicit	yes	yes/no[1]	yes/no[2]	no
Explicit	yes	no	no	yes

Table 1: Overview of features used for implicit/explicit classification.

We consider the embedding models which lead to two different types of intermediate representations. The relational phrase embedding model considers the dependency within words uniformly without considering the second-order effect. The word-pair embedding model considers the second-order effect of specific combinations within the word-pairs in $Arg1$ and $Arg2$. If we plug in a paragraph vector model for the relational phrase embedding model, the model considers the effect of uni-gram within a sentence as a sequence. If we plug in a RNN-LSTM model (Le and Zuidema, 2015), the model considers the effect of uni-gram within a sentence as a tree.

2.1 Relational Phrase Embedding Features

Phrase embeddings (or sentence embeddings) are distributed representation in a higher level than a word level. We used a paragraph vector model to obtain these phrase embeddings (Le and Mikolov, 2014). Upon obtained the phrase embeddings for

[2]For the official score, we did not use production features due to the timing constraint. We write the result for the development set.

[3]For the official score, we did not use the word-pair feature due to the timing constraint. We write the result for the development set.

Proceedings of the Nineteenth Conference on Computational Natural Language Learning: Shared Task, pages 71–77,
Beijing, China, July 26-31, 2015. ©2014 Association for Computational Linguistics

$Arg1$, $Arg2$ (and Connectives), we used the relational phrase embedding from these triples (or pairs) based on their phrase embeddings (Bordes et al., 2013).

The first type of embedding we used in this paper is a combination of paragraph vector (Le and Mikolov, 2014) and translational embeddings (Bordes et al., 2013). First, the abstraction of each variable $Arg1$ and $Arg2$ was built independently in a vertical way, and then the relation among these ($Arg1$,$Conn$,$Arg2$) and ($Arg1$,$Arg2$) are examined in a collective way. This is shown in Figure 3. This model has two intermediate embeddings: paragraph vector embeddings of $Arg1$, $Arg2$, and $Conn$, and translational embedding of ($Arg1$,$Conn$,$Arg2$) and ($Arg1$,$Arg2$).

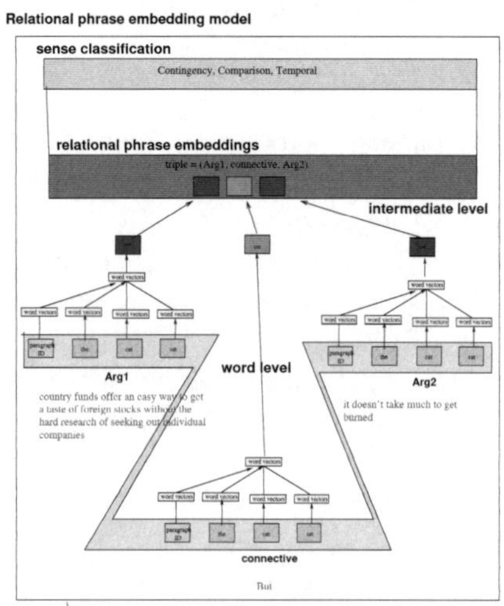

Figure 1: Figure shows relational paragraph embeddings.

We use a paragraph vector model to obtain the feature for $Arg1$ and $Arg2$ (Le and Mikolov, 2014). The paragraph vector model is an idea to obtain a real-valued vector in the similar construction with the word vector model (or word2vec) (Mikolov et al., 2013b) where the detailed explanation can be obtained.

In implicit/explicit sense classification, the participated items related to this classification are two for implicit relations of a pair $(Arg1, Arg2)$ and three for explicit relations of a triple $(Arg1, Conn, Arg2)$. This is by nature a multiple-instance learning setting (Dietterich et al., 1997), which receives a set of instances which are labeled collectively instead of individually labeled where each contains many instances. All the more, linguistic characteristics of discourse relations support this: meaning/sense is attached not to a single argument $Arg1$ or $Arg2$ but to a pair $(Arg1, Arg2)$ or a triple $(Arg1, Conn, Arg2)$.

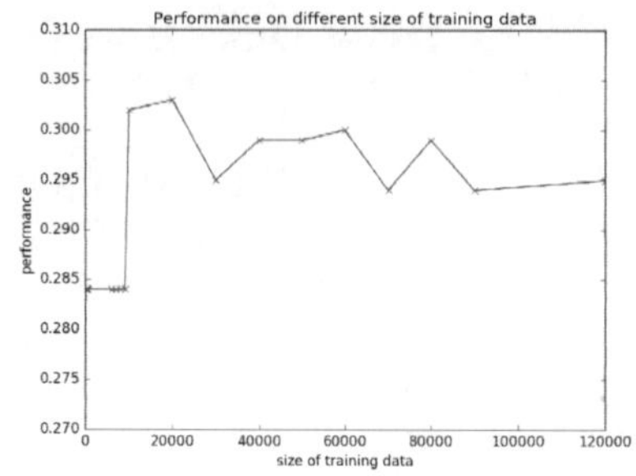

Figure 2: Figure shows a scalability of implicit classification performance based on the size of additional training data. We used dev set and used resources from WestBurry version of wikipedia corpus[6]and WMT14[7].

Followed by Bordes et al. (Bordes et al., 2011; Bordes et al., 2013), we minimized a margin-based ranking criterion over the pair of embeddings:

$$\mathcal{L} = \sum_{(Arg1,Arg2)\in S} \sum_{(Arg1,Arg2)\in S'} [\gamma + d(Arg1', Arg2) - d(Arg1, Arg2')]_+$$

where $[x]_+$ denotes the positive part of x, $\gamma > 0$ is a margin hyperparameter. S' denotes a set of corrupted pair where $Arg1$ or $Arg2$ is replaced by a random entity (but not both at the same time). Readers should see the detailed explanation in (Bordes et al., 2013).

It is noted that we tried indicator function (alternatively called discrete-valued vector, bucket function (Bansal et al., 2014), binarization of embeddings (Guo et al., 2014)) for embeddings which are converted from real-valued vector. Although we have not tested sufficiently due to the timing constraint, we did not include this method in our experiments since we could not have any gain.

2.2 Production Features for Constituent Parsing

(Lin et al., 2014) describes the method using the production features based on the parsing results.

[6]www.psych.ualberta.ca/ westburylab.
[7]www.statmt.org/wmt14.

Subtree extract	extracted		not extracted	
Exact match	16582	0.347	31265	0.653
+-1 position	39096	0.817	8751	0.183
Combi 2 elem	43031	0.899	4816	0.101
Combi 3 elem	45102	0.943	2745	0.057
Combi 4 elem	45872	0.959	1975	0.041

Table 2: Extraction of production features for constituent parsing results.

In this paper, we further process and treat these as the phrase embeddings. The algorithm is as follows. First, the subset of (constituent) parsing results which correspond to $Arg1$ and $Arg2$ are extracted. Then, all the production rules for these subtrees are derived. Third, we apply these production rules into the relational phrase embedding model that we described in 2.1. We replace all the words in 2.1 with production rules.

2.3 Word-Pair Features

Word-pair features in discourse parsing indicate the Cartesian products of all the combinations of words in $Arg1$ and $Arg2$. This feature is used in (Lin et al., 2014; Rutherford and Xue, 2015). (Rutherford and Xue, 2015) further developed this method combined with Brown clustering (Brown et al., 1992). We use this by word-pair embedding.

The second type of embedding we used in this paper is an abstraction of word-pair embedding in $Arg1$, $Arg2$ (and $Conn$) in a horizontal way. This is shown in Figure 4. The word grows their bi-gram in terms of Cartesian product of elements in different $Arg1$ and $Arg2$ which has a order from $Arg1$ to $Arg2$ where this bi-gram is embedded in the word embedding. Followed by Pitler et al. (Pitler et al., 2008) we use the 100 frequent word-pairs in training set for each category of relation. We did not delete function words/stop-words.

2.4 Heuristic Features for Explicit Connectives

Heuristic features in this paper indicate the specific features used in the explicit sense classification: (1) connective, (2) POS of connective, and (3) connective + previous word (Lin et al., 2014). These three features are employed in order to resolve the ambiguity in discourse connectives, and practically work fairly efficiently.

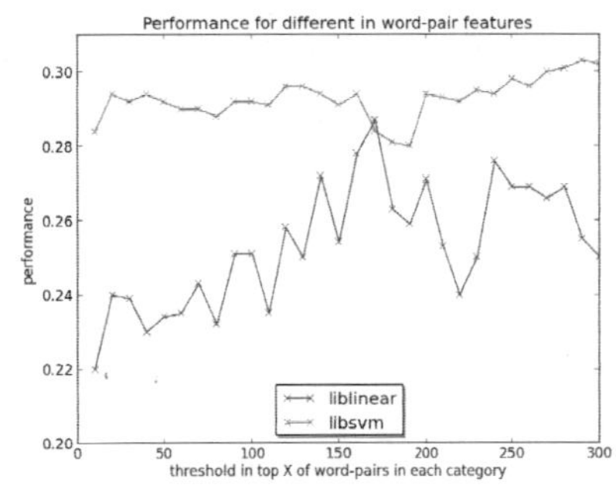

Figure 3: Figure shows the variation of the threshold in top X of word-pairs in each category. Most of the frequent word-pairs are functional word pairs, such as *the-the*, but we did not remove them.

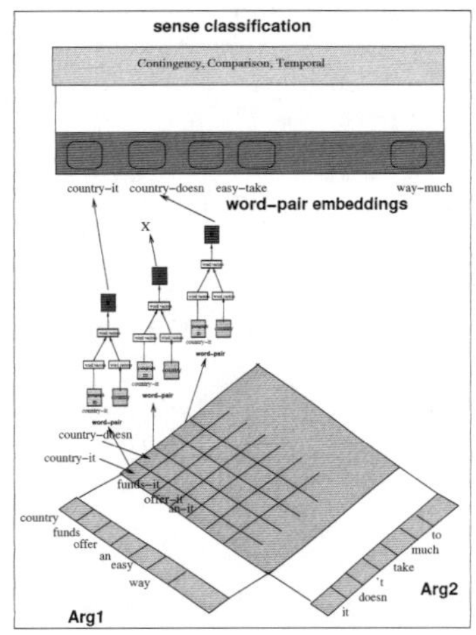

Figure 4: Figure show word-pair embeddings.

3 Experimental Settings

For the dataset, we used the CoNLL 2015 Shared task data set, i.e. LDC2015E21 (Xue et al., 2015) and Skip-gram neural word embeddings (Mikolov et al., 2013a)[8]). For the unofficial run, we used westbury version of English wikipedia dump (such as Figure 2) and WMT14 data set.[9]

We choose python as the language to develop our discourse parser. We use external tools such as libSVM (Chang and Lin, 2011), liblinear (Fan et al., 2008), wapiti (Lavergne et al., 2010), and maximum entropy model[10] for a classification task described as Section 2. Among these off-the-shelf classifiers, we used libSVM for the official re-

[8]https://code.google.com/p/word2vec

[9]www.statmt.org/wmt14.

[10]http://homepages.inf.ed.ac.uk/lzhang10/maxent.html

	Overall Task									Sense Classification					
	dev			test			blind			dev			test		
	f1	pr	rec	f1	pr	rec	f1	pr	rec	f1	pr	rec	f1	pr	rec
Overall															
Arg12	.291	.250	.348	.246	.210	.297	.215	.188	.252	1	1	1	1	1	1
Arg1	.392	.336	.469	.357	.304	.431	.317	.276	.371	1	1	1	1	1	1
Arg2	.422	.362	.505	.398	.339	.480	.382	.333	.448	1	1	1	1	1	1
conn	.863	.904	.827	.881	.903	.859	.794	.849	.746	1	1	1	1	1	1
parser	.154	.132	.184	.123	.105	.149	.107	.093	.125	.492	.812	.474	.466	.804	.458
sense	.081	.270	.099	.083	.207	.112	.041	.047	.065	.546	.546	.546	.531	.531	.531
Explicit Only															
Arg12	.186	.195	.178	.147	.150	.143	.111	.119	.104	1	1	1	1	1	1
Arg1	.263	.275	.252	.211	.216	.206	.167	.178	.157	1	1	1	1	1	1
Arg2	.373	.391	.357	.382	.392	.373	.281	.301	.264	1	1	1	1	1	1
conn	.863	.904	.827	.881	.903	.859	.794	.849	.746	1	1	1	1	1	1
parser	.158	.166	.152	.132	.136	.129	.079	.084	.074	.707	.882	.694	.727	.726	.838
sense	.138	.263	.142	.108	.175	.110	.077	.077	.084	.838	.838	.838	.873	.873	.873
Implicit Only															
Arg12	.355	.275	.501	.307	.237	.436	.276	.217	.378	1	1	1	1	1	1
Arg1	.453	.351	.640	.430	.332	.610	.392	.309	.538	1	1	1	1	1	1
Arg2	.451	.349	.638	.407	.314	.578	.441	.347	.603	1	1	1	1	1	1
conn	1	1	1	1	1	1	1	1	1	1	1	1	1	1	1
parser	.151	.117	.213	.117	.091	.166	.123	.097	.169	.283	.283	.283	.221	.221	.221
sense	.019	.699	.052	.025	.667	.061	.016	.598	.046	.105	.803	.136	.112	.891	.149

Table 3: Official results for task of identification of connectives and arguments. Table shows the results for dev set, test set and blind test set.

sults. Additionally we use word2vec (Mikolov et al., 2013b) and Theano (Bastien et al., 2012)[11] in the pipeline.

One bottleneck of our system was in a training procedure. Since a paragraph vector is currently not incrementally trainable, we were not able to separate training and test phases. Hence, we need to run it all on TIRA,[12] whose computing resource is powerless which took a considerable time such as 15 to 30 minutes where most of other participants only finish their run in 30 seconds or so.

4 Experimental Results

Table 3 shows our results. There are fifteen columns where the nine columns in the left show the overall task while the six columns in the right shows the supplementary task.[13]

In terms of the evaluation for explicit connectives, we obtained F score of 0.138, 0.108, and 0.077 for dev/test/blind sets for overall task (the lowest low in the second group) while we obtained F score of 0.707 for sense classification task. For the connectives, F score was 0.863 while Arg 1-2 was 0.186 which was fairly low. This may be result in the policy of the evaluation script which checks the correct classification results together with the correct identification of triples $(Arg1, Conn, Arg2)$. Hence, even if the classification results were correct if the triples $(Arg1, Conn, Arg2)$ were not correctly identified, the results were not correct. Thus, this explains why there is a big difference between the overall task (left nine columns) and the sense classification task (right three columns), as well as the low scores of 0.138, 0.108 and 0.077.

For the implicit only evaluation, on contrast, we obtained F score of 0.019, 0.025, and 0.016 (the lowest row in the third group) for overall task and 0.105 for sense classification task. Here, precision was high (precision of these which were 0.699, 0.667, and 0.598) for overall task and 0.803 and 0.891 for sense classification task; while recall

[11] http://deeplearning.net/tutorial/rnnslu.html

[12] http://www.tira.io

[13] Due to the unforeseen errors occurred on TIRA, we could not obtain the results for blind test set.

		dev set (official results)						dev set (unofficial results)								
		Explicit			Implicit			Implicit(30m)			Implicit (prod)			Implicit (wp)		
		pr	rec	f1	pr	rec	f1	pr	rec	f1	pr	rec	f1	pr	rec	f1
1	Comp	1	0	0	1	0	0	1	0	0	1	0	0	1	0	0
2	Comp.Conc	.13	.17	.14	1	0	0	1	0	1	0	0	0	0	0	0
3	Comp.Cont	.79	.84	.82	1	0	0	1	0	0	.05	.02	.03	.16	.2	.18
4	Cont.Cau.Rea	.96	.58	.72	1	0	0	1	0	0	.09	.10	.03	.24	.10	.14
5	Cont.Cau.Res	1	.84	.91	1	0	0	1	0	0	.08	.08	.08	.15	.08	.10
6	EntRel	–	–	–	.28	.95	.44	.29	.98	.45	.24	.91	.43	.36	.69	.47
7	Exp	–	–	–	1	0	0	1	0	0	1	0	0	1	0	0
8	Cont.Cond	1	.89	.94	–	–	–	–	–	–	–	–	–	–	–	–
9	Exp.Alt	.86	1	.92	1	0	0	1	0	0	1	0	0	1	0	0
10	Exp.Alt.C alt	1	.83	.91	1	0	0	1	0	0	0	0	0	1	0	0
11	Exp.Conj	.96	.96	.96	.26	.04	.07	.54	.11	.18	.17	.15	.16	.35	.26	.30
12	Exp.Inst	.90	1	.95	0	0	0	.75	.06	.12	.09	.23	.13	.43	.06	.11
13	Exp.Rest	1	.33	.50	.50	.04	.07	.33	.01	.02	.14	.16	.15	.11	.06	.08
14	Temp.As.Pr	.94	.96	.95	1	0	0	1	0	0	.13	.04	.06	0	0	0
15	Temp.As.Su	.95	.73	.82	1	0	0	1	0	0	0	0	0	1	0	0
16	Temp.Syn	.62	.97	.76	1	0	0	1	0	0	.08	.10	.09	0	0	0
17	Average	.88	.69	.71	.80	.14	.11	.86	.14	.11	.21	.14	.07	.39	.16	.09
18	Overall	.84	.84	.84	.28	.28	.28	.30	.30	.30	.16	.16	.16	.29	.29	.29

Table 4: Results for devset (Official and unofficial results). Implicit only includes Implicit, EntRel, and AltLex. This experiment uses the development set. The right most column *Implicit only(30m)* shows the results with additional data of 30M sentence pairs using the same setting of Figure 2.

was very low.

Table 5 shows the detailed results for sense classification under the setting that identification of connectives and arguments are correct. The first group (the left three columns) show the results for explicit classification. On contrast to implicit classification all the figures are considerably good except Comp.Conc whose F score was 0.14. The second group to the fifth group (the rightmost three columns) show four configurations of implicit classification. The third group shows the 30 million additional sentence pairs for training, the fourth group uses production feature, and the fifth group uses word-pair feature. These three groups exposed each characteristics quite clearly. Relational phrase embeddings (Implicit and Implicit(30m)) works for Expansion group (Exp.Conj, Exp.Inst, Exp.Rest), the production feature (marked as Implicit(prod)) worked for Temporal group (Temp.As.Pr and TempSyn), and the word-pair feature (marked as Implicit(wp)) worked for Comparison/Contingency groups. The effect of additional data was shown in the third group (marked as Implicit(30m)). This group was given additional data of 30M sentence pairs which improved the performance on Exp.Conj (from F score 0.07 to 0.18), and Exp.Inst (from F score 0.00 to 0.12) while Exp.Rest was down from fi score 0.07 to 0.02. The effect was limited to these categories.

It is easily observed that if the surface form of connective does not share multiple senses, such as *if* (67%) in Cont.Cond and *instead* (87%) in Exp.Alt.C, the results of sense classification performed good where Cont.Cond was F score of 0.94 and Exp.Alt.C was F score of 0.91. If the surface form of connective share multiple senses, they tend to be classified unbalancedly and one sense tends to be collected many votes. (For example, *But* has multiple senses, including Comp.Conc, Comp, and Comp.Cont. Comp.Cont collected many votes. As a result, the classification results for Comp.Cont was good but for others they were bad).

5 Discussion

A paragraph vector is proven useful for the sentiment analysis-typed task (Le and Mikolov, 2014). The word embedding is propagated towards the parent node and averaged. Our intension was that

	test set					
	Explicit			Implicit		
	pr	rec	f1	pr	rec	f1
1	1	0	0	–	–	–
2	.41	.59	.48	1	0	0
3	.91	.83	.87	1	0	0
4	1	.75	.86	1	0	0
5	1	.97	.99	1	0	0
6	–	–	–	.22	.96	.35
7	–	–	–	1	0	0
8	1	.81	.89	–	–	–
9	.83	1	.91	–	–	–
10	1	1	1	1	0	0
11	.98	.98	.98	.25	.09	.13
12	1	1	1	1	.04	.08
13	1	.29	.44	1	0	0
14	.92	1	.96	1	0	0
15	.94	.69	.79	1	0	0
16	.58	.98	.73	1	0	0
17	.84	.73	.73	.89	.15	.11
18	.87	.87	.87	.22	.22	.22

Table 5: Official results for explicit/implicit sense classification for test set.

the averaged embedding in a sentence will perform meaning establishment in the intermediate representation which capture the characteristics of $Arg1$, $Arg2$, and $Conn$. First, Comp.Cont or Comp.Conc may include sentence polarity with some additional condition that these polarities may be reversed. Against our expectation only a handful of examples were classified in these categories. However, if they are classified in these categories they were correct, i.e. precision 1. Second, if $Arg1$ and $Arg2$ are required to expose the causal relation such as Cont.Cau.Rea and Cont.Cau.Res this may be beyond the framework of a paragraph vector. Third, our implicit classification tried to classify Exp.Conj and Exp.Rest. Both of these categories of relation can be found some similarities with sentiment analysis/polarities, which can be reasonable that it worked for these categories. Four, interestingly, the word-pair feature works for Comparison/Contingency sense group while the production feature works (only slightly though) for Temporal sense group.

We used a margin-based ranking criteria to obtain relations over a paragraph vectors. First, (Mikolov et al., 2013b) observed a linear relation on two word embeddings. However, it might be too heavy expectation for two paragraph embeddings which can capture the similar phenomenon. Even if $Arg1$ consists of many words, a paragraph vector will average their word embeddings. In this sense this approach may have a crucial limit together with the fact that this is unsupervised learning. Second, we do not know yet but some small trick may improve the relation of Comp.Cont or Comp.Conc since these relations are quite similar relations with Exp.Conj, Exp.Instantiation, and Exp.Rest except that these relations are the polarities reversed.

6 Conclusion

This paper describes the discourse parsing system developed at Dublin City University for participation in the CoNLL 2015 shared task. We take an approach based on a paragraph vector. One shortcoming was that our classifier was effective only Exp.Conj, Exp.Inst and Exp.Rest despite our expectation that this model will work for Comp.Cont and Comp.Conc as well. The relation of the latter is in an opposite direction. We provided the word-pair model which works for these categories but in a different perspective.

Further work includes the mechanism how to make it work for Comp.Cont and Comp.Conc. Although a paragraph vector did not work efficiently, our model has a tentative model which does not have interaction between relational, paragraph, and word embeddings such as in (Denil et al., 2015), which is one immediate challenge. Then, other challenge includes replacement of a paragraph vector model with a convolutional sentence vector model (Kalchbrenner et al., 2014) and RNN-LSTM model (Le and Zuidema, 2015). The former approach is related to the supervised learning instead of unsupervised learning. The latter approach is to employ the structure of tree instead of a sequence.

Acknowledgment

This research is supported by the Science Foundation Ireland (Grant 12/CE/I2267) as part of the ADAPT at Dublin City University. We would also like to thank ICHEC, the CoNLL 2015 Shared Task Committee, and Martin Potthast.

References

Mohit Bansal, Kevin Gimpel, and Karen Livescu. 2014. Tailoring continuous word representations for dependency parsing. *In Proceedings of the Association for Computational Linguistics (ACL 2014).*

Frédéric Bastien, Pascal Lamblin, Razvan Pascanu, James Bergstra, Ian J. Goodfellow, Arnaud Bergeron, Nicolas Bouchard, and Yoshua Bengio. 2012. Theano: new features and speed improvements. *Deep Learning and Unsupervised Feature Learning NIPS 2012 Workshop.*

Antoine Bordes, Jason Weston, Ronan Collobert, and Yoshua Bengio. 2011. Learning structured embeddings of knowledge bases. *In Proceeding at the Learning Workshop.*

A Bordes, N Usunier, A Garcia-Duran, J Weston, and O Yakhnenko. 2013. Translating embeddings for modeling multi-relational data. *Advances in Neural Information Processing Systems*, pages 2787–2795.

Peter F. Brown, P.V. deSouza, Robert L. Mercer, Vincent J.D Pietra, and J.C. Lai. 1992. Class-based n-gram models of natural language. *Computational Linguistics*, pages 467–479.

C.-C. Chang and C.-J. Lin. 2011. Libsvm : a library for support vector machines. *ACM Transactions on Intelligent Systems and Technology*, 2:27:1–27:27.

Misha Denil, Alban Demiraj, and Nando de Freitas. 2015. Extraction of salient sentences from labelled documents. *Technical Report at Oxford University.*

Thomas G. Dietterich, Richard H. Lathrop, and Tomas Lozano-Perez. 1997. Solving the multiple instance problem with axis-parallel rectangles. *Artificial Intelligence*, 89(12):3171.

R. E. Fan, K. W. Chang, C. J. Hsieh, X. R. Wang, and C. J. Lin. 2008. Liblinear: A library for large linear classification. *Journal of Machine Learning Research*, 9:1871–1874.

Jiang Guo, Wanxiang Che, Haifeng Wang, and Ting Liu. 2014. Revisiting embedding features for simple semi-supervised learning. *In Proceedings of the Conference on Empirical Methods in Natural Language Processing (EMNLP 2014).*

Nal Kalchbrenner, Edward Grefenstette, and Phil Blunsom. 2014. A convolutional neural network for modelling sentences. *Proceedings of the 52nd Annual Meeting of the Association for Computational Linguistics*, June.

Thomas Lavergne, Olivier Cappé, and François Yvon. 2010. Practical very large scale CRFs. *Proceedings the 48th Annual Meeting of the Association for Computational Linguistics (ACL)*, pages 504–513, July.

Quoc V. Le and Tomas Mikolov. 2014. Distributed representations of sentences and documents. *In Proceedings of ICML.*

Phong Le and Willem Zuidema. 2015. Compositional distributional semantics with long short term memory. *In Proceedings of SemEval (*SEM 2015).*

Ziheng Lin, Min-Yen Kan, and Hwee Tou Ng. 2009. Recognizing implicit discourse relations in the penn discourse treebank. *In Proceedings of the 2009 Conference on Empirical Methods in Natural Language Processing (EMNLP 2009).*

Ziheng Lin, Hwee Tou Ng, and Min-Yen Kan. 2014. A pdtb-styled end-to-end discourse parser. *Natural Language Engineering (Cambridge University Press)*, pages 151–184.

Tomas Mikolov, Quoc V. Le, and Ilya Sutskever. 2013a. Exploiting similarities among languages for machine translation. *ArXiv:1309.4168.*

Tomas Mikolov, Ilya Sutskever, Kai Chen, Greg Corrado, and Jeffrey Dean. 2013b. Distributed representations of words and phrases and their compositionality. *In Proceedings of NIPS conference.*

Emily Pitler, Annie Louis, and Ani Nenkova. 2008. Automatic sense prediction for implicit discourse relations in text. *In Proceedings of the 14th Conference of the Association for Computational Linguistics (ACL 2009).*

Attapol Te Rutherford and Nianwen Xue. 2015. Improving the inference of implicit discourse relations via classifying explicit discourseconnectives. *In Proceedings of the NAACL-HLT.*

Langyue Wang, Chris Hokamp, Tsuyoshi Okita, Xiaojun Zhang, and Qun Liu. 2015. The dcu discourse parser for connective, argument identification and explicit sense classification. *In Proceedings of the Nineteenth Conference on Computational Natural Language Learning: Shared Task.*

Nianwen Xue, Hwee Tou Ng, Sameer Pradhan, Rashmi Prasad, Christopher Bryant, and Attapol Rutherford. 2015. The conll-2015 shared task on shallow discourse parsing. *In Proceedings of the Nineteenth Conference on Computational Natural Language Learning: Shared Task.*

Improving a Pipeline Architecture for Shallow Discourse Parsing

Yangqiu Song Haoruo Peng Parisa Kordjamshidi Mark Sammons Dan Roth

Cognitive Computation Group, University of Illinois at Urbana-Champaign
{yqsong,hpeng7,kordjam,mssammon,danr}@illinois.edu

Abstract

We present a system that implements an end-to-end discourse parser. The system uses a pipeline architecture with seven stages: preprocessing, recognizing explicit connectives, identifying argument positions, identifying and labeling arguments, classifying explicit and implicit connectives, and identifying attribution structures. The discourse structure of a document is inferred based on these components. For NLP analysis, we use Illinois NLP software[1] and the Stanford Parser. We use lexical and semantic features based on function words, sentiment lexicons, brown clusters, and polarity features. Our system achieves an F1 score of 0.2492 in overall performance on the development set and 0.1798 on the blind test set.

1 Introduction

The Illinois discourse parsing system builds on existing approaches, using a series of classifiers to identify different elements of discourse structures such as argument boundaries and types along with discourse connectives and senses. In developing the components of this pipeline, we investigated different kinds of features to try to improve abstraction while retaining sufficient expressivity. To that end, we investigated a combination of parse and lexical (function word) features; brown clusters; and relations between verb-argument structures in consecutive sentences.

2 System Description

In this section, we describe the system we developed, and introduce the features we used in each component. For our starting point, we implemented a pipeline architecture based on the description in Lin et al. (2014), then investigated features and inference approaches to improve the system. The pipeline includes seven components. After a preprocessing step, the system identifies explicit connectives, determines the positions of the arguments relative to the connective, identifies and labels arguments, classifies explicit and implicit connectives, and identifies attribution structures. The system architecture is presented in Figure 1. All the classifiers are built based on LibLinear (Fan et al., 2008) via the interface of Learning Based Java (LBJava) (Rizzolo and Roth, 2010).

2.1 Preprocessing

The preprocessing stage identifies tokens, sentences, part-of-speech (Roth and Zelenko, 1998), shallow parse chunks (Punyakanok and Roth, 2001), lemmas[2], syntactic constituency parse (Klein and Manning, 2003), and dependency parse (de Marneffe et al., 2006). This stage also generates a mapping from our own token indexes to those provided in the gold standard data, to allow evaluation with the official shared task scoring code.

2.2 Recognizing Explicit Connectives

To recognize explicit connectives, we construct a list of existing connectives labeled in the Penn Discourse Treebank (Prasad et al., 2008a). Since not all the words of the connective list are necessarily true connectives when they appear in text, we build a binary classifier to determine when a word matching an entry in the list represents an actual connective. We only focus on the connectives with consecutive tokens and ignore the non-consecutive connectives. We generate lexico-syntactic and path features associated with the

[1] http://cogcomp.cs.illinois.edu/page/software

[2] http://cogcomp.cs.illinois.edu/page/software_view/illinois-lemmatizer

Proceedings of the Nineteenth Conference on Computational Natural Language Learning: Shared Task, pages 78–83,
Beijing, China, July 26-31, 2015.

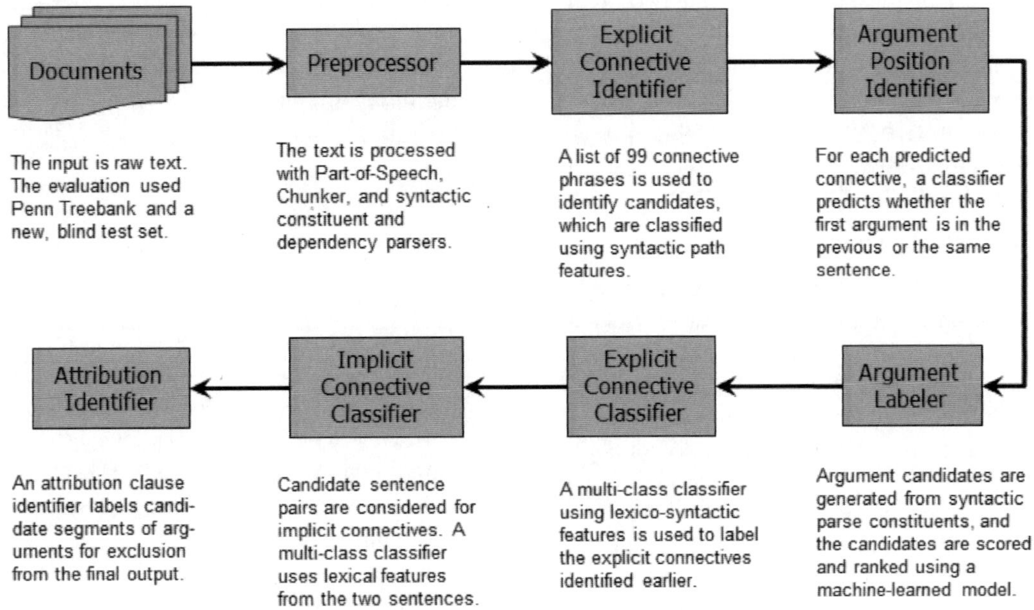

Figure 1: System architecture

connectives following Lin et al. (2014).

2.3 Identifying Arguments and Argument Positions

For each explicit connective, we first identify the relevant argument positions – whether Arg1 is in the previous sentence relative to the connective or in the same sentence. We build a classifier incorporating the contextual lexico-syntactic features. We then detect the spans of Arg1 and Arg2 based on these two decisions. The features used are similiar to those of Lin et al. (2014).

To generate candidate arguments, we enumerate all subtrees in the parse tree of each sentence. We then classify the subtrees to be Arg1, Arg2, or None. In addition to the features used by Lin et al. (2014), we also add function words to the path features. If we detect a word which is in the lexicon of function words, we replace the corresponding tag used in the path with the word's surface string.

2.4 Classifying Explicit Connectives

To classify explicit connectives, we build a multi-class classifier to identify the senses. In addition to the features used by Lin et al. (2014), we also incorporate Brown cluster (Brown et al., 1992) features generated by Liang (2005). The Brown clustering algorithm produces a binary tree, where each word can be uniquely identified by its path from the root, and this path can be compactly represented with a bit string. Different lengths of the prefix of this root-to-leaf path provide different levels of word abstraction. In this implementation, we set the length of the prefix to 6.

2.5 Classifying Implicit Connectives

We classify the sense of implicit connectives based on four sets of features. We follow Lin et al. (2014) to generate the product rules of both constituent parse and dependency parse features, and to generate the word pair features to enumerate all the word pairs in each pair of sentences. In addition, similar to Rutherford and Xue (2014), we incorporate Brown cluster pairs by replacing each word with its Brown cluster prefixes (length of 4) in the way described in Section 2.4. We also use another rich source of information - the polarity of context, which has been previously shown to be useful for coreference problems (Peng et al., 2015). We extract polarity information using the data provided by Wilson et al. (2005) given the predicates of two discourse arguments. The data contains 8221 words, each of which is labeled with a polarity of *positive*, *negative*, or *neutral*. We use the extracted polarity values to construct three features: Two individual polarities of the two predicates and the conjuction of them. We also implement feature selection to remove the features that are active in the corpus less than five times. As a result, we have 16,989 parse tree features, 4,335 dependency tree features, 77,677 word pair features, and 67,204 Brown cluster features.

2.6 Identifying Attribution Structures

We train two classifiers for attribution identification based on the original PDTB data (sections 2-21). The first classifier is similar to that developed by Lin et al. (2014). We use the patterns proposed by Skadhauge and Hardt (2005) to enumerate all the candidate attribution spans. The coverage of our implementation is 59.8%, which means that we can only enumerate the candidates that contain the attribution covering 59.8% of the annotation. We then build a classifier following Lin et al. (2014) to decide whether the candidate is a valid attribution or not. Using the sentences that contain the attribution(s), we also train a tagger. The tagger is designed following the features used in Illinois Chunker (Punyakanok and Roth, 2001).

3 Evaluation and Results

In this section, we present the data we used and results of the evaluation based on both cross-validation on the training data (computed within our software) and using the official CoNLL 2015 Shared Task evaluation framework of Xue et al. (2015).

3.1 Data

The data we used is provided through the CoNLL-2015 shared task (Xue et al., 2015), which is a modification of Penn Discourse Treebank (PDTB) (Prasad et al., 2008b) sections 2 through 21. The training data for attribution identification is obtained from the original PDTB release, also sections 2 through 21.

3.2 Cross-Validation Results

We first present the cross validation results for each component using the training data (Table 1). All the results are averaged over 10-fold cross validation of all the examples we generated, using our own predicted features and our own evaluation code. Each component is evaluated in isolation, assuming the inputs are from gold data (for example: for connective classification, it is assumed we have the correct connective and arguments provided as input). This means that these results are higher than they would be if evaluated using inputs generated by previous stages of the system, although in this evaluation they still use the predicted part-of-speech, chunk, and parse information.

Table 1: Cross validation results of all the components.

	P	R	F1
Explicit Connectives	92.97	93.91	93.44
Argument Positions	98.15	98.15	98.15
Exact Arg1	64.41	64.95	64.68
Exact Arg2	87.06	86.06	86.56
Partial Arg1	77.02	77.66	77.34
Partial Arg2	94.74	93.65	94.19
Explicit Sense	83.18	83.18	83.18
Implicit Sense	34.58	34.58	34.58
Attribution Identification	82.94	58.02	68.27
Attribution Tagger	59.75	56.49	58.08

3.3 CoNLL Results

We also present the results evaluated by the CoNLL-2015 shared task scorer on dev, test, and blind sets in Tables 2, 3, and 4. The results are consistent with the cross validation results, allowing for the fact that components are working with predicted inputs rather than gold annotations. The sense performance reported here is the macro-average of explicit and implicit senses.

Compared with the best results on the blind set, which is shown in Table 5, our main weaknesses lie in the sense classifier and argument detector. Since we presently ignore the disjoint connectives, our results can be improved if we incorporate those missing connectives. We do not presently incorporate the argument information in connective detection and sense classification for the explicit parser. Connective detection and classification can be improved if we also incorporate more features from arguments or perform joint learning.

4 Discussion

In this section we point to some types of errors in our system's predictions and the complications of working on the provided corpus.

Table 2: CoNLL results on dev set.

	P	R	F1
Explicit connective	93.27	89.71	91.45
Exact Arg1	50.88	56.62	53.59
Exact Arg2	62.27	69.29	65.59
Exact Arg1 & Arg2	41.24	45.89	43.44
Sense	33.88	17.87	21.27
Parser	23.65	26.32	24.92

Table 3: CoNLL results on test set.

	P	R	F1
Explicit connective	92.33	91.33	91.83
Exact Arg1	45.93	52.71	49.09
Exact Arg2	58.97	67.66	63.02
Exact Arg1 & Arg2	35.73	41.00	38.18
Sense	27.01	17.54	15.72
Parser	18.97	21.76	20.27

Table 4: CoNLL results on blind set.

	P	R	F1
Explicit connective	89.11	86.87	87.98
Exact Arg1	49.52	51.61	50.55
Exact Arg2	66.83	69.64	68.21
Exact Arg1 & Arg2	40.48	42.18	41.31
Sense	21.02	16.81	16.49
Parser	17.62	18.36	17.98

Table 5: CoNLL best results on blind set.

	P	R	F1
Explicit connective	93.48	90.29	91.86
Exact Arg1	55.12	56.58	55.84
Exact Arg2	73.49	75.43	74.45
Exact Arg1 & Arg2	45.77	46.98	46.37
Sense	23.29	20.56	20.27
Parser	23.69	24.32	24.00

4.1 Error Analysis

We provide examples of the errors in the systems's predictions that show where the system can be improved, but also some that may indicate possible improvements in the task annotations themselves.

The argument boundaries in our system are predicted based on parse tree constituents. Some mistakes occur when an argument is non-contiguous, and some extraneous content is included. However, the UI-CCG system also generated correct arguments with erroneous token offsets due to tokenization differences.

> **Predicted Argument:**
> Golden West Financial Corp. , riding above the turbulence that has troubled most of the thrift industry , posted a 16 % increase of third-quarter earnings to $41.8 millon , or 66 cents a share .
> **Gold Argument:**
> Golden West Financial Corp posted a 16% increase of third-quarter earnings to $41.8 millon, or 66 cents a share

Although the shared task specification indicates that attribution detection is not evaluated, our results suggest that it is helpful for some cases in order to obtain the correct argument boundaries.

> **Predicted Argument:**
> In savings activity , Mr. Sandler said consumer deposits have enjoyed a steady increase throughout 1989 , and topped $11 billion at quarter 's end for the first time in the company 's history .
> **Gold Argument:**
> consumer deposits have enjoyed a steady increase throughout 1989, and topped $11 billion at quarter's end for the first time in the company's history

In some cases, there seems to be a legitimate alternative explanation. The issue of whether connectives should be included in arguments seems somewhat hard to pin down.

> **Prediction:**
> *argument1* then giving up some of its gains
> *connective/sense* as (Contingency.Cause.Reason)
> *argument2* the dollar recovered
> **Gold:**
> *argument1* **and** then giving up some of its gains
> *connective/sense* as (Temporal.Synchrony)
> *argument2* the dollar recovered

We also found examples where it is hard to make sense of the gold token offsets.

> **Prediction – argument 1:**
> *text:* The more active December delivery gold settled with a gain of $3.90 an ounce at $371.20
> *tokens:* 267, 268, 269, 270, 271, 272, 273, 274, 275, 276, 277, 278, 279, 280, 281, 282
> **Gold – argument 1:**
> *text:* The more active December delivery gold settled with a gain of $3.90 an ounce at $371.20
> *tokens:* 267, 268, 269, 270, 271, 272, 273, 274, 275, 276, 277, 278, 279, 280, 281, 282, 283, 284

4.2 Task-specific Complications

Since we wanted to use our own NLP software and to build a general-purpose system that will process raw text from new sources, we parsed the raw text files provided for the PDTB data. However, the shared task formulation requires outputs to be specified in terms of token indexes. We must therefore align our tokenization to that of the task-provided parse files, which were based on the gold tokenization of the Penn Treebank. We found some disagreements in tokenization decisions by our NLP tools with the gold standard which introduced unwelcome complications and consequent errors. Possibly, character spans from the original text might provide an accurate but less constraining basis for evaluating system outputs, although the gold standard tokenization appears to omit terminal periods from abbreviated words.

5 Extending the Submitted System

Comparing the experimental results of other participating systems in the shared task to our model, it seems that sense disambiguation is the critical step in our pipeline that requires further improvements. We designed an initial model for making global decisions for the sequence of senses that can occur in a paragraph. The idea is to consider the label of the neighboring senses when predicting the sense of any implicit or explicit discourse relation candidate. To implement this idea we designed a constrained conditional model (CCM) (Chang et al., 2012) in LBJava. In this model two basic classifiers are trained. A first classifier, $C1$, is trained to predict the sense of each candidate explicit/implicit relation and a second classifier $C2$ is trained to predict the cooccurrence of the senses of any neighboring pair of candidate explicit/implicit relations. These classifiers are trained independently using features similar to those in the previous pipeline model. At prediction time, using $C1$ and $C2$ we make a global decision for the whole paragraph by modeling the component decisions as a sequence tagging task formulated as a CCM. In this model, the sequential joint prediction is made by adding two global constraints on the predictions made by $C1$ and $C2$: a) $C2$ is applied on all pairs of neighboring relation candidates contained in a paragraph and the label assignments to any pair should be consistent with the label assignments made by $C1$ to the relations in that pair. b) For any two neighboring pairs in a paragraph that share a relation, the label assignments should be consistent; that is, if a pair $p1$ contains relation i and relation $i+1$ and the next pair $p2$ contains relation $i+1$ and relation $i+2$ then the assignments to the shared relation, $i+1$, should be the same. This constraint should hold for the whole paragraph. Using this model, we consider both emission and transition factors in making a global decision for the whole sequence of senses in a paragraph. However, this initial experiment on joint inference did not yield a significant improvement when tested on the sense prediction layer given all ground-truth labels of the previous layers in the pipeline.

6 Conclusions and Future Work

We have built a reasonably effective discourse parser using a pipeline architecture, and identified some features that improve performance over the previous reported state-of-the-art, including features based on Brown Clusters and on argument polarity information. We have also begun investigating the use of constrained conditional models for global inference.

Two natural extensions are: a) Improved features for sense classification. Our sense classification accuracy is relatively low. We need to improve the features we extract from the candidate arguments, and ideally these will reflect a higher level of semantic abstraction than the brown cluster features we used here. b) Global inference over multiple component decisions using Constrained Conditional Models.

Acknowledgments

This work builds on a core implementation developed by Yee Seng Chan. We thank the reviewers for their helpful advice, and the Shared Task organizers for their hard work and support. This work is supported by DARPA under agreement number FA8750-13-2-0008; by grant 1U54GM114838 awarded by NIGMS through funds provided by the trans-NIH Big Data to Knowledge (BD2K) initiative (www.bd2k. nih.gov); and by the Multimodal Information Access & Synthesis Center at UIUC, part of CCICADA, a DHS Science and Technology Center of Excellence. The U.S. Government is authorized to reproduce and distribute reprints for Governmental purposes notwithstanding any copyright notation thereon. The views and conclusions contained herein are those of the authors and should not be interpreted as necessarily representing the official policies or endorsements, either expressed or implied, of any of the organizations that supported the work.

References

P. Brown, V. Della Pietra, P. deSouza, J. Lai, and R. Mercer. 1992. Class-based n-gram models of natural language. *Computational Linguistics*, 18(4):467–479.

M. Chang, L. Ratinov, and D. Roth. 2012. Structured learning with constrained conditional models. *Machine Learning*, 88(3):399–431, 6.

M. de Marneffe, B. MacCartney, and C. Manning. 2006. Generating typed dependency parses from phrase structure parses. In *Proceedings of the Fifth International Conference on Language Resources and Evaluation (LREC'06)*.

R.-E. Fan, K.-W. Chang, C.-J. Hsieh, X.-R. Wang, and C.-J. Lin. 2008. Liblinear: A library for large linear classification. *Journal of Machine Learning Research*, 9:1871–1874.

D. Klein and C. D. Manning. 2003. Fast exact inference with a factored model for natural language parsing. In *The Conference on Advances in Neural Information Processing Systems (NIPS)*, volume 15. MIT Press.

P. Liang. 2005. Semi-supervised learning for natural language. Master's thesis, Massachusetts Institute of Technology.

Z. Lin, H. T. Ng, and M.-Y. Kan. 2014. A PDTB-styled end-to-end discourse parser. *Natural Language Engineering*, 20(2):151–184.

H. Peng, D. Khashabi, and D. Roth. 2015. Solving hard coreference problems. In *Proceedings of the 2015 Conference of the North American Chapter of the Association for Computational Linguistics*, Denver, Colorado, June. Association for Computational Linguistics.

R. Prasad, N. Dinesh, A. Lee, E. Miltsakaki, L. Robaldo, A. Joshi, and B. Webber. 2008a. The penn discourse treebank 2.0. In *Proceedings of the Sixth International Conference on Language Resources and Evaluation (LREC'08)*.

R. Prasad, N. Dinesh, A. Lee, E. Miltsakaki, L. Robaldo, A. Joshi, and B. Webber. 2008b. The penn discourse treebank 2.0. In Nicoletta Calzolari (Conference Chair), Khalid Choukri, Bente Maegaard, Joseph Mariani, Jan Odijk, Stelios Piperidis, and Daniel Tapias, editors, *Proceedings of the Sixth International Conference on Language Resources and Evaluation (LREC'08)*, Marrakech, Morocco, May. European Language Resources Association (ELRA). http://www.lrec-conf.org/proceedings/lrec2008/.

V. Punyakanok and D. Roth. 2001. The use of classifiers in sequential inference. In *Proc. of the Conference on Neural Information Processing Systems (NIPS)*, pages 995–1001. MIT Press.

N. Rizzolo and D. Roth. 2010. Learning based java for rapid development of nlp systems. In *Proc. of the International Conference on Language Resources and Evaluation (LREC)*, Valletta, Malta, 5.

D. Roth and D. Zelenko. 1998. Part of speech tagging using a network of linear separators. In *Coling-Acl, The 17th International Conference on Computational Linguistics*, pages 1136–1142.

A. Rutherford and N. Xue. 2014. Discovering implicit discourse relations through brown cluster pair representation and coreference patterns. In *Proceedings of the 14th Conference of the European Chapter of the Association for Computational Linguistics*, pages 645–654. Association for Computational Linguistics.

P. R. Skadhauge and D. Hardt. 2005. Syntactic identification of attribution in the rst treebank. In *Proceedings of the Sixth International Workshop on Linguistically Interpreted Corpora (LINC-2005)*.

T. Wilson, P. Hoffmann, S. Somasundaran, J. Kessler, J. Wiebe, Y. Choi, C. Cardie, E. Riloff, and S. Patwardhan. 2005. Opinionfinder: A system for subjectivity analysis. In *Proceedings of HLT/EMNLP on interactive demonstrations*, pages 34–35. Association for Computational Linguistics.

N. Xue, H. T. Ng, S. Pradhan, R. Prasad, C. Bryant, and A. Rutherford. 2015. The conll-2015 shared task on shallow discourse parsing. In *Proceedings of the Nineteenth Conference on Computational Natural Language Learning: Shared Task*, Beijing, China.

A Shallow Discourse Parsing System Based On Maximum Entropy Model

Jia Sun, Peijia Li, Weiqun Xu, Yonghong Yan
The Key Laboratory of Speech Acoustics and Content Understanding
Institute of Acoustics, Chinese Academy of Sciences
No. 21 North 4th Ring West Road, Haidian District, 100190 Beijing, China
{sunjia,lipeijia,xuweiqun,yanyonghong}@hccl.ioa.ac.cn

Abstract

This paper describes our system for Shallow Discourse Parsing - the CoNLL 2015 Shared Task. We regard this as a classification task and build a cascaded system based on Maximum Entropy to identify the discourse connective, the spans of two arguments and the sense of the discourse connective. We trained the cascaded models with a variety of features such as lexical and syntactic features. We also report the results achieved by our team.

1 Introduction

Discourse parsing is one of the most challenging tasks in natural language processing (NLP) field. It focuses on parsing the structure of a piece of text into a set of discourse relations between inter sentences. There is considerable interest in discourse parsing, both as an end in itself and as an intermediate step in a variety of NLP applications like question answering (Verberne et al., 2007), text summarization (Louis et al., 2010), sentiment analysis and opinion mining (Somasundaran, 2010).

There are many approaches working on identifying the discourse relations and data-driven approaches are dominated. A number of pioneers take the discourse relations identification as a classification task (Marcu and Echihabi, 2002; Pitler et al., 2009; Duverle and Prendinger, 2009) by the construction of features like lexical, syntactic and constituent features. Some take the argument segmentation task as a semantic role detection task (Wellner and Pustejovsky, 2007) and a sequence labeling task (Ghosh et al., 2011). However, some of the previous research is based on different corpus, lacking an common evaluation data set. This has been addressed with the release of Penn Discourse Treebank (PDTB) 2.0 corpus (Prasad et al., 2008) which provides detailed annotations about the discourse relations and argument spans addresses this problem. Besides, much research about discourse parsing working on the PDTB appears (Prasad et al., 2010; Lin et al., 2009) and they put more attention on the "harder" part - labelling the arguments. Lin (Lin et al., 2014) designed an end-to-end discourse parser with the PDTB including the explicit, implicit sense and the argument spans identification.

Shallow Discourse Parsing (Xue et al., 2015) is the CoNLL shared task this year[1] which takes a piece of newswire text as input and returns all the discourse relations in the form of a discourse connective (explicit or implicit) taking two arguments (which can be clauses, sentences, or multi-sentence segments) in JSON format. A relation will be parsed as correct if the explicit discourse connective (e.g., "because", "however") once it has, the spans of text that serve as the two arguments for each discourse connective and the sense (e.g., "Comparison") are all correct. The F1 score of the parser's performance is the evaluation metric.

In this paper, we describe our system details in Section 2, the evaluation result and subsequent experiments in Section 3. Finally, we draw some conclusions in Section 4.

2 Our System

2.1 Resources

The resources used in our system are as follows:
Labeled training and development data: The training and development (dev) data is derived from the PDTB 2.0 Section 2-21 and Section 22 in JSON format . There are 32535 relations and 1436 relations annotated in the training data and the dev data respectively. Table 1 shows the distribution of the four types in the data. There are

[1] http://www.cs.brandeis.edu/ clp/conll15st/

Proceedings of the Nineteenth Conference on Computational Natural Language Learning: Shared Task, pages 84–88,
Beijing, China, July 26-31, 2015.

Type	Train data	Dev data
Explicit	14,727	680
Implicit	13,163	522
EntRel	4,133	215
AltLex	524	19
all	32,535	1,436

Table 1: Distribution of the four discourse relation types in the data sets.

Sense level 1	Sense level 2or3	Train	Dev
Temporal	A.P	1,277	78
	A.S	1,014	55
	Synchrony	499	100
Contingency	Cause.Reason	3,344	147
	Cause.Result	2,137	81
	Condition	1,197	52
Comparison	Contrast	4,714	257
	Concession	1,293	17
Expansion	Conjunction	7,817	310
	Instantiation	1,403	58
	Restatement	2,699	110
	Alternative	210	6
	A.C	241	6
	Exception	15	0
	EntRel	4,133	215

Table 2: Distribution of the 15 senses from the different data sets. A.P, A.S, A.C are the abbreviations of "Asynchronous.Precedence", "Asynchronous.Succession", "Alternative.Chosen alternative" respectively .

15 valid senses including the second-level "types" as well as a selected number of third-level "subtypes". Table 2 shows the distribution of the 15 senses in the data.

Test data: There are two test data sets. One is the blind set which contains 20,000 to 30,000 words of newswire text annotated following the PDTB annotation guidelines. The other test set is Section 23 of the PDTB which is used for comparison with previous work.

The connectives list: A list contains 100 discourse connectives in the PDTB and three syntactic categories form (Knott, 1996).

Opennlp-maxent: We used the open source package Opennlp-maxent[2] to construct the classification models.

[2]http://sourceforge.net/projects/maxent/files/

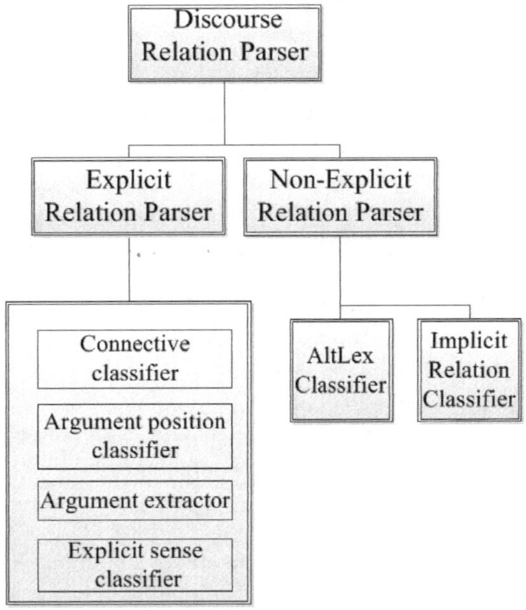

Figure 1: The structure of the system.

2.2 System overview and Features

Our system mainly follows the work of (Lin et al., 2014), which consists of two parts: the explicit relation parser and the non-explicit relation parser. The explicit relation parser is composed of the connective classifier, the argument position classifier, the argument extractor and the explicit sense classifier while the non-Explicit relation parser contains the AltLex classifier and the implicit classifier. The structure of our system is shown in Figure 1.

The set of features used in our system are listed in Table 3. All the features fall into four classes: lexical features, part-of-speech (POS) features, syntactic features and positional features.

- **Lexical features:** The lexical features (F1-F10) contain the connectives C, their contextual words and word-pair features (i.e., F7 (w_i,w_j) where w_i is a word from Arg1 and w_j is a word from Arg2) .
- **POS features:** F11-F17 belong to the POS features .
- **Syntactic features:** The syntactic features (F18-F26) include the connectives' syntactic category (F18): subordinating, coordinating, or discourse adverbial, the path of syntactic trees (F19, F20, F23), the number of siblings

Feature	Description
F1.	C string
F2.	the first word before C
F3.	the second word before C
F4.	F2 + C
F5.	F3 + C
F6.	C + the next word after C
F7.	word-pair
F8.	the first word of Arg2
F9.	the second word of Arg2
F10.	the third word of Arg2
F11.	the POS of C
F12.	the POS of F2
F13.	F11 + F12
F14.	the POS of the word after C
F15.	F11 + F14
F16.	the POS of F3
F17.	F11 + F16
F18.	the syntactic category of C
F19.	the path of C's parent to root
F20.	the compressed path of F19
F21.	the number of left siblings of C
F22.	the number of right siblings of C
F23.	the path of C's parent to N
F24.	whether the C's left sibling number is greater than 1
F25.	the constituent rules
F26.	the dependency rules
F27.	the relative position of N to C
F28.	the position of C in the sentence

Table 3: The features used in our system. "C" denotes the connectives. N means a current node in the constituent tree used in Section 2.3.2.

(F21, F22, F24), constituent rules (F25) and dependency rules (F26).

- **Position features:** F27 is the relative position in the syntactic tree structure (left, middle or right), while F28 is the connectives' positions in the sentence (start, middle or end).

2.3 Training

2.3.1 The Connective Classifier

All the 100 connectives that appeared in one discourse were extracted whether it functioned as a connective or not. We converted all upper case letters in connective to lower case ones.

The connective classifier decides whether a connective is functioned as a discourse connective. The features used were F4, F6, F11-F15, F19-F20 in Table 3.

2.3.2 The Argument Labeller

Once the connective is identified, the argument labeller identifies the Arg1 and Arg2 spans of this instance. This is accomplished in two steps: (1) Classifying the locations of Arg1 by the Argument Position Classifier. (2) Labelling the spans of Arg1 and Arg2 by the Argument Extrator.

The Argument Position Classifier: Normally Arg2 immediately follows the connective while the position of Arg1 is uncertain. In this model, we classified the Arg1's locations into two classes: Arg1 was located within the same sentence of the connective (SS) or in the previous sentence of connective (PS) (Prasad et al., 2008).

We implemented this as a binary classification task. In this step, features F1-F5, F11, F13, F16-F17, F28 in Table 3 were adopted to train the model. After the position label of Arg1 was determined, the result was passed to the argument extractor.

The Argument Extractor: In this module, our classifier labelled the previous sentence as Arg1 immediately for the PS case. The argument spans for the SS case were extracted described as below.

- Classify each internal node N in the constituent tree as Arg1-node, Arg2-node, or None with features F1, F18, F21-F24, F27 in Table 3.
- Label a node as Arg1-node once its Arg1-node predicted probability is greater than 0.1 (which is tuned on the dev data set).
- Select only one Arg1-node and one Arg2-node in one instance with the maximal probability of the respective label.
- Extract the Arg1 and Arg2 spans by tree subtraction. If the Arg1 node is the ancestor of the Arg2 node, the span of Arg1 should be subtracted from the Arg2 span, and vice versa.
- Remove punctuation tokens and connectives out of the exact argument spans.

2.3.3 The Explicit Sense Classifier

After recognizing the discourse connective and its two arguments spans, the next step is to decide the

Data	Connective	Span	Sense	Parser
Dev	0.9152	0.2668	0.1367	0.1814
Test	0.9064	0.2336	0.1191	0.1505
Blind	0.826	0.2195	0.1232	0.1262

Table 4: The results F1 score obtained by our team

sense of the connective. We trained this model using features F1, F4, F11 in Table 3. We picked the output whose maximal sense probability is greater than 0.45 which was experientially determined on dev data set.

2.3.4 The AltLex classifier

We extracted all adjacent sentence pairs within each paragraph and removed the pairs that were identified by the explicit relation parser. Then we trained the AltLex Classifier which decided whether the pairs were AltLex pairs and classified the senses with features F8-F10 in Table 3. The pairs labelled as non-AltLex relations were passed to the next implicit relation classifier.

2.3.5 The Implicit relation classifier

The implicit relation classifier classified the sense of each pair into one of the 15 valid senses or NoRel with F7, F25-F26 in Table 3. After predicting, we kept the implicit discourse relations whose maximal sense probability were greater than a threshold (0.25 in our case) which was determined on the dev data set .

3 Experiments and Results

There are two test data sets this year as described in Section 2.1 and the organizers reported the results on the two test data sets and the dev data set. The results of our system obtained are shown in Table 4. We ranked the 10th on every data set.

After the deadline of evaluation, we made some improvements in the module of implicit relation classifier inspired by (Lin et al., 2009). We selected the word-pair features (F7) while the experiments showed a little degradation in F1 score through selecting the constituent rules and the dependency rules (F25, F26) on the dev data set.

We computed the mutual information between each word-pair feature and the 15 valid senses and then selected the top N as the features. Table 5 shows the improvement of different N.

N	Non-Explicit	Overall
50	0.0683	0.1876
100	0.0683	0.1876
200	0.0614	0.1870
300	0.0603	0.1870
Baseline	0.0435	0.1814

Table 5: The F1 score in non-explict and overall parser when selecting features F7 using different N on dev data set.

4 Conclusion

We divided the complex task of discourse parsing into a set of classification subtasks and glued them together. A variety of features, including lexical, part-of-speech, syntactic and positional feature were employed to train the baseline with open Maximum Entropy package, then the system was improved by setting probability-output threshold. We did not utilize any additional resources and only used the annotations the official provided. Our system ranked the 10th among seventeenth teams on the two test data sets.

Acknowledgments

We would like to thank the shared task organizers for their support throughout this work. This work is partially supported by the National Natural Science Foundation of China (Nos. 11161140319, 91120001, 61271426), the Strategic Priority Research Program of the Chinese Academy of Sciences (Grant Nos. XDA06030100, XDA06030500), the National 863 Program (No. 2012AA012503) and the CAS Priority Deployment Project (No. KGZD-EW-103-2).

References

David A Duverle and Helmut Prendinger. 2009. A novel discourse parser based on support vector machine classification. In *Proceedings of the Joint Conference of the 47th Annual Meeting of the ACL and the 4th International Joint Conference on Natural Language Processing of the AFNLP: Volume 2-Volume 2*, pages 665–673. Association for Computational Linguistics.

Sucheta Ghosh, Richard Johansson, and Sara Tonelli. 2011. Shallow discourse parsing with conditional random fields. In *In Proceedings of the 5th International Joint Conference on Natural Language Processing (IJCNLP 2011)*.

Alistair Knott. 1996. A data-driven methodology for motivating a set of coherence relations.

Ziheng Lin, Min-Yen Kan, and Hwee Tou Ng. 2009. Recognizing implicit discourse relations in the penn discourse treebank. In *Proceedings of the 2009 Conference on Empirical Methods in Natural Language Processing: Volume 1-Volume 1*, pages 343–351. Association for Computational Linguistics.

Ziheng Lin, Hwee Tou Ng, and Min-Yen Kan. 2014. A pdtb-styled end-to-end discourse parser. *Natural Language Engineering*, 20(2):151–184.

Annie Louis, Aravind Joshi, and Ani Nenkova. 2010. Discourse indicators for content selection in summarization. In *Proceedings of the 11th Annual Meeting of the Special Interest Group on Discourse and Dialogue*, pages 147–156. Association for Computational Linguistics.

Daniel Marcu and Abdessamad Echihabi. 2002. An unsupervised approach to recognizing discourse relations. In *Proceedings of the 40th Annual Meeting on Association for Computational Linguistics*, pages 368–375. Association for Computational Linguistics.

Emily Pitler, Annie Louis, and Ani Nenkova. 2009. Automatic sense prediction for implicit discourse relations in text. In *Proceedings of the Joint Conference of the 47th Annual Meeting of the ACL and the 4th International Joint Conference on Natural Language Processing of the AFNLP: Volume 2-Volume 2*, pages 683–691. Association for Computational Linguistics.

Rashmi Prasad, Nikhil Dinesh, Alan Lee, Eleni Miltsakaki, Livio Robaldo, Aravind K. Joshi, and Bonnie L. Webber. 2008. The penn discourse treebank 2.0. In *Proceedings of the International Conference on Language Resources and Evaluation, LREC 2008, 26 May - 1 June 2008, Marrakech, Morocco*.

Rashmi Prasad, Aravind K. Joshi, and Bonnie L. Webber. 2010. Exploiting scope for shallow discourse parsing. In *Proceedings of the International Conference on Language Resources and Evaluation, LREC 2010, 17-23 May 2010, Valletta, Malta*.

Swapna Somasundaran. 2010. *Discourse-level relations for Opinion Analysis*. Ph.D. thesis, University of Pittsburgh.

Suzan Verberne, Lou Boves, Nelleke Oostdijk, and Peter-Arno Coppen. 2007. Evaluating discourse-based answer extraction for why-question answering. In *Proceedings of the 30th annual international ACM SIGIR conference on Research and development in information retrieval*, pages 735–736. ACM.

Ben Wellner and James Pustejovsky. 2007. Automatically identifying the arguments of discourse connectives. In *Proceedings of the 2007 Joint Conference on Empirical Methods in Natural Language Processing and Coumptational Natural Language Learning (EMNLP- CoNLL)*, pages 92–101.

Nianwen Xue, Hwee Tou Ng, Sameer Pradhan, Rashmi Prasad, Christopher Bryant, and Attapol Rutherford. 2015. The CoNLL-2015 shared task on shallow discourse parsing. In *Proceedings of the Nineteenth Conference on Computational Natural Language Learning*.

The DCU Discourse Parser for Connective, Argument Identification and Explicit Sense Classification

Longyue Wang, Chris Hokamp, Tsuyoshi Okita, Xiaojun Zhang, Qun Liu
ADAPT Centre
School of Computing, Dublin City University
Glasnevin, Dublin 9, Ireland
{lwang, chokamp, tokita, xzhang, qliu}@computing.dcu.ie

Abstract

This paper describes our submission to the CoNLL-2015 shared task on discourse parsing. We factor the pipeline into sub-components which are then used to form the final sequential architecture. Focusing on achieving good performance when inferring explicit discourse relations, we apply maximum entropy and recurrent neural networks to different sub-tasks such as connective identification, argument extraction, and sense classification. The our final system achieves 16.51%, 12.73% and 11.15% overall F1 scores on the dev, WSJ and blind test sets, respectively.

1 Introduction

The task of discourse parsing is generally conceived as a pipeline of steps, corresponding to: i) locating explicit discourse connectives, ii) identifying the spans of text that serve as the two arguments for each discourse connective, and iii) predicting the sense for both explicit and implicit relations. Understanding such discourse information is clearly an important component of natural language understanding that impacts a wide range of downstream natural language applications.

Since Penn Discourse Treebank was released, a number of data driven approaches have been proposed to deal with different challenging subtasks of discourse parsing. As explicit arguments may be intra-sentential or inter-sentential, Lin et al. (2012), Xu et al. (2012), Stepanov and Riccardi (2012) propose to employ argument position classification as heuristic and then apply separated models for argument extraction. Ghosh et al. (2011) regarded argument extraction as a token-level sequence labeling task, applying conditional random fields (CRFs) to label each token in a sentence. Following on this work, Ghosh et al. (2012) designed many global features to help distinguish Argument1 and Argument2 within the same sentence. Lin et al. (2014) formulated the task as finding the nodes in the constituent parse that are Argument1 or Argument2. However, the performance of this approach is heavily dependent upon the quality of the input parse trees. The different characteristic of implicit and explicit discourse relations are another important consideration. Lin et al. (2009) apply three feature classes: the constituent parse, the dependency parse and word-pair features for implicit relation classification. Rutherford and Xue (2014) exploit Brown cluster pairs to represent discourse relations in naturally occurring text. Considering the whole task, Lin et al. (2014) introduce a pipeline framework including several sub-tasks (connective classifier, argument labeler, explicit classifier and non-explicit classifier) to handle both explicit and non-explicit relations based on the PDTB corpus using maximum entropy.

In our work, we design the framework of our system based on Lin et al. (2014). The task is split the into seven components: connective classifier, argument positions classifier, three argument extractors, explicit sense classifier and implicit sense classifier. We approach argument extraction as a sequence labelling task, employing recurrent neural network (RNN) to classify each candidate token. We use distributional representations via word embeddings to decrease the out-of-vocabulary words (OOVs) problem which result from the scarcity of training data. After a post-precessing step which resolves label conflicts, we extract the spans of arguments. For other components, we use a classification via maximum entropy, and explore diverse features. In this system, we mainly focus on explicit relations, thus we only apply a simple majority function for the non-explicit component.

The remainder of this paper is organized as fol-

Proceedings of the Nineteenth Conference on Computational Natural Language Learning: Shared Task, pages 89–94,
Beijing, China, July 26-31, 2015.

lows: Section 2 describes the framework and each component of our proposed system. Then we discuss the results, including the official results and post-task results, in Section 3. Finally, we summarize our conclusions in Section 4.

2 Proposed System

The framework of our system is shown in Figure 1. In the first step, the connective classifier is used to identify connectives according to the occurrences of the predefined connectives. Once a candidate is labelled as a connective, an explicit relation is created. The next step is then to find the argument positions (*arg1* and *arg2*) for each explicit relation. Here we use a classifier to label two cases: 1, *arg1* and *arg2* are in the same sentence (SS), or 2, *arg1* and *arg2* are not in the same sentence (OT). Then we train and apply different argument extraction models for these two cases. After labelling the argument span, we use a sense classification component to classify them to predefined sense types.

After processing the explicit relations, the non-explicit part extracts all the adjacent sentence pairs which are not explicit relations and then infers implicit relations. As we mainly focus on explicit relations, in this part, we only apply a simple majority function to give all candidate pairs the same results.

2.1 Connective Classifier

As words which can be discourse connectives do not always function as discourse connectives, we need to identify if an instance of a connective candidate is a functional connective each time it occurs. Pilter and Nenkova (2009) showed that syntactic features extracted from constituent parse trees are very useful in disambiguating discourse connectives from other functions. Lin et al. (2014) tackled this problem by first using the connective list to identify the candidates and then using a combination of simple POS-based features and tree-based features, an approach which also achieved good performance. To model the syntactic relation, they also propose a path feature, which is the combined tags of sub-tree nodes from connective to the root. Compressed path means the adjacent identical tags are combined (e.g., -NP-NP- is combined into -NP-).

Based on above work, we extract the 99 types of connectives defined in the PDTB training corpus. As shown in Table 1, we use three feature classes: lexical, syntactic and others. Especially, we employ the position of connection as a new feature (i.e., beginning or not), because we observe that the candidates occurring at the beginning are always the connectives. Then a ME model is applied to classify each connective candidate as a connective or not. After exploring 14 features and combinations, we finally found that the feature set {2-10,13, 14} which yields the best performance on dev set. The final score is shown in Section 3.

2.2 Argument Position Classification

arg2 is the argument with which the connective is syntactically associated, and its position is fixed once we have located the connective from the previous component (Section 2.1). Thus, the challenging step for this task is to identify the location of *arg1*.

Prasad et al. (2008) show that *arg1* may be located in various positions to the connective, such as within the same sentence (SS), before (PS), or after (FS) the sentence containing the connective. Furthermore, *arg1* may be adjacent or non-adjacent with connective sentence. *arg1* may also contain one or more sentences. Table 2 shows the statistics of each of above scenarios.

Relative Position	**1 Sent**	**n Sents**
SS	60.38%	-
FS	0.01%	0.03%
PS	27.93%	1.89%
Other Scenarios	9.79%	

Table 2: Statistics of *arg1*'s Positions. (Percentage (%) is computed as the number of the scenario divided by the total relations; n>1)

As SS and PS constitute 90.20% of all explicit relations, our system mainly focus on these two cases. Therefore, we use a argument position classifier to classify a relation as SS or PS. In our experiment, we compared 17 features and their combinations, which are shown in Table 3. Finally, we use the feature set {1-3, 5, 7, 9, 11-14, 17} since it achieves the highest accuracy (97.78%) on dev set.

2.3 Argument Extraction

One of the key problems in discourse parsing is the task of extraction of argument spans of discourse relation. In the light of the recent success

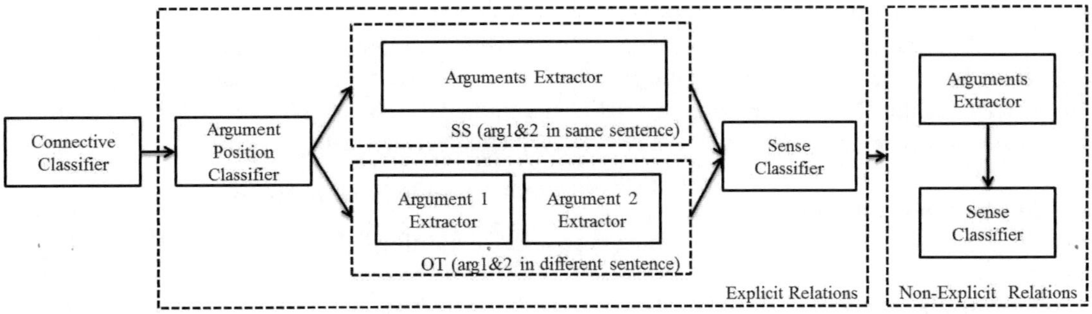

Figure 1: Framework of Our System

Type	ID	Features
Lexical Features	1	Connective Word
	2	Connective POS
	3	1st Previous Word of Connective
	4	1st Next Word of Connective
	5	1st Previous Word + Connective Word
	6	Connective Word + 1st Next Word
	7	1st Previous POS + Connective POS
	8	Connective POS + 1st Next POS
	9	1st Previous Word + Connective Word + 1st Next Word
	10	1st Previous POS + Connective POS + 1st Next POS
Syntactic Features	11	Path of Connective to the Root
	12	Path of Connective's Parent to the Root
	13	Compressed Path of Connective's Parent to the Root
Others	14	Low-Cased Connective Word

Table 1: Features for Connective Classification

Type	ID	Features
Lexical Features	1	Connective Word
	2	Connective POS
	3	1st Previous Word of Connective
	4	1st Next Word of Connective
	5	1st Previous POS of Connective
	6	1st Next POS of Connective
	7	1st Previous Word + Connective Word
	8	Connective Word + 1st Next Word
	9	1st Previous POS + Connective POS
	10	Connective POS + 1st Next POS
	11	2nd Previous POS of Connective
	12	2nd Previous Word of Connective
	13	2nd Previous POS + Connective POS
	14	2nd Previous Word + Connective Word
	15	1st Previous Word + Connective Word + 1st Next Word
	16	1st Previous POS + Connective POS + 1st Next POS
Others	17	Position of Connective

Table 3: Features for Argument Position Classification

of applying deep neural network technologies in natural language processing, we carried out an investigation of the use of recurrent neural network (RNN) for this difficult task (Mesnil et al., 2013; Raymond and Riccardi, 2007).

After determining the likely position of *arg1*, we split the explicit relations into two sets: SS and OT. We apply token-level sequence labeling approach with the separate models for arguments of intra-sentential and inter-sentential explicit discourse relations (Ghosh et al. 2011; Stepanov and Riccardi, 2012). As shown in Figure 1, we apply two components to deal with these two cases. Besides, in OT, we also train separated models to deal with Arg1 and Arg2 extraction.

Since for sequence labeling we use IOBE (Inside, Out, Begin, End) notation as the labels for both Arg1 and Arg2. For example, the set of classes for the SS case is {arg1-B, arg1-I, arg1-E, arg2-B, arg2-I, arg2-E and None}. The sets of classes for OT are {arg1-B, arg1-I, arg1-E and None} and {arg2-B, arg2-I, arg2-E and None}.

As input features, we use the word embeddings for Arg1 and Arg2 in order to infer the argument labels. We use RNNs to learn a word embedding on the part of training data. As the official scorer will give points only when the whole argument span is right, we employ this scorer to calculate the performance in each iteration of training. Furthermore, we compare the performance with different parameters: number of context windows, hidden layers, iterations and word embeddings. Finally, we set number of context windows as 5, hidden layers as 300, iterations as 10 and word embeddings as 100 to achieve the highest performance.

Besides, we only extract the relations in the corresponding scenario as the training data, thus OOVs may harm the models. We use distributional representations via word embeddings to alleviate the problem, which results from the scarcity of training data.

2.4 Explicit Sense Classification

One method that has previously been employed to resolve the ambiguity in discourse connectives is to build a classifier with some very simple features. They are the connective (one or more words), the connectives POS, and the connective + its previous word (Lin et al., 2014). This approach achieves an F1 score of 86.77, which is quite impressive compared the human agreement score of 84%.

Therefore, for this component, we still employ the similar feature set, which is shown in Table 4. Finally, we apply the feature set {1-3, 5-6} to obtain the best scores on dev set.

2.5 Non-Explicit Relations

The non-explicit relation includes Implicit , AltLex, EntRel and NoRel relations.

The non-explicit relations are annotated for all adjacent sentence pairs within paragraphs. If there is already an explicit relation from the previous step between two adjacent sentences, they are exempt from this step. In our system, we just apply a majority classifier, labeling all non-explicit relation candidates as EntRel.

3 Experiments and Results

3.1 System Setup

All available training data, development set, test sets from CoNLL 2015 (LDC2015E21)[1] are used in this study. Besides, we use the Skip-gram Neural Word Embeddings[2] for RNNs. All the used syntactic information are automatically predicted by the Berkeley Parser[3].

We use Maxent toolkit[4] for the ME method. And we apply Theano[5] (Bastien et al., 2012; Bergstra et al., 2010) for the RNNs. We use the Python programming language to develop all the compontents and divided each component into two parts: one is training which is processed in our CPU and GPU servers and the other is decoding which is run on TIRA server[6].

3.2 Official Results

The official results are shown in Table 5. The performance of connective classifier is around 80%, which is not good enough. There are two reasons: 1, we skip some separated connectives such as either or, neither nor etc. and 2, the current feature set missed some syntactic information. For argument extraction, the reasonable scores show our proposed method can really work for this part. However, it does not work well for OT case, because the span is always located the whole sentence. It may be helpful by adding structure fea-

[1] Available at https://www.ldc.upenn.edu
[2] Available at https://code.google.com/p/word2vec
[3] Description at http://www.cs.brandeis.edu/ clp/conll15st/rules.html
[4] Available at https://github.com/lzhang10/maxent
[5] Available at http://deeplearning.net/tutorial/rnnslu.html
[6] Available at http://www.tira.io

Type of Feature	ID	Features
Lexical Features	1	Connective Word
	2	Connective POS
	3	Connective + 1st Previous Word
	4	Connective + 2st Previous Word
	5	Connective + 1st Previous POS
Others	6	Low-Cased Connective

Table 4: Features for Explicit Sense Classification.

tures into RNNs. The sense classifier is the worst component, which only obtained about 8% F1 scores. It is because 1, the errors from previous components are propagated, which is also the limitation of the pipeline architecture; 2, we apply a simple non-explicit component and miss a lot implicit relations, which result in the low recall. On the whole, our system can still be improved in many ways.

4 Conclusions and Further Work

This paper describes the discourse parsing system we implemented for the CoNLL-2015 shared task. We build a pipeline system which focuses on achieving good performance when inferring explicit discourse relations. We apply maximum entropy and recurrent neural networks to different sub-tasks.

This is our ongoing work, and we will keep on improving the system by employing novel neural network methods.

Acknowledgments

This work is supported by the Science Foundation of Ireland (SFI) CNGL project (Grant No.: 12/CE/I2267), and partly supported by the DCU-Huawei Joint Project (Grant No.:201504032) and the Open Projects Program of National Laboratory of Patter Recognition (Grant No.: 201407353), and also by the European Commission FP7 EXPERT project.

References

Ziheng Lin, Hwee Tou Ng and Min-Yen Kan. 2014. *A PDTB-styled End-to-End Discourse Parser*, volume 1-34. Natural Language Engineering.

Sucheta Ghosh, Richard Johansson and Sara Tonelli. 2011. *Shallow Discourse Parsing with Conditional Random Fields*. In Proceedings of the 5th International Joint Conference on Natural Language Processing.

Sucheta Ghosh, Giuseppe Riccardi and Richard Johansson. 2012. *Global Features for Shallow Discourse Parsing*, 150-159. In Proceedings of the 13th Annual Meeting of the Special Interest Group on Discourse and Dialogue. Association for Computational Linguistics

Emily Pitler and Ani Nenkova. 2009. *Global Features for Shallow Discourse Parsing*, 150-159. In Proceedings of the ACL-IJCNLP 2009 Conference Short Papers. Association for Computational Linguistics.

Attapol T. Rutherford and Nianwen Xue. 2014. *Discovering Implicit Discourse Relations Through Brown Cluster Pair Representation and Coreference Patterns*, 645. In Proceedings of EACL 2014.

Rashmi Prasad, Nikhil Dinesh, Alan Lee, Eleni Miltsakaki, Livio Robaldo, Aravind Joshi, Bonnie Webber. 2008. *The Penn Discourse TreeBank 2.0*. In Proceedings of the LREC.

Grgoire Mesnil, Xiaodong He, Li Deng and Yoshua Bengio. 2013. *Investigation of Recurrent-Neural-Network Architectures and Learning Methods for Spoken Language Understanding*. In Proceedings of the Interspeech 2013.

Christian Raymond and Giuseppe Riccardi. 2007. *Generative and discriminative algorithms for spoken language understanding*. In Proceedings of the Interspeech 2007.

Frdric Bastien, Pascal Lamblin, Razvan Pascanu, James Bergstra, Ian Goodfellow, Arnaud Bergeron, Nicolas Bouchard, David Warde-Farley, Yoshua Bengio. 2012. *Theano: new features and speed improvements*. In Proceedings of the Python for Scientific Computing Conference (SciPy).

James Bergstra, Olivier Breuleux, Frdric Bastien, Pascal Lamblin, Razvan Pascanu, Guillaume Desjardins, Joseph Turian, David Warde-Farley, Yoshua Bengio. 2010. *Theano: a CPU and GPU math expression compiler*. In Proceedings of the Python for Scientific Computing Conference (SciPy).

Evgeny A. Stepanov and Giuseppe Riccardi. 2013. *Comparative evaluation of argument extraction algorithms in discourse relation parsing*. In Proceedings of 13th International Conference on Parsing Technologies (IWPT 2013).

	Dev Set			Test Set			Blind Set		
Components	**Precision**	**Recall**	**F1**	**Precision**	**Recall**	**F1**	**Precision**	**Recall**	**F1**
Connectives	0.9010	0.8162	0.8565	0.9040	0.8570	0.8799	0.8487	0.7464	0.7943
Arg1	0.3437	0.4770	0.3995	0.3100	0.4384	0.3632	0.2794	0.3755	0.3204
Arg2	0.3778	0.5244	0.4392	0.3559	0.5034	0.4170	0.3489	0.4690	0.4001
Arg1 & Arg2	0.2559	0.3552	0.2975	0.2174	0.3074	0.2546	0.1926	0.2589	0.2209
Sense	0.3194	0.1080	0.0938	0.2257	0.1124	0.0849	0.0905	0.0701	0.0481
Overall	0.1420	0.1971	0.1651	0.1087	0.1537	0.1273	0.0972	0.1307	0.1115

Table 5: Official Results.

Xu Ming, Zhu Qiao and Zhou Guo Dong. 2012. *A Unified Framework for Discourse Argument Identification via Shallow Semantic Parsing*. In Proceedings of 24th International Conference on Computational Linguistics.

Hybrid Approach to PDTB-styled Discourse Parsing for CoNLL-2015

Yasuhisa Yoshida, Katsuhiko Hayashi, Tsutomu Hirao and **Masaaki Nagata**
NTT Communication Science Laboratories, NTT Corporation
2-4, Hikaridai, Seika-cho, Soraku-gun, Kyoto, 619-0237, Japan
{yoshida.y,hayashi.katsuhiko,
hirao.tsutomu,nagata.masaaki}@lab.ntt.co.jp

Abstract

This paper describes our end-to-end PDTB-styled discourse parser for the CoNLL-2015 shared task. We employed a machine learning-based approach to identify discourse relation between text spans for both explicit and implicit relations and employed a rule-based approach to extract arguments of the discourse relations. In particular, we focus on improving the implicit discourse relation identification. First, we extract adjacent pairs of sentences that have some discourse relationships by exploiting a two-class classifier from an entire document. Second, we assign sense labels for them by utilizing a multiple-class classifier. Our system achieved a 0.316 overall F-score for the development set, 0.249 for the testset and 0.157 for the blind testset.

1 Introduction

In this paper, we describe our end-to-end PDTB-styled discourse parsing system for CoNLL-2015. Our system is an extension of Ziheng et al.'s discourse parser (Ziheng et al., 2014). Our explicit connective-argument structure parser consists of three modules: (1) a connective classifier that classifies connective candidates into discourse connective or not, (2) an argument position classifier that classifies whether $Arg1$ and the discourse connective co-occur in the same sentence or not. (3) a rule-based argument extraction that extracts both $Arg1$ and $Arg2$ using rules derived from a syntactic tree. The implicit parser consists of two modules: (1) argument pair identification that finds the pair of adjacent sentences that have some discourse relation, (2) sense labeler assigning the role of the discourse relation between the sentences.

In addition, we introduce a new evaluation measure for argument extraction. Since exact matching between arguments used in "scorer.py" provided by the organizers of CoNLL-2015 is too strict, we introduce relaxed matching for the task. The evaluation metric measures how close arguments provided by the system are to the gold arguments.

The evaluation results provided by the CoNLL-2015 official scorer show that our system achieved 5th rank in the $Arg1$ extractor, 6th rank in the $Arg2$ extractor, 4th rank in the $Arg1\&Arg2$ extractor, and 8th rank in overall performance.

2 Explicit Connective-Argument Identification

The explicit connective-argument parser consists of three steps. First, we identify discourse connectives for an entire document. Second, we determine whether $Arg1$ is contained in the same sentence that includes the discourse connective. Third, we assign a sense label for each discourse connective.

2.1 Connective Classification

The connective classifier classifies ambiguous connective candidates such as "and" into discourse connective or not. We exploit lexical features and features obtained from parse trees by extending (Ziheng et al., 2014). Note that connective candidates were extracted from the PYTHON script "conn_head_mapper.py" provided by the organizers of CoNLL-2015. Features that we utilized are shown in Table 1.

We trained the classifier by using SVM with second-order polynomial kernel.

2.2 Argument Position Classification

By following (Ziheng et al., 2014), we implemented an argument position classifier that classifies the location of the arguments of arbitrary

Proceedings of the Nineteenth Conference on Computational Natural Language Learning: Shared Task, pages 95–99,
Beijing, China, July 26-31, 2015.

Type	Features
Context	C_s, POS$_s$, {Word$_u$}, {POS$_u$}
Parse Tree	Path(C_s,root), Parent(C_s), depth(C_s), RightSib(C_s), LeftSib(C_s)
	$u = s-5, \ldots, s-1, s+1, \ldots, s+5$

Table 1: Features used in connective classifier

discourse connective into "same sentence" (SS) or "previous sentence" (PS). SS indicates both $Arg1$ and $Arg2$ are located in the same sentence that contains the discourse connective. PS indicates $Arg1$ is located in the sentence previous to that containing both the discourse connective and $Arg2$. We utilized context features in Table 1 and the position of the connective C_s: start, middle, or end.

We also trained the classifier by using SVM with second-order polynomial kernel.

2.3 Sense Classification

We assign majority sense ℓ^* for each discourse connective C_s as follows:

$$\ell^* = \text{arg max}_{\ell \in L} \text{freq}(C_s, \ell). \quad (1)$$

L is a set of sense labels used in training data and freq returns the frequency of co-occurrences of the discourse connective and sense label.

3 Implicit Connective-Argument Relationship Identification

The implicit parser consists of two steps. First is the argument identification step. In this step, we examine whether an adjacent sentence pair in the same paragraph has a discourse relation or not. Second is the sense classification step. Given a pair of sentences, we classify it into a predefined sense label.

3.1 Argument Position Identification

In the argument identification step, following Ghosh et al. (2011), the identifier examines all adjacent sentence pairs within each paragraph. For each pair of sentences (S_i, S_{i+1}), we identify the existence of a discourse relation. To identify the existence of the relation (binary classification), we used SVM with the following features.

- First unigram, last unigram, and first trigram of S_i and S_{i+1}.
- S_i (or S_{i+1}) contains modality words or not.
- Word pairs $(w_i, w_{i+1}) \in S_i \times S_{i+1}$
- Brown cluster pairs feature defined in Rutherford and Xue (2014)
- Sentence-to-sentence discourse dependency tree features including existence of dependency edges and rhetorical relation labels. Discourse dependency trees are defined in Li et al. (Li et al., 2014).

If the identifier identifies that a pair of sentences (S_i, S_{i+1}) has the discourse relation, we heuristically regard S_i as $Arg1$ and S_{i+1} as $Arg2$.

3.2 Sense Classification

In the sense classification step, we classify the discourse relation between a pair of sentences (S_i, S_{i+1}) into five senses: "Expansion", "Contingency", "Temporal", "Comparison", and "EntRel". To classify the sense of a pair of sentences, we used multi-class SVM. We used the same features described in the argument position identification step. To increase the number of training data, we used the (inter-sentential) explicit training data as the additional training data (Rutherford and Xue, 2015). We removed a connective from each instance in the explicit training data and treated them as implicit training data. The accuracy of classification into five senses is still low because the distribution of the senses is imbalanced. Following Rutherford and Xue (2014), we resampled the instances in the training data of sense classification to balance the distribution of the senses.

4 Argument Extractor

We utilized two rule-based argument extractors. One extracts both $Arg1$ and $Arg2$ from the same sentence (SS). The other extracts $Arg1$ and $Arg2$ from adjacent sentences respectively (PS).

4.1 SS Cases

4.1.1 Subordinating Conjunctions

We adopted Dinesh et al. (2005)'s tree subtraction method for subordinating conjunctions. This method takes a constituent parse tree as an input and detects argument spans as follows:

(1) set a node variable x to the last word of the target connective,

(2) set x to the parent node of x and repeat until x has label SBAR or S and set a node variable $Arg2$ to the node of x,

	Dev			Test			Blind		
	P	R	F	P	R	F	P	R	F
Con.	.924	.857	.889	.918	.866	.891	.925	.353	.510
$Arg1$	.658	.549	.599	.719	.584	.644	.638	.330	.435
$Arg2$	.768	.640	.698	.587	.477	.526	.765	.395	.521
$Arg1\&Arg2$	.566	.471	.514	.488	.397	.438	.522	.269	.356
Overall	.348	.290	.316	.279	.226	.249	.230	.119	.157

Table 2: Official evaluation results.

(3) set x to the parent node of x and repeat again until x has label SBAR or S and set a node variable $Arg1$ to the current node of x,

(4) consider $span(Arg2)$ as the span of argument2 and $span(Arg1) \setminus span(Arg2)$ as that of argument1, where $span(\cdot)$ is a function mapping a node $\cdot$ to a set of words dominated by the node.

4.1.2 Coordinating Conjunctions

For coordinating conjunctions, we also define a rule-based method that works on a constituent tree:

(1) set a node variable x to the last word of the target connective,

(2) set a node variable y to x and x to the parent node of x, and repeat while the leftmost word in $span(x)$ is equal to that in $span(y)$, and after the process, add y and the more right child nodes of x into a set $Arg2\_set$,

(3-1) if a node labeled with S or SBAR is contained in the set of the more right child nodes of x than y, set a node variable $Arg1$ to the node,

(3-2) otherwise, set x to the parent node x and repeat until x has label SBAR or S, and set a node variable $Arg1$ to the node of x,

(4) consider $union\_span(Arg2\_set)$ as the span of argument2 and $span(Arg1) \setminus union\_span(Arg2\_set)$ as that of argument1, where $union\_span(\cdot)$ is a function mapping a node set $\cdot$ to the union of each word set $span(Arg2)$ for $Arg2 \in Arg2\_set$.

4.1.3 Discourse Adverbials & Implicit Argument Structures

We did not treat the discourse adverbial connective-argument and inter-sentential implicit argument structures because their frequencies are not high in the training data.

4.2 PS Cases

In the PS cases, our rule-based extraction method is very simple and has only two processes: (1) remove sentence end symbols such as . ! ?. and (2) remove brace expressions enclosed in sentence start and end brackets like “”. This method repeats (1) and (2) until unchanged.

5 Evaluation Results

Table 2 shows the official evaluation results. From the results, explicit connective identification and the $Arg2$ extractor performed well, but performance of the $Arg1$ extractor and sense classification was not very good. Thus, the overall performance is significantly degraded. Table 3 shows the official evaluation results for explicit relations. Compared with the testset, the accuracies for the blind testset drastically dropped. This is because our programs might failed to identify some connectives. Table 4 shows the official evaluation results for implicit relations. Among the participants, our implicit parser performed well (1st rank in the $Arg1\&Arg2$ extractor and 2nd rank in the overall performance). Previous study like Ghosh et al. (2011) jointly extracted the argument and classified the sense with a single classifier. Our system performed well since we split our system into the argument extractor and the sense classifier.

“scorer.py” employs exact matching for argument extraction, and when the span of the argument provided by systems exactly matches the span of the human annotated argument, the scorer evaluates the system's tuples. However, the boundaries of human annotated arguments are blurry. The span of the argument may differ from the span annotated by another human. Thus, we evaluate our argument extractor with relaxed

	Dev			Test			Blind		
	P	R	F	P	R	F	P	R	F
Con.	.924	.857	.889	.918	.866	.891	.924	.353	.510
$Arg1$	.578	.537	.557	.475	.448	.461	.509	.194	.281
$Arg2$	.749	.696	.722	.705	.664	.684	.689	.263	.380
$Arg1\&Arg2$	.498	.462	.479	.400	.377	.388	.392	.149	.216
Overall	.447	.415	.430	.355	.335	.345	.307	.117	.169

Table 3: Official evaluation results for explicit relations.

	Dev			Test			Blind		
	P	R	F	P	R	F	P	R	F
$Arg1$	.729	.546	.625	.708	.491	.579	.692	.438	.537
$Arg2$	.788	.589	.675	.733	.509	.601	.804	.508	.623
$Arg1\&Arg2$	.641	.480	.549	.596	.413	.488	.588	.372	.456
Overall	.237	.177	.203	.184	.128	.151	.191	.121	.148

Table 4: Official evaluation results for implicit relations.

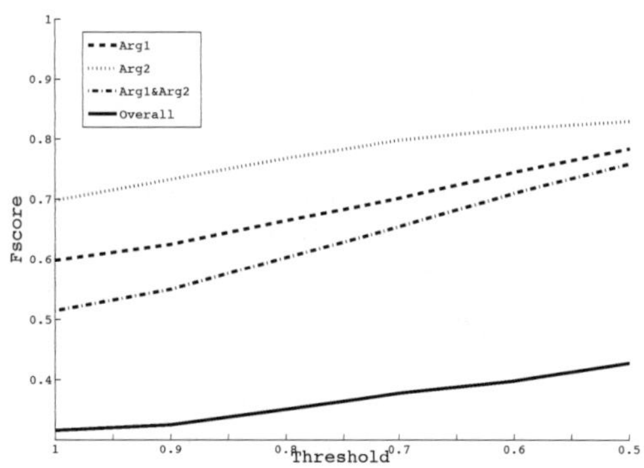

Figure 1: Evaluation results with relaxed matching.

matching. We compute token-based arg-Fscore between the system argument and the gold argument that is defined as follows:

$$\text{Prec.} = \frac{|A_s \cap A_g|}{|A_s|}, \tag{2}$$

$$\text{Rec.} = \frac{|A_s \cap A_g|}{|A_g|}, \tag{3}$$

$$\text{arg-Fscore} = \frac{2 * \text{Prec.} * \text{Rec.}}{\text{Prec.} + \text{Rec.}}. \tag{4}$$

A_s indicates a set of tokenIDs obtained from the system argument. A_g indicates a set of tokenIDs obtained from the gold argument. Then, we regard the system argument that has a certain threshold arg-Fscore as the correct argument.

Figure 1 shows evaluation results with thresholds from 1.0 to 0.5. When we set the threshold to 0.5, $Arg1\&Arg2$ Fscore achieved 0.7. This implies that our system can detect most of the correct positions of both explicit and implicit connectives but can not extract the correct span of the arguments. Moreover, overall performance is still low because of error caused by the sense classification modules.

6 Conclusion

In this paper, we presented our PDTB-styled full discourse parser for CoNLL-2015. We extended the work by (Ziheng et al., 2014). The experimental resulted show that our performed well on explicit connective identification and $Arg1$ extraction, but not on $Arg2$ extraction and sense classification.

References

Nikhil Dinesh, Alan Lee, Eleni Miltsakaki, Rashmi Prasad, Aravind Joshi, and Bonnie Webber. 2005. Attribution and the (non-) alignment of syntactic and discourse arguments of connectives. In *Proceedings of the Workshop on Frontiers in Corpus Annotations II: Pie in the Sky*, pages 29–36. Association for Computational Linguistics.

Sucheta Ghosh, Sara Tonelli, Giuseppe Riccardi, and Richard Johansson. 2011. End-to-end discourse parser evaluation. In *Fifth IEEE International Conference on Semantic Computing (ICSC), 2011; September 18-21, 2011; Palo Alto, United States*, pages 169–172.

Sujian Li, Liang Wang, Ziqiang Cao, and Wenjie Li. 2014. Text-level discourse dependency parsing. In *Proceedings of the 52nd Annual Meeting of the Association for Computational Linguistics (Volume 1: Long Papers)*, pages 25–35, Baltimore, Maryland, June. Association for Computational Linguistics.

Attapol Rutherford and Nianwen Xue. 2014. Discovering implicit discourse relations through brown cluster pair representation and coreference patterns. In *Proceedings of the 14th Conference of the European Chapter of the Association for Computational Linguistics*, pages 645–654, Gothenburg, Sweden, April. Association for Computational Linguistics.

Attapol Rutherford and Nianwen Xue. 2015. Improving the inference of implicit discourse relations via classifying explicit discourse connectives. In *Proc. of the 2015 NAACL*. Association for Computational Linguistics.

Lin Ziheng, Ng Hwee Tou, and Kan Min-Yen. 2014. A PDTB-styled End-to-End Discourse Parser. *Natural Language Engineering*, 20:151–184.

Author Index

Bayer, Ali Orkan, 25
Bryant, Christopher, 1

C.S., Malarkodi, 50
Chen, Changge, 37
Chiarcos, Christian, 42

Davoodi, Elnaz, 56

Gopalan, Sindhuja, 50
Gupta, Mohit, 61

Hayashi, Katsuhiko, 95
Hirao, Tsutomu, 95
Ho, Quoc, 66
Hokamp, Chris, 89

Kong, Fang, 32
Kordjamshidi, Parisa, 78
Kosseim, Leila, 56
Kumar Singh, Anil, 61

Laali, Majid, 56
Lalitha Devi, Sobha, 50
Lan, Man, 17
Li, Peijia, 84
Li, Sheng, 32
Liu, Qun, 71, 89

Mukherjee, Shubham, 61

Nagata, Masaaki, 95
Ng, Hwee Tou, 1
Nguyen, Minh, 66
Nguyen, Son, 66

Okita, Tsuyoshi, 71, 89

Peng, Haoruo, 78
Pradhan, Sameer, 1
Prasad, Rashmi, 1

Riccardi, Giuseppe, 25
RK Rao, Pattabhi, 50
Roth, Dan, 78
Rutherford, Attapol, 1

S, Lakshmi, 50
Sammons, Mark, 78
Schenk, Niko, 42
Song, Yangqiu, 78
Stepanov, Evgeny, 25
Sun, Jia, 84
Sundar Ram, Vijay, 50

Tiwari, Abhishek, 61

Wang, Jianxiang, 17
Wang, Longyue, 71, 89
Wang, Peilu, 37

Xu, Weiqun, 84
Xue, Nianwen, 1

Yan, Yonghong, 84
Yoshida, Yasuhisa, 95

Zhang, Xiaojun, 89
Zhao, Hai, 37
Zhou, Guodong, 32